GRACE ON CRUTCHES

also by Walter J. Burghardt, S.J.
published by Paulist Press

TELL THE NEXT GENERATION
SIR, WE WOULD LIKE TO SEE JESUS
SEASONS THAT LAUGH OR WEEP
STILL PROCLAIMING YOUR WONDERS
CHRISTIAN TRADITION (videocassette)

GRACE ON CRUTCHES

Homilies for Fellow Travelers

WALTER J. BURGHARDT, S.J.
Theologian in Residence
Georgetown University

PAULIST PRESS
New York/Mahwah

Acknowledgments
The publisher gratefully acknowledges use of the following
materials:

Excerpts from *The Unicorn and Other Poems* © 1956 by Anne
Morrow Lindbergh. Reprinted by permission of Pantheon
Books, a Division of Random House, Inc.

Excerpts from "In Praise of Diversity" from *Times Three* by
Phyllis McGinley, © 1954 by Phyllis McGinley, renewed © 1981
by Julie Elizabeth Hayden and Phyllis Hayden Blake. Reprinted
by permission of Viking Penguin Inc.

Selections from *Monsignor Quixote* © 1982 by Graham Greene.
Reprinted by permission of Simon & Schuster, Inc.

Illustrations by Wendy Mahin.

Library of Congress
Catalog Card Number: 85-62930

ISBN: 0-8091-2782-2

Published by Paulist Press
997 Macarthur Boulevard, Mahwah, N.J. 07430

Printed and bound in the
United States of America

TABLE OF CONTENTS

MEDLEY

for Mary Margaret and Albert W. Tegler,

    whose living homilies are
17 children,
75 grandchildren,
7 great-grandchildren,

    all of whom have learned from them,
as I too have learned,
how to wed wisdom to silence as well as to words,
how to love the unloved as we love ourselves,
how to give without counting the cost,
how to fashion a Christlife merry with laughter
and walk on crutches with grace.

PREFACE

Unlike the biblical Melchizedek, "without father or mother or genealogy" (Heb 7:3), *Grace on Crutches* has an ancestry. The tree began to grow in Maryland: my first sermon book, *All Lost in Wonder* (Westminster, Md.: Newman, 1960), a set of 37 radio talks that stressed dogma rather than morality, belief rather than conduct, thought rather than action. This was followed five years later by *Saints and Sanctity* (Englewood Cliffs, N.J.: Prentice-Hall, 1965), an effort to reveal, through the life experiences of 20 saints, the significance which the sanctity of the past might have for the holiness of the present. A third volume, *Tell the Next Generation* (New York/ Ramsey: Paulist, 1980), gathered together 36 "homilies and near homilies" delivered between 1964 and 1979; a number of these reflect the growing influence of Vatican II, especially a return to the Bible for homiletic inspiration and content.

It is, however, in the two most recent collections, *Sir, We Would Like To See Jesus* and *Still Proclaiming Your Wonders* (New York/Ramsey: Paulist, 1982, 1984), that the link between liturgy, Scripture, and the homily comes consistently to the fore, together with an increasing concern for the movement from faith to social justice. These are the linkages that carry over prominently into the present volume.

The title *Grace on Crutches* reproduces my recent characterization of the Catholic novelist and short-story writer Flannery O'Connor (1925–64). Only 25 when her incurable lupus erythematosus was diagnosed, she is a remarkable example of the human and Christian struggle to "accept with passion, possibly with joy," what

1

cannot be changed, plus a quiet conviction that "You will have found Christ when you are concerned with other people's sufferings and not your own." The subtitle *Homilies for Fellow Travelers* may strike some as uncomfortably reminiscent of an older expression for those who walked too close to the Russian Bear. In point of fact, it is intended to remind the reader that we Christians are a pilgrim people, ceaselessly journeying to God and His Christ. Together, title and subtitle suggest our halting yet graced steps toward Jerusalem and beyond, the dying/rising that is our paschal mystery.

It would be less than gracious not to acknowledge my mounting debts to the Jesuit community at Georgetown University, to scores of students and faculty at the University, to the clergy and laity of Holy Trinity parish in Washington, D.C., and Dahlgren Chapel's 12:15 congregation. The community is a living library, the campus ceaseless inspiration, the parish and chapel grace-filled contradictions to the congregations I describe in my prelude "Preacher and Parishioner." I am indeed a fortunate man.

Walter J. Burghardt, S.J.

PROLOGUE

PREACHER AND PARISHIONER:
THE VIEW FROM THE PEW

For the most part, preaching presupposes a parish. A parish that should be shaped, in large measure, by preaching. A parish that normally comes together on Sundays in congregations. So then, three stages to my development: the parish, the congregation, the preacher.

I

First, what ought to be our vision of a parish? Here the word "vision" is dreadfully vague. Certain dictionary definitions do not concern us here. For example, we are not talking about "an imaginary, supernatural, or prophetic sight beheld in sleep or ecstasy." We are not interested in the mystics' "direct awareness of the supernatural." I suggest that we mean, quite simply, "a way of seeing" something. If, for instance, you think of Jesuits as a crafty, insidious, well-disciplined, tightly-knit, 007-type of male creaturehood creeping stealthily into the power structures of church, state, and society, you have a "vision" of the Jesuits. You may not be totally accurate; you may be a bit biased; but you do have a way of looking at that curious amalgam of men a retired soldier organized almost four and a half centuries ago. Green Berets of the Spirit?

Here we are talking about a vision of parish: How should we see, how should we envision, a parish? Technically, the vision is simple enough. A parish is a segment of a diocese under the direction of a priest known as the pastor or parish priest, who is charged with the care of the people in that area who have been officially entrusted to him. This is clear, canonical; and it will help you if you are taking a parish census or an envelope collection. But we are concerned with far more than a definition. What is a parish, a congregation, all about? Why does it exist? What is supposed to happen there?

You can speak of it, as Matthew Fox does so eloquently, as a journey, "becoming a people." You can speak of it as a ceaseless process of conversion. You can speak of it as a continuing development in faith. These are different aspects of a single reality, ways of focusing on a reality too rich and complex to be imprisoned in a definition. I suggest that it is all of these. Putting them together in a bit of a synthesis, I conclude: A [Catholic] parish is a group of Catholic Christians who are in process of becoming a people by deepening and expanding their faith through a ceaseless process of conversion.

The group is in process of becoming a people, a community. They are, therefore, at once a community and not a community. They are indeed a community; for all acknowledge Christ as Lord and Savior, all profess the same basic beliefs, are sanctified by the same sacramental system, are bound by the same code of laws—and all this in obedience to the bishop of Rome and the bishop at home. And still they are not the community they should be. A parish is fashioned initially out of individuals who love God but normally do not particularly love one another. They do not hate one another; they simply do not know one another. And many parishes stay that way. Isolated individuals, or at best isolated family units, congregate in the one place once a week, do their solitary thing, and go back home pretty much as they were when they came. Nourished indeed individually, but to all appearances no more a community than before.[1]

Tragic, for a parish is the Church in miniature; it is the single Body of Christ localized. And so it must be fashioned into a oneness where, as St. Paul puts it, "The eye cannot say to the hand, 'I have no need of you,' nor again the head to the feet, 'I have no need of you' " (1 Cor 12:21), where "If one member suffers, all suffer together; if one member is honored, all rejoice together" (v. 26). The problem is, we rarely have the social structure for this in a city parish, a Saturday-evening and Sunday-morning affair where the hearts that go up to heaven hardly go out across the pews.

Still, this is part of the parish pilgrimage. The parishioners of St. Martin-on-the-Rocks are not journeying to a better life with blinders. They are part and parcel of a process: They have to become a people, a little church, where grace is not a narrow pipeline from heaven to each parishioner but flows through all to each, where every man, woman, and child strives consciously to be a channel of grace for the whole, where, as Karl Rahner phrased it, all of us are mediators for one another.

How do they become a people? By deepening and expanding their faith. Catholic faith, you see, is not primarily a matter of propositions: "I believe in one God the Father almighty; I believe in His Son, who became man, died for our sins, and rose from the dead; I believe in the Holy Spirit, the Lord, the Giver of life; I believe in the Catholic Church, the forgiveness of sins, the resurrection of the body, and life everlasting." It includes all that, of course; but faith is more than the acceptance of propositions. Remember the New Testament Letter of James: "You believe that God is one; you do well. Even the demons believe—and shudder" (Jas 2:19).

Catholic faith surrenders to God and His Christ not only the mind: "I accept as true whatever you say." No, I surrender my whole self. And I do so within a community that is the Body of Christ. In saying a total yes to the risen Christ, I am saying yes to the total Christ, head and members, vine and branches. True faith, therefore, is a loving faith. And the love, to be faith-full, must go out to every limb that forms part of the whole Christ. That is how faith builds community: Our love goes not only up but out. It sounds the death knell for the me-and-Jesus spirituality.

How is such faith deepened and expanded? Through a ceaseless process of conversion. I mean a constant turning to Christ . . . through Christ. It is relatively rare, I believe, that a Christian has turned totally from Christ, is alienated from God, is in rebellion against Him. My experience of Christians is very much my experience of myself: turned radically to Christ in mind and will, but dreadfully weak in living the logic of that primal conversion. You cannot call me sinner, because my face is set towards Christ. But you can call me sinful, because so many of the actions that should express who I am, a committed lover of Christ, give the lie to that person. So much of my life is superficial. I mean, so many of my human acts are not fully human, do not commit me as a total person. They are neither sin in the radical sense nor conversion. They do not enslave me to Satan, they do not commit me to Christ. The danger in such semi-Christian living was strongly stated in the last book of the Bible: "I know your works: You are neither hot nor cold. Would that you were cold or hot! So, because you are lukewarm, and neither cold nor hot, I will spew you out of my mouth" (Rev 3:15–16).

Christian parish living is a continual movement towards the risen Christ. Not simply as individuals—as a single body that resonates to the indwelling Christ it is trying to image, resonates to St. Paul's cry to the Christians of Galatia: "There is neither Jew nor Greek, there is neither slave nor free, there is no male-and-female; for you are all one in Christ Jesus" (Gal 3:28).

II

Which brings me to the second stage in my development: We move from the parish to the congregation, from the people as an amorphous group in "low cost" and condo to the highly visible audience resting restlessly on its haunches as I begin to homilize. They are indeed what I have described: a group of Catholic Christians who are in process of becoming a people by deepening and expanding their faith through a ceaseless process of conversion. My homily should promote that process. But to do that effectively, I must recognize that, at this specific moment in the history of homiletics, I rarely face an audience drooling in anticipation of my message. Even *God's* word on my lips has trouble making it out of the sanctuary.

What keeps God's word from getting through to a congregation or to an individual believer? Obstacle number 1: You are here because you have to be, because Sunday Mass is a serious obligation, because otherwise there's a chance you may blister in hell. Little or no openness here, either to the preacher or to God. With this cast of mind, you don't expect God to speak to you; you want the homily to be short; you are easily distracted; you simply put up with the whole bloody thing; you'd rather be somewhere else, anywhere else. Little wonder Jesuit William O'Malley's sixth commandment for preachers reads: "*Presume disinterest....* [W]hile you are poring over the readings for next Sunday's homily, presume a cold audience. Presume that they would rather feed their children to crocodiles than listen to you."[2]

Obstacle number 2: You approach the liturgy with a prejudice. Prejudice *a*: You don't like the liturgy. The vernacular Mass is for the birds; "To Jesus' Heart All Burning" has been supplanted by "I Wanna Hold Your Hand"; and oh, that kiss of peace! Prejudice *b*: You don't care for sermons. From sheer temperament or Sundays of sickening experience, sermons turn you off. Prejudice *c*: You can't take that priest. He mumbles, rambles, stumbles; or he sports a scraggly beard straight out of the late sixties; or he's a young whip-persnapper still wet behind the ears; or he's old enough to know better. Prejudice *d*: You've had it "up to here" with a Church in politics: bishops sounding off on nuclear arms or withholding taxes in protest, Marxist priests toting Russian rifles in Nicaragua, sisters disbursing tax monies for abortions, ceaseless collections for shiftless minorities.

Obstacle number 3: You come here to be alone with your God. You used to be able to, for you came into a house of God hushed in reverence. Now everything is noise, activity, hustle and bustle, "everybody sing!" You can't even kneel—there aren't any kneelers, no Communion rails, no vigil lights. And the statue of our Lady is straight out of *Glamour*.

Obstacle number 4: You're not going to learn anything. After all, you've had eight to 16 years of Catholic education, and there's nothing new sounding from that pulpit; it's all like a TV repeat. Recently I heard a young priest say to several relatives at dinner: "What did you get out of the bishop's letter at Mass this morning?" "Oh," one replied, "I didn't really listen. It was on abortion, and we know all about that."

Imagine what would happen if you went to *Swan Lake* or to the *Return of the Jedi* in some such frame of mind. Someone made you come; you can't stand Tchaikovsky or George Lucas; you really want to be alone with your psyche; or you know everything there is to know about ballet or outer space. You have to use the ticket, but let no one ask you to like it. Oh, you might accidentally be caught and ravished by the performance; but not likely. You'd be distracted, bored; you'd yawn, pick your nose, sneak looks at your Timex, doze off. You would hardly leave the theatre a different person, uplifted, carried out of your small self. You might even be irritated, resentful, angry.

So with the liturgy, so with the homily. If you come with a grudge or a bias, irritated or indifferent, then I, the homilist, am your enemy. I'm part of the conspiracy: canon law, bishop, pastor, celebrant, preacher. Get the homily over with; get to the Consecration. I'm interrupting your Sunday—sleep or golf, TV or crab feast, whatever. If you were one of the old-timers, you'd sneak out the back for a smoke during the sermon. How can God possibly speak to your heart?

So much for the negative. But almost anyone can analyze what is awry in an attitude; the positive poses the greater problem. What should characterize a Christian congregation if it is to profit from a homily, if it is to hear and respond to the word of God from the lips of a man?

Basic to it all is a living faith. By faith I do not mean simply that you "believe all that the holy Catholic Church teaches," or even simply that you have committed yourself totally to our Lord and Savior. I mean a special something that should flow from this belief, from this commitment. I mean, first, that you come to the Eucharistic celebration because you are convinced that you are about to celebrate the most important social act in Christian history: The Christian community is about to worship its God in the primary way the Lord commanded. Here is the center of divine life, of grace, of forgiveness and conversion, of thanksgiving and praise. Here is where God meets His people as nowhere else. Here is where the New Covenant is confirmed, where we memorialize, as no place else, the death of the Lord until he comes. Here is what Vatican II called "the outstanding means by which the faithful can express in their lives, and manifest to others, the mystery of Christ and the real nature of the true Church."[3] Nothing you do this day, or any day, outstrips in its potential for grace the act you will place in common with your fellow worshipers on that holy spot. Such should be your frame of mind, your mindset.

Within that facet of your faith, within the conviction that in the Eucharistic action God meets His people not exclusively but in privileged fashion, what worshipful attitude is best calculated to let you hear what the Lord is saying, what your Lord wants from you? I suggest . . . openness. The obstacles I have outlined are all features of a closed mind, a closed heart. What is needed is the boy Samuel's response when the Lord called "Samuel! Samuel!" He answered: "Speak, Lord, for your servant is listening" (1 Sam 3:9–10).

The trouble is, such a response is not automatic, is not triggered by some psychological open-sesame. It calls for a faith at once profound and practical. I mean a conviction that, somewhat as God's sacraments work their power in you through the instrumentality of a weak human being, God's word speaks to you through the mouth of even a bungling homilist. I am not contending that everything he says to you, every word he utters however inept or foolish, becomes God's word. I *am* saying that in this fellow's liturgical preaching, God is trying to tell you something.

This is not magic, but neither is the liturgical homily a William Buckley show, where human learning and rhetorical skill, dramatic flair and ready wit, are the highest factors. Here God must be allowed to work His grace. My own homiletic experience humbles me.

Some of the most effective, grace-producing remarks I have emitted are those I was not personally smitten by. "It was so wonderful, Father, when you said 'God loves you.' " Not a particularly original observation. But someone was ready for it, needed it, was open to it.

And remember—at least in my own theory of preaching—you are listening not so much to what *I* have to say as to what *God* has to say through me. Oh yes, you hear me (no way of escaping it); but actually the question is, what is God trying to tell you through my feeble language?

Another way of putting it: You dare not listen to a sermon the way you watch TV, ready to tune out as soon as it gets dull, as soon as *The Edge of Night* loses its soap, or Quincy starts raving and ranting for justice' sake, or Kojak's lollypop gets on your nerves.[4] I am not applauding mediocrity, settling for inferiority. I've been as caustic as the laity in my criticisms, am known to many a reader of religious news for one syndicated sentence: "We homilists mount the pulpit or approach the podium with the imagination of a dead fish." I simply insist that you will miss much of God's own whispering to you if you focus sheerly on the humanity or inhumanity of the preacher.

You may remember the story of Balaam in the Book of Numbers (chap. 22). The Moabites were in deadly fear of the Israelites, newly freed from Egypt, who threatened to overrun them. So Balak, king of Moab, sent for Balaam, a priest-diviner from Mesopotamia, and asked him to lay a curse on the Israelites. Balaam refused to do so, but still went along with the princes of Balak, riding on his ass. Three times the ass refused to go on when an angel with drawn sword would have slain Balaam; three times Balaam struck the ass to make him move ahead. The ass finally spoke to him, rebuked him for his anger and violence. As the popular story saw it, God Himself spoke through Balaam's beast: "The Lord opened the mouth of the ass" (v. 28). Now if God can speak through a harassed ass, He can surely speak through the dullest and most plodding of preachers. Not an ideal, just a fact.

III

All of which leads to my pregnant third point: the preacher. How does a homilist address effectively a congregation composed in large measure of men and women who expect little or nothing from a sermon, or confront him with all sorts of prejudices, or just want to be left alone—Catholic Christians who do not look for their faith to be deepened or expanded, do not anticipate any kind of conversion?

If such you are, I approach you much as I would approach a congregation hanging on my lips, panting in feverish expectation. I approach you as a people of faith, a people drawn here by God—if not quite by Augustine's cords of love. Oh, I know that apathy and bias are obstacles to grace: Teresa of Avila burning with yearning for Christ is richer promise for grace than the three-piece suit wrinkling spastically on the pew, anxious for the whole blessed thing to end. But I do not change an apathetic audience, a prejudiced people, by assailing its apathy, by pummeling its prejudice. I convert by being converted.

What do I mean? Negatively, I mean it is not enough that I preach the gospel by divine or ecclesiastical commission, that I have the right to say to you "Thus says the Lord." This by itself will shake no one's apathy, dispel no one's prejudice, save perhaps the scrupulous or the neurotic. Positively, I mean that, far from occupying a position atop the parish, "far from the madding crowd's ignoble strife" (Thomas Gray), I come through to you as one who shares your struggle—the struggle to become a people, a living community. I am part of the people, part of you. In harmony with my description of a parish, this makes at least three demands on me.

First, it should become clear to you from my preaching that I too am a pilgrim, I too am "on the way." Put another way, when preaching to you I am preaching first to myself. In a sense, this reverses, or at least reinterprets, the ageless homiletic commandment "Know your audience." Of course the people in front of me make a difference. I agree wholeheartedly with Augustine as he speaks of his own catechetical instructions: "It . . . makes a great difference . . . whether there are few present or many; whether learned or unlearned, or a mixed audience made up of both classes; whether they are townsfolk or countryfolk, or both together; or a gathering in which all sorts and conditions of men are represented."[5] Without denying this, I am confessing that I preach most effectively when I am acutely aware of the prophet Nathan's accusation to King David: "You are the man" (2 Sam 12:7).

Let me make this uncommonly concrete. Several years ago I gave the homily during the Holy Thursday liturgy at the Franciscan Renewal Center in Scottsdale, Arizona. The title: "I Have Given You an Example." In the latter half of the homily I asked how we become eucharists for the life of the world. Right where we are, I answered, right where we live. As Jesus did. He did not move past Palestine, did not look to see what he could do for Lebanon. He helped people as they crossed his path, seemed even to choose his special friends as he found them. And so for you and me. The distance, for most of us, is not geographical. People can occupy the same space as we do and still be as far away as the Lebanese or Japanese. We create our own distances. And I went on to say:

> The other day, right out of the blue, I indulged in a fantastic fantasy: "A Day in the Life of Jesus." It begins with breakfast. While his mother is preparing his bagels and cream cheese, Jesus is reading the Jerusalem *Post*—comics first, then the sports pages. A few grunts in response to Mary's tries at conversation, then he bolts a bagel, grabs another on the flight from table, a hurried peck on the cheek with his mouth full—and off he goes to meet the Twelve outside the Sheraton Sinai.
>
> All day long they run across people; people are his job. But the "kitchen cabinet," Peter, James, and John, have their instructions. "Keep the scribes and Pharisees away; they're as bad as *Post* reporters, always trying to catch me in a contradiction. Watch out for that woman who hemorrhages; she'll get blood all over my new tunic. Remember, I don't like Samaritans; they don't like us, and they're just not our kind of folk. If you accept an invitation to dinner, make sure it's with a respectable host like Simon; tax collectors and adulterers give me a bad name. And, for the Lord's sake, don't promise any more cures on the Sabbath; I've had enough trouble with the local officials. When that centurion asks about his sick kid, tell him in a nice way that I'm tied up; better say "overcommitted." By all means, get an SRO crowd for my next sermon, but don't let them touch our boat; and make sure they go home by sundown, else we'll have to send Judas with all our money to the nearest Deli. By the way, John and James, if your mother comes around once more asking seats for you on the dais in my kingdom, I'm going to tell her flat-out to "buzz off." And Peter: I know I agreed to eat at your house tonight. But your mother-in-law has this high fever; she'll want me to sit by her all evening, soothe her burning brow with my cool hand, give her one of those endless blessings. We'll never get to the Manischewitz."
>
> Fantasy? Yes—about Christ. No more than a modest satire about many Christians. I thought it was real funny—till I changed the title to "A Day in the Life of Walter Burghardt." Then, as we youngsters used to say in a simpler age, it was as funny as a rubber crutch.[6]

I am not claiming that, to arouse an audience from apathy or to abate its bias, I have to identify myself expressly as a culprit among culprits. I do claim that, to shape a pilgrim people, I must preach precisely as a pilgrim. Not simply in the secret chambers of my mind, my intention. The pilgrim in me should be palpable to you: I do not stand above you, I sit beside you.

A second demand. I have said that a parish is a group of Catholic Christians who are in process of becoming a people by deepening and expanding their faith. And I insisted that faith is more than the acceptance of propositions. To be genuinely faith-full, you surrender to God and His Christ not only your mind but your whole self. Living faith, loving faith, is a total yes to the total Christ, head and members.

The pertinent point here is this: If liturgical preaching is to contribute to your growth in faith, it is not enough that my *homily* be a resounding call to self-surrender, an eloquent challenge to an unreserved yes. *I* must come through to you as a man of faith. Not indeed without my infidelities; no more than Paul am I "already perfect" (Phil 3:12). And still, what you must sense in my sermon is that these are not disembodied words, syllables floating in space, eternal verities in a Platonic world of ideas. For all my reliance on the word of God, ultimately *I* am the word I preach. Herein lies the power of the word and its weakness. Its power? The Christ who speaks through me. Its weakness? The human vessel through whom Christ has to flow.

Hence the risk, the glorious Christian risk, in any live homily. A cassette is not quite I, not by half. In the assembly you see *me*—every gesture or lack thereof, every change of expression. You hear *me*—not just a voice from the past. In the seeing and the hearing, you touch me, you scrape beneath my skin. Oh yes, if I'm a consummate actor, Laurence Olivier or Woody Allen, I might deceive you. I might spout a message that moves your hearts despite my disbelief, gives life even though I do not live it. But most of us are not such accomplished Thespians. Most of us are open to the devastating remark a very young teen-ager made to his mother on leaving a Sunday Mass: "Mother, I don't think that priest believes what he was saying."

More positively, I am not so much concerned about the ability of a perceptive Christian to see my Christian infidelities. More positively, I have to, I must want to, speak in such a way that this congregation can react: "Wow! He really believes this stuff. He really believes that Jesus is alive and well, that to save your life you have to lose it, that to live humanly you ought to love God above all else, love everyone else as much as you love yourself. The words are flowing from his life; he seems to be suffering to live them."

A third demand. I have said that a parish is a group of Catholic Christians who are in process of becoming a people by deepening and expanding their faith through a ceaseless process of conversion. Conversion. Now conversion, a ceaseless turning to Christ, is not a process which a preacher simply recommends to a needy congregation, somewhat as Johnny Carson might recommend the latest in gentle laxatives. No. When I repeat John the Baptist's "Repent" (Mt 3:2), I ought, like John, to be "preaching in the wilderness" (v. 1). In my wilderness. Calvin Klein may have replaced "camel's hair," a Lacoste belt John's "leather girdle," beef fondue his "locusts and wild honey" (v. 4). Such details, though not impertinent to conversion, can be incidental. What is indispensable, if preaching is to contribute to congregational conversion, is that my homily be part and parcel of my constant turning to Christ. It should proceed from conversion, express conversion, promote conversion.

Not necessarily radical conversion, casting off the slough of deadly sin to be clothed anew in amazing grace. Not so much Augustine's "Your right hand had regard to the profundity of my death and drew out the abyss of corruption that was in the bottom of my heart."[7] More commonly, the slow, sluggish, day-to-day, up-and-down, frustrating effort to grow into Christ, to get to be in his image. Aware of this, experiencing this, I can speak to the heart of a people—strong at times but never harsh, sweetly reasonable but never saccharin. It is my own story my homily should retell, even when that perilous "I" is not pronounced expressly. And that story is most effective when my turning to Christ reflects the conversion experience of the community, when it reproduces daily the prayer of the publican, the toll collector: "Lord, be merciful to me *the* sinner" (Lk 18:13).

It's a liberating experience, believe me. I no longer have to mount the pulpit as one who dwells with God in light inaccessible, remote from "the perils of Pauline" on earth. But genuinely liberating only if, like St. Paul, I continually carry the marks of Christ's passion in my flesh. Only if I share in some way the poverty of the poor to whom I preach so trippingly the poverty of Christ. Only if the love I would have lavished on wife and children is spent on all the loveless and unlovable who cry out to me. Only if my vow of obedience delivers me from a damnable preoccupation with my own wants, my own good pleasure, my own satisfaction, rather than the will of God and the agonizing needs of God's people.

As I close this essay on the preacher and the parish, I realize how little I've said about the "nuts and bolts" of homiletics. It's been with malice aforethought. I see no point in eye contact unless "my eye is sound" (Mt 6:22; Lk 11:34). No sense projecting my voice if my sound waves are disembodied. No use constructing a classical sentence if the phrases are not charged with the Christ in me.

The view from the pew may be jaundiced in part, colored by all manner of morbidity. And that's a problem indeed. But what our parishioners see in the pulpit is not quite as important for the parish as what they do *not* see. Too often, I fear, they do not see a pilgrim who walks beside them, a man of faith who loves God and them with a crucifying passion, a constant convert reaching out to touch the hem of Jesus' garment.

To help fashion a parish after the mind of Christ, we have a long way to walk—preacher and parishioner. I have only one exhortation: Let's walk together.

ADVENT

1

HOPE FOR THE HUNGRY?
First Sunday of Advent (B)

- Isaiah 63:16–17, 19; 64:2–7
- 1 Corinthians 1:3–9
- Mark 13:33–37

Dear friends in Christ: I come before you today perplexed—perplexed by a paradox. A paradox, you know, is an apparent contradiction. My particular paradox this Christian season is simple to state: Advent is a season of hope, and I—I am profoundly discouraged. Not to keep you in unbearable suspense, let me develop three motifs: the hope that is Advent, the discouragement that is mine, and the solution that is Christ.

I

First, the hope that is Advent. Advent is a wreath of evergreen, symbol of life, of growth, of hope. It's the overture to the Church's year. The theme, the focus, is salvation. Not some abstract, flimsy pie-in-the-sky. The message is startling: God Himself will come to save.

To recapture that truth, the liturgy rushes us back 2500 years, back to Isaiah and the Exile. We experience the expectation of Israel. Jerusalem and its temple are in ruins; thousands have been deported to Babylonia, must live amid false gods. The community is politically impotent; its public worship is emasculated; its sacrifice is a thing of the past. And still they keep their faith alive, their hope, their identity, their consciousness of continuity—more alive than do their brothers and sisters back home in Jerusalem. God will come, will return them to sacred soil.

Half a century later, God does just that. But what do the exiles return to? Brothers and sisters who have changed, practice nature cult and fertility cult, burn incense to idols, consult the dead, eat the forbidden flesh of swine; and still no temple. Even here Isaiah[1] preaches hope. Life is discouraging, yes; but remember, your hope lies not in inconstant man and woman but in God, a Yahweh for ever faithful. So, confess your sins and proceed with confidence to the task at hand. A glorious future beckons. "The Lord will be your everlasting light, and your God will be your glory" (Isa 60:19). From Sion shall come forth salvation for all the world.

The Advent liturgy cuts back to a little town named Nazareth. We experience the expectation of teen-age Mary. She too is waiting in hope, waiting for the Promised One to come. But not like any other Jew, peering anxiously into a clouded future, sure that salvation is coming but unsure how. For Mary, the salvation for which she is waiting is nestling within her, a living fetus in her flesh. Her hope is simply that she will bring salvation to birth, wrap him in swaddling clothes, offer him to you and me.

The Advent liturgy flashes back to a prison cell in Palestine. We experience the expectation of John the Baptist. He too is living in hope, but the hope is shadowed by confusion. He has heard about "the deeds of the Christ" (Mt 11:2), but where is the fiery social reformer the prophets have led him to expect? The Jews still chafe under the heel of Rome; the poor still lie like Lazarus at the gates of the rich; sickness and death refuse to take a holiday. Perplexed, John sends his own disciples to ask Jesus: "Are you he-who-is-to-come [the Messiah], or shall we look for another?" (v. 3). Jesus opens John's eyes, invites him to compare what he sees and hears with the prophecy of Isaiah: "The blind receive their sight and the lame walk, lepers are cleansed and the deaf hear, the dead are raised up and the poor have good news preached to them" (v. 5). No need to look for another; hope is here. Hope is . . . Jesus.

II

An incredible hope, this hope that is Advent: God Himself will come to save His people. For four weeks we shall relive that anxious expectation: Israel waiting, Mary waiting, the Baptist waiting. We shall relive that expectation, but with a difference. We know that hope has come. Our hope was born in Bethlehem, sealed with the kiss of Mary. Bethlehem tells us that the Christ who came to earth in a feeding trough comes now to our hearts, tells us that he will come again, tomorrow or a thousand years hence, to take us to himself for ever.

Why, then, am I discouraged? Why has my hope been shaken? Very simply, because 20 centuries after hope was born, for uncounted millions hope is dead. I shall not speak of the unspeakable numbers whose hope has perished in the ruins of war. I shall not speak of the 50 million in a given year whose hope is literally aborted. I shall target only one enemy of hope. I mean . . . hunger.

Ten years ago, then Secretary of State Henry Kissinger delivered a message of hope to the World Food Conference in Rome:

> The profound promise of our era is that for the first time we may have the technical capacity to free mankind from the scourge of hunger. Therefore, today we must proclaim a bold objective— that within a decade no child will go to bed hungry, that no family will fear for its next day's bread and that no human being's future and capacities will be stunted by malnutrition.[2]

The ten years have come and gone. On the African continent more than 150 million men, women, and children face starvation. 150 million—almost two thirds of the U.S. population. In a single country, Ethiopia, six million are existing on the edge of starvation; a million may die this year alone; 16 million are malnourished; over two million have left home to search for food. "You can tell," said a British nurse of Bati children, "who will live and who will die. The dying ones have no light left in their eyes."[3] Where is their Advent, where their hope?

Across the world, the number of people seriously malnourished has been put at 500 million; some say a billion. Each day 40,000 children die from diseases related to hunger, diseases we know how to prevent: diarrhea and diphtheria, measles and polio. And do you know how many children will die in the Third World this year? 21 million—equal to all the children under five in the United States.[4] Where is their Advent, where their hope?

And you know, you need not jet to Africa to uncover bellies bloated by hunger. In our own land of plenty, one out of every four children under the age of six is living in poverty.[5] Not starving perhaps, but growing up dangerously—mind and heart and flesh—on the deficient diet of the poor.

My friends, this is not a "secular" issue, divorced from the love of God preachers are expected to proclaim. The skin-and-bones child on TV, eyes blank, tongue limp and dry, is not just hungry, simply starving. He has *no* hope. He is not just stunted intellectually; he will never hear the Word of God. He is not simply starved for bread; he will never taste our Supper. He will share Christ's cross without ever having known his love.

III

So then, Advent is hope, but hope is far from the hungry of our world. The solution? It falls easily from our lips. The solution is . . . Christ. After all, he is the hope of *all* humankind; in him, as we shall sing at Christmas, "the hopes and fears of all the years are met." So, he will take care of the hungry in his own inimitable way. Not much *I* can do about it. And since I did not dry up the sub-Sahara, don't hang a guilt trip on me. Don't spoil my Christmas.

I'm afraid it will not wash; the solution is not that simple. The solution is indeed Christ, but not Christ in glorious isolation, at the right hand of the Father. Christ does not rain down manna from heaven on starving refugees; he no longer multiplies loaves and fishes. And it's a cop-out to mouth the Beatitude "Blessed are you that hunger now, for you *shall* be satisfied" (Lk 6:21). The problem is . . . now. There has to be "good news" for the hungry now.

The solution is the whole Christ, head and members. Unless *we* act, the most effective solution to hunger is our present solution: death. The hungry die. But for every one who dies, two will be born hungry. The hungry must have hope.

I know, hope is not a promise of middle-class prosperity. Christ did not promise a chicken in every pot and a two-car garage for every family. But he did expect that life would be human enough so that every child could grow up to think about him and love him. He did expect that we would feed the hungry and slake their thirst. He did expect the hopeful to lend hope to the hopeless. In fact, he said that our own hope, our own salvation, depends on whether we do or not.

The problem, of course, is what to do; world hunger baffles the experts. I do not come to you with answers; theology does not make arid lands fertile, prevent droughts, distribute grain to rural areas. But this I do say: Unless we whose bellies are full make hunger a priority in our lives, a quarter of the world may perish.

We dare not lay the burden or the blame on governments alone. Still, I am dismayed when I discover that not a single world leader "has given consistent public attention to the problem of hunger in the past decade."[6] I am distressed when I find that in 1980 a Presidential Commission on World Hunger recommended that "the United States Government make the elimination of hunger the primary focus of its relationship with the developing countries," and four years later a high Agriculture official whose job it is to know admitted "he was unaware of the report's existence."[7] I bleed when I read that governments play politics with bread.

But democracies will not act if their people are indifferent, are not disturbed, furious, up in arms. And I ask myself: Is it true what sociologists tell us—that 19th-century rugged individualism is on the loose again in our land, that a new "me generation" has sprung up, that a primary passion between 18 and 25 is money, that Catholics, who claim Africans as sisters and brothers in one body, are no different in their priorities than their unbelieving neighbors? I ask myself: Do I really believe what Jesus said—that this child with flies buzzing about her carcass is Christ?

Much is indeed being done by Christians. In the District, on Rhode Island Avenue, Bread for the World has for ten years kept hunger alive in the halls of Congress. 45,000 U.S. Christians, 600 churches, fuel its efforts. From Cambodia's hunger through Somalia and Ethiopia to America itself, these Christians committed to Advent hope have goaded Congress and galvanized it, move it to alter its priorities, urge it to spend less on weapons and more on people. Christians are coming awake. The agonizing question is: Is it too little and too late?

My friends, do you want to live Advent? Then *be* Advent. Be a sign of hope to the hopeless. Today's Gospel warns us to be alert, on watch for the Messiah. Don't look for him in a Christmas crib; he left that 20 centuries ago. He's heaving dry on the dried-up soil of the sub-Sahara.

Dahlgren Chapel
Georgetown University
and
Holy Trinity Church
Washington, D.C.
December 2, 1984

LENT

2

YOU ARE DUST
Ash Wednesday

> ♦ Joel 2:12–18
> ♦ 2 Corinthians 5:20—6:2
> ♦ Matthew 6:1–6, 16–18

Lent is something of a paradox, a seeming contradiction. One part of the paradox protrudes today. When I cross your head with ashes, one of the formulas the Church recommends is: "Remember, man, you are dust and to dust you will return." That body of yours, man, that body you pamper with pizza and Pabst, that's gonna crumble, man; you'd better believe it, and start making with the tears. And yet, during next Sunday's liturgy, the priest will open the Preface with: "Father, all-powerful and ever-living God, . . . each year you give us this joyful season." This joyful season. Well, which is it to be? Will the real Lent kindly emerge from the closet? Are you supposed to weep and mourn with the prophet Joel or give ear to Jesus, douse your face with Dove, slap on some Brut or Chanel N° 5, and come out smelling like Joe Namath or Brooke Shields?

The paradox is real, but you do not solve it with an either/or, by eliminating one panel of the paradox. As with any good paradox, so with the paradox that is Lent: The solution is a both/and. Both sorrow and joy; tears and laughter. In a word, the paschal mystery: dying/rising, intertwined. Let's see how it works out, by plumbing the twin symbols on your forehead: dust and the sign of the cross.[1]

I

The first symbol: dust. The formula stems from Genesis, God's judgment on humanity after His first human images have rejected Him: "In the sweat of your face you shall eat bread till you return

27

to the ground, for out of it you were taken; you are dust and to dust you will return" (Gen 3:19). It's an image that dots the Old Testament: the Psalms, Ecclesiastes, Job. Even Abraham, "father of a multitude of nations" (Gen 17:4), pleads with the Lord for Sodom from the stance of Adam: "I who am but dust and ashes" (Gen 18:27).

But what does the symbol symbolize? What does dust say to us? With his uncommon insight, the German theologian Karl Rahner phrased it starkly:

> Dust . . . is the image of the commonplace. There is always more than enough of it. One fleck is as good as the next. Dust is the image of anonymity: one fleck is like the next, and all are nameless.
>
> It is the symbol of indifference: what does it matter whether it is this dust or that dust? It is all the same. Dust is the symbol of nothingness: because it lies around so loosely, it is easily stirred up, it blows around blindly, is stepped upon and crushed—and nobody notices. It is a nothing that is just enough to be—a nothing. Dust is the symbol of coming to nothing: it has no content, no form, no shape; it blows away, the empty, indifferent, colorless, aimless, unstable booty of senseless change, to be found everywhere, and nowhere at home.[2]

Now precisely this is what God says to me: "You are dust." It is not the only thing God says to me; He does not say I am only dust. What else He says we shall see shortly. But to understand what else He says, to grasp it in all its glory, I have to accept, experience, endure the dust I am. Like dust, I'm commonplace. I'm ordinary. I'm Scripture's blade of grass, puff of wind. I'm a speck in the universe. I'm one of uncounted billions who have blown about this planet. If a handful of people see me as different—keen mind, rich voice, deep tan—a billion Chinese have never heard my name. And if they did hear it, they couldn't care less.

Each day I experience my dust. From the moment I struggled from my mother's flesh, I've been in process of dying. I'm a creature of pain: From adolescent acne through malignant growth to senile forgetfulness, I sense how near to nothing I am. I'm a creature of sin: not always sinning but blowing hot and cold, dreadfully small, wrapt in the strait jacket of my selfishness, desperately far from the God I ought to love above life itself. I'm so anxious, so perplexed: about myself, about people, about life—frequently losing my way, often adrift like the dust I cannot capture.

Is it any wonder that, for all too many, despair is just around the corner? Little wonder the French novelist Georges Bernanos could say it is not easy for man not to hate himself.

II

Pretty grim, isn't it? Only if you stop there; only if you stop with the symbol that is dust. But that symbol is incomplete. When I dust your forehead, I dust it with another symbol: the sign of the cross. And that symbol declares that dust has been redeemed. Redeemed not in some shadowy sense but with startling realism. The sign of the cross tells us that, in taking flesh, the Son of God became dust, that save for sin his dust was the same as ours. It tells us that, in an outrageous reversal, we can say to God's Son what God told us in Paradise: "You are dust and to dust you will return." His dust was as short-lived, as fleeting, as ours. For a few brief years his feet scuffed the dust of Palestine; his sweat bloodied the dust of Gethsemane; with a last loud cry his body joined ours in the dust of death.

Precisely here is the bone and marrow of our belief; here joy transmutes sorrow, ecstasy weds pain, as nowhere else in history. When God's Son became the dust we are and nailed it to a cross, God's judgment "You are dust" was transformed. I do not mean that you cease to be dust. You will always be men and women of flesh and blood. You can expect to experience in every fiber of your being the anguish, the tears, the daily dying, the sense of nothingness that fragile dust can never quite escape. The new thing, the redeeming feature, is that the Son of God experienced every bit of that—for us. And so, ever since Bethlehem and Calvary, this speck of humanity that is you, this is now "charged with the grandeur of God."[3] You are brothers and sisters of God-in-flesh. Your dust is literally electric with God's own life; your nothingness is filled with God's eternity. Your nothingness has Christ's own shape.

With this new shape, the sentence "You are dust and to dust you will return" ought no longer terrify us. We no longer have to despair at our ceaseless downward movement to death. Of course we shall die; and I, for one, am not anxious to die—I love this life with a passion that is perhaps unchristian. But the sign of the cross cries to us that death is not the end of our dust. The cross is indeed a sign. It signifies what Paul proclaimed without ceasing: "If the Spirit of Him who raised Jesus from the dead dwells in you, He who raised Christ Jesus from the dead will give life to your mortal bodies also through His Spirit which dwells in you" (Rom 8:11).

So then, back to our original question. Is Lent for laughter or for tears? Lent is for laughter *and* for tears. Lent plays out, in memory and in symbol, what the whole of Christian living is all about. It is a dying/rising. Not simply at the end of your days; all your days. On the one hand, you must journey to Jerusalem with Jesus. It is a journey that mingles gladness and sadness, satisfaction and frustration, high hopes and sometimes near despair. On the other hand, you walk that dusty journey with Jesus, and you walk it as risen Christians. You don't wait for Easter to rise with Christ; you don't wait for your very last death. You have risen! From the moment that water flowed over your forehead in the shape of a cross, the life of the risen Christ has been thrilling through your dust like another bloodstream. You can be incredibly alive—if you will only let yourself feel that life, live it.

For your Lenten penance, therefore, force yourself to come alive—alive in Christ. Focus on those twin symbols. When you leave here to continue your journey to Jerusalem, wear those symbols with awareness, with pride, with hope, with love. Even when the dust disappears, remember the reality: Remember, man/woman, remember that you are dust—dust redeemed by a cross.

Dahlgren Chapel
Georgetown University
Washington, D.C.
February 20, 1985

3

LIVING WATER OR MILLER LITE?
Third Sunday of Lent (A)

+ Exodus 17:3–7
+ Romans 5:1–2, 5–8
+ John 4:5–42

I suspect you are puzzled by today's Gospel. Here it is the third Sunday of Lent, and what do we hear? A conversation between Jesus and a woman with five husbands. A setting bizarre enough for a Fellini film. Or a splendid spot for a homily on woman in the Church: "[The disciples] marveled that he was talking with a woman" (Jn 4:27). But what has this to do with Lent?

We have much to learn from today's liturgy: much to learn about Lent, about Jesus, about ourselves. Three points right there! First, what is Lent all about? Second, how does the Gospel of the Samaritan woman fit into this understanding of Lent? Third, what does Lent's Samaritan woman say to us?

I

First, what is Lent all about? For some Christians, it means you turn sad for 40 days. From the ashes on your forehead ("Remember, man, you're dust and, man, you're gonna be dust again") to the anguished cry of Christ on the cross ("My God, my God, why have you forsaken me?"), Lent is a downer. You're dirt and God will die. So, get all the joy, all the beer, all the sex out of your system by Mardi gras, "fat Tuesday," because for 40 days you're supposed to be a sad sack.

For liturgy and for living, this is nonsense. The first Preface for Lent proclaims "this joyful season." We dare not divide the paschal mystery into a season of dying (Lent) and a season of rising (Easter).

31

Indeed there was a chronological sequence to the events in Jesus' life. But to stress the history is to miss the mystery. Jesus Christ is risen; even in Lent we may not pretend he has not. Lent is our increasingly intense initiation into the *whole* paschal mystery—and that is the mystery of dying/rising: his and ours. One mystery: life in and through death.

Each Sunday Gospel this Lent plays on that theme, but with different images. First Sunday: the desert (Mt 4:1–11). The biblical desert was at once a "terrible wilderness" (Deut 1:19) where death was ever a threat *and* the place where the people of God was born. It was the locus of testing and suffering, but also of discovery and covenant, of intimacy and love and new life. "I will allure her," the Lord said of Israel, "and bring her into the wilderness, and speak tenderly to her" (Hos 2:14). Here a hungry Jesus told the tempter what makes for life: "not bread alone . . . but every word" that God speaks (Mt 4:4).

Last Sunday: the Transfiguration (Mt 17:1–9). On the journey of death, Jesus is revealed as the man of life. On the death march, the disciples glimpse his glory. But they miss the death/life duality. Not on this mountain, Peter, do you set up your condo—not till you've mounted the hill of Calvary.

Next Sunday: darkness and light—the man born blind (Jn 9:1–41). Hopelessly sightless, sight is given him. The second reading, from Paul to the Ephesians, will express the miracle's deeper meaning: "Once you were darkness, but now you are light in the Lord" (Eph 5:8).

The fifth Sunday: Lazarus "dead four days" called from death's cave (Jn 11:1–45). Here you have dying/rising in its supreme paradox, the promise of Jesus: "I am the resurrection and the life; he who believes in me, though he die, yet shall he live, and whoever lives and believes in me shall never die" (vv. 25–26).

So, too, for the sixth Sunday, Passion/Palm Sunday (Mt 21:1–11; 26:14—27:66). Not palms *or* passion; both. Not triumph *or* tragedy; triumph *in* tragedy. Not a dying *or* a rising Christ; a dying/rising Christ. Life leaps *from* death.

II

Which brings me to my second point: today's Gospel. How does the Samaritan woman fit into Lent, into dying/rising? As on the other Sundays, so here: an image, a striking image, for the life that comes through death. When the woman wonders aloud how a Jew can ask a Samaritan for water, Jesus responds: "If you knew the gift of God, and who it is that is saying to you 'Give me a drink,' you would have asked him, and he would have given you living water" (Jn 4:10).

But what does the image mean? What is this "living water," water that slakes your thirst forever, that becomes in you "a spring of water welling up to eternal life" (v. 14). In John's theology two thrilling ideas come together here: Living water is the revelation Jesus gives us, and living water is the Spirit Jesus gives us.[1]

Water as symbol for God's life-giving wisdom has rich biblical roots. Listen to Proverbs: "The teaching of the wise is a fountain of life, that one may avoid the snares of death" (Prov 13:14). Listen to Yahweh inviting men and women to hear, that their souls might live: "All you who thirst, come to the waters" (Isa 55:1; cf. v. 3). Listen to Wisdom singing her own praises: "Those who eat me will hunger for more, and those who drink me will thirst for more" (Sir 24:21). Read the Dead Sea Scrolls: The Jewish law is "living water."[2] In this context Jesus can well call his own revelation "living water"; for in John Jesus is divine Wisdom in flesh and he replaces the law.

If you would see living water as the Spirit Jesus gives us, recall his impassioned outburst to the people: "If anyone thirst, let him come to me and drink. He who believes in me, as the Scripture has said, 'Out of his heart shall flow rivers of living water.' Now this [John adds] he said about the Spirit, which those who believed in him were to receive" (Jn 7:37–39).

In sum, living water is at once the life-giving word of God Jesus speaks and the Spirit of truth who interprets the word Jesus speaks. This is what Jesus calls "the gift of God" (Jn 4:10).

Now this story of living water is a drama about faith: John dramatizes how an individual and a community come to believe in Jesus. As always, the Lord takes the initiative. He speaks, and a woman begins to sip living water—without knowing it. In the power of the Spirit, she is hearing God's word—without knowing it. Not yet does she know who Jesus is. She knows only that "Messiah is coming" (v. 25)—for her, the prophet-like-Moses promised of old (cf. Deut 18:15). Jesus asserts flatly: "I who speak to you am he" (v. 26). He even uses of himself the venerable title of divinity: "I am."

Still not sure who Jesus is, the woman rushes from the well to the city, crying breathlessly to all she meets: "Come, see a man who told me all that I ever did. Can this be the Christ?" (v. 29). Not certainty, but a touch of hope. And the drama of belief expands. Someone who knows everything this much-married woman ever did? The citizens of Sychar hasten to the well to see this prodigy for themselves. Seeing, they ask him "to stay with them"; he stays "two days" (v. 40). Many of the Samaritans have already believed in him on the woman's witness; "many more" believe "because of *his* word . . . : 'we have heard for ourselves, and we know that this is indeed the Savior of the world' " (vv. 41–42).

III

My third point: What does Lent's Samaritan woman say to us? I recommend two responses. First, it is not only Samaritans who should recognize Jesus and ask him for living water. Every man and woman must; you and I must. Oh yes, you have already tasted it; otherwise you would not be here. You have been touched by God's word, and the Holy Spirit lives in you. Well then, preacher, what more do you want of us? Lots more.

You see, most of us have only *sipped* God's living water; few thirst for it the way they thirst for a Miller Lite. For Lent, try this one-question quiz: What are you thirsty for? If you can trust a survey in *Psychology Today,* a central passion between 18 and 25 is money. If you can credit your peers, you worry about it, fantasize about it, much of the time, think of it more than you think of work or family.[3] But if it's not money that turns you on, what does? Michael Jackson or Chrissy Hine, Bob's ice cream or Armand's pizza, Hoya hoops? No protest there from my theology—only from fragile ears and a spastic colon. But my Christian sense does protest when the Son of God, in history's most amazing act of love, is nailed to a bloody cross for us, and we—we are so bored that we fling frisbees on Good Friday.

Somehow the Christ who mesmerized the woman at the well must grab us, turn us on. It's not a matter of academic knowledge: He is God's Son as no other is Son, very God in our flesh. Good, but not enough. Not enough for a disciple. You must know *him,* not only *about* him. I mean the knowledge that is love—the kind of love you experience when you want to surrender all else in wild abandon. The type of love that links two persons—where your whole being, flesh and spirit, thrills to the presence of the other. The sort of love the Psalmist sang:

> As a hart longs
>   for flowing streams,
> so longs my soul
>   for thee, O God.
> My soul thirsts for God,
>   for the living God.
>   (Ps 42:1–2)

What earlier Christians called a "divine and sober intoxication." Holy Roller stuff? Not at all; just living water. If this has not been your drink, spend the rest of Lent asking for it. "If you knew the gift of God . . . you would have asked him [Jesus], and he would have given you living water" (Jn 4:10). Ask!

A second suggestion. The Samaritan woman did not hide her living water in some private, do-not-touch water jar. She "left her water jar," jetted back to the city, grabbed everyone she spied: "Come, see" this amazing man! Could be he's the prophet we've been waiting for. The consequence? The Gospel is clear: "Many Samaritans from that city believed in him because of the woman's testimony" (v. 39). The point is, she became an apostle. I mean, she brought the message of Jesus to the people she knew; she shared with them her own experience of him; she urged them to go see for themselves. They went; they brought him back with them; they spent two days in his company; they heard the word from his very lips; and many believed. Because of her.

Do I want you to drop what you're doing, go back to Bayonne or Bayamón, and buttonhole your friends: "Come and see"? Not quite; not yet. I do regret that on the lips of many Catholics "Jesus Christ" is more likely to be a cuss word than a source of living water. I wish you felt as free to talk about Jesus as thousands of young Mormon missionaries do. But naked words will rarely move the human heart. I suspect that what impelled the Samaritans pell-mell to the well was not simply the woman's confession, he "told me all that I ever did." Over and above that, something had happened to her; she had changed; she was different. This woman with five husbands had all the excitement, all the glow, of someone who has fallen in love for the first time.

And so for you. Apostles you must be, but in the mold of Mother Teresa. A woman of few words, she speaks Christ most powerfully when her arms open literally to the world's unwanted children, when she cradles one of them and a smile of unbearable bliss caresses each wrinkle on that careworn face. She has drunk deeply of living water; she lives each day the dying/rising of her Lord.

My friends, when you ask for living water, you are taking a giant risk. It's not like giving up Spritzers or Doritos for Lent; you're asking God to change you, to transform you in the image of His Christ, to redirect your tomorrow on to roads you cannot map. If that frightens you, I commend to you an episode in Graham Greene's novel *Monsignor Quixote*.[4] It is a bit of dialogue, in a Spanish monastery church, between an American professor and a Trappist monk. Professor Pilbeam confesses:

> "I haven't read Cervantes since I was a boy. Too fanciful for my taste. I haven't much time for fiction. Facts are what I like. . . . Now you, Father Leopoldo, you are a student of Descartes. That's hardly likely to open many doors for you. What brought you here?"
>
> "I suppose Descartes brought me to the point where he brought himself—to faith. Fact or fiction—in the end you can't distinguish between them—you just have to choose."
>
> "But to become a Trappist?"
>
> "I think you know, professor, that when one has to jump, it's so much safer to jump into deep water."

It's so much safer to jump into deep water. . . .

Dahlgren Chapel
Georgetown University
and
Holy Trinity Church
Washington, D.C.
March 25, 1984

4

LAUGH WITH ME!
Fifth Sunday of Lent (A)

♦ Ezekiel 37:12–14
♦ Romans 8:8–11
♦ John 11:1–45

On the fifth Sunday of Lent each year, I raise a glass to playwright Eugene O'Neill. Not for Pulitzer-winning *Anna Christie;* not for the brutal *Desire under the Elms;* not for the pessimistic *Iceman.* Rather for a lesser play, muddled in many ways but with an unexpected insight. It deals with the life of Lazarus after the Son of God has summoned him from the grave. O'Neill called his play *Lazarus Laughed.* It is the story of a lover of Christ who has tasted death and sees it for what it is—the story of a man whose one invitation to all is his constant refrain:

> Laugh with me!
> Death is dead!
> Fear is no more!
> There is only life!
> There is only laughter![1]

And O'Neill tells us: Lazarus "begins to laugh, softly at first," then full-throated—"a laugh so full of a complete acceptance of life, a profound assertion of joy in living, so devoid of all fear, that it is infectious with love," so infectious that, despite themselves, his listeners are caught by it and carried away.

At the root of O'Neill's play lies John's Gospel just proclaimed. From that Gospel O'Neill has captured dramatically a Christian truth that Martha recognized, but he has failed to capitalize on a corresponding reality that Martha herself missed. In consequence, three stages to my homily. First, what is it that lies clearly before our eyes—the obvious lesson, the patent truth, of the Lazarus story? Second, what is Jesus saying on a deeper level—the reality even dear Martha failed to grasp? Third, what might the risen Lazarus say to you and me now—especially as Lent draws on to Easter, and we move more and more intensively into the paschal mystery, the mystery of dying/rising?

I

First, what is the Lazarus story obviously about? Recall the basic facts. A dear friend of Jesus falls ill. His sisters send word to Jesus: "Lord, he whom you love is ill" (Jn 11:3). What does Jesus do? Speed to Bethany and heal his friend? As he had healed the military officer's son, the paralytic, the hemorrhaging woman, lepers, Peter's fever-ridden mother-in-law—a hundred others he hardly knew? Against all our expectations, he delays two days. Finally he goes, only to find that his friend has been in his tomb four days. Lazarus' sister Martha is more than a little upset: "Lord, if you had been here, my brother would not have died" (v. 21). And some of the grieving Jews are not particularly impressed by Jesus' tears: "Could not he who opened the eyes of the blind man have kept this man from dying?" (v. 37).

But Jesus' love for Lazarus goes beyond what his sisters had been silently asking: "Don't let him die." That love is revealed in the dialogue with Martha. Jesus: "Your brother will rise again." Martha: "I know that he will rise again in the resurrection on the last day." Jesus: "*I* am the resurrection . . . ; he who believes in me, even if he dies, will come to life . . ." (v. 25). Yes indeed, the believer too will go to the grave, as surely as the unbeliever. But the life that Jesus gives through the Spirit will conquer sheer physical death. As Paul put it to the Christians of Corinth, "When the perishable puts on the imperishable, and the mortal puts on immortality, then shall come to pass the saying that is written: 'Death is swallowed up in victory.' 'O death, where is your victory? O death, where is your sting?' " (1 Cor 15:54–55; cf. Isa 25:8; Hos 13:14).

After the dialogue, a sign and a promise. As a sign of his power to give eternal life, and as a promise that on the last day he will raise our mortal flesh, Jesus calls Lazarus back to this life, to physical life, to life in Bethany, to life with Martha and Mary: "Lazarus, come out!" (v. 43). And out Lazarus comes, to eat and drink, to dance and weep, to play and pray, to believe and hope and love—living witness to Jesus' astonishing claim "I am the resurrection. . . ."

II

If this were all, it would surely be enough: to rise from the dead and share God's life forever. But there is something still deeper, even more remarkable. More remarkable than resurrection unto eternal life? Isn't this our Christian hope? Isn't this what Paul proclaimed with such passion: "If for this life only we have hoped in Christ, we are of all men and women most to be pitied" (1 Cor 15:19)?

Yes, of course! But there is much more to our Christian hope than dying at eight or 80 and rising again like Lazarus. To Martha Jesus said not simply "I am the resurrection" but "I am the resurrection and the life." Not only "he who believes in me, even if he dies, will come to life," but "everyone who is alive [in me] and believes in me shall never die" (vv. 25–26).[2] *Never* die? Exactly. Never? Uh-huh. Never.

But how can this be? You just said that even the believer must bite the dust. Not a jesuitical contradiction, only a thrilling Christian mystery. Eternal life does not begin with death; eternal life has its beginning now. That is why Jesus consoled a mourning Martha as he did. He was not satisfied with her belief in *another* life, her conviction that her dead brother would "rise again in the resurrection on the last day." Jesus not only *has* life, he *is* life—because the Holy Spirit, that Spirit who gives life, is his Spirit; and this Spirit, this life, this Spirit of life, he gives to us. Now. In Jesus' teaching, in Christian believing, I die the death that ultimately matters, spiritual death, only if and when the Spirit of life leaves me. Eternal death is not separation of soul from body, but separation of soul from God. That is why, at the very moment Jesus "bowed his head and handed over his spirit [to the Father]" (Jn 19:30), he was gloriously alive, because the Spirit of life, the Holy Spirit, was still and forever his Spirit, his life.

This is not pious pap, not abstract theology for ivory-tower theologians. This is the most significant facet, the pith and marrow, of your Christian existence. Eternal life is not simply a gift you hope for, yearn for, the life you *will* live beyond the grave. Eternal life is the life you are living now, if through love you and God are one. For to be one with God is not the same as being one with a lover on earth, however intimate that oneness. When you are one with God, there is a presence of God to you so incredibly close that to express it the Son of God Himself had to resort to a metaphor. If you love me, he promised, my Father will love you, and we will come to you and make our "home" with you (cf. Jn 14:23).

This is the beginning of eternal life. It is life because a new Principle of being and acting has been given you; it is eternal in that the Principle is literally divine. You share in the very life that God lives. Not that you live a double life, natural and supernatural. No, human spirit and divine Spirit are marvelously intertwined in you, a bit like the divine and human in the one person that is Jesus Christ. In consequence, you are a different person—so different that Paul dares to call you "a new creation" (2 Cor 5:17). You have a fresh dignity: daughter of God or son of God, by gracious adoption what Christ is by very nature, with his life coursing through you like another bloodstream. And because you *are* different, you can *act* differently, on a level utterly human yet above the human. You can believe as Jesus believed: I mean, you can surrender all you are to the Father without reserve. You can hope as Jesus hoped: I mean, you can confidently expect God from God from here to eternity. You can love as Jesus loved: I mean, you can love God above all else, love man and woman as you love your own self. And all this *now!*

III

This leads with fair logic to my third point: What might the risen Lazarus say to you and me now—especially as these next two weeks involve us ever more intensely in the mystery of dying/rising? I suggest he would repeat the refrain O'Neill put on his lips:

> Laugh with me!
> Death is dead!
> Fear is no more!
> There is only life!
> There is only laughter!

I would only add: You and I can echo that refrain with deeper understanding than O'Neill's Lazarus could command; for the Lazarus who laughed is terribly confused and confusing about his risen life—perhaps because his playwright was a morose stoic for whom "man's fate is in his genes and hormones," who "could be counted on to find the worm in the apple of life."[3] But you and I know why "death is dead": Christ has conquered death by his own dying/rising. You and I know why "fear is no more": for "neither death nor life nor angels nor principalities nor things present nor things to come nor powers nor height nor depth nor anything else in all creation will be able to separate us from the love of God in Christ Jesus our Lord" (Rom 8:38–39). You and I know why "there is only life": Right now our spirits are aquiver with the life of the risen Christ. You and I know why "there is only laughter": because Christian laughter is not hysteria, not a belly explosion over a vulgar joke, but sheer joy in living, in coming alive.

The trouble is, few live fully the logic of that divine life. Here we are, men and women who are shrines of the Holy Spirit, men and women whose Principle of life is a dancing God, Life itself, Love divine, and we resemble a leading character in O'Neill's *The Great God Brown*: "Why am I afraid to dance, I who love music and rhythm and grace and song and laughter? Why am I afraid to live, I who love life and the beauty of flesh and the living colors of earth and sky and sea? Why am I afraid of love, I who love love?"[4]

Oh, I know you do dance, you are alive, you do love—but in the power of the Spirit? Believe me, I marvel at your rock and roll, I envy your vitality, I am moved beyond telling by the love of man and maid. What distresses me is that so many seem insensible to the Power that hides within you, the Spirit that needs only your yes to be released, to charge your acre of the world with God's own energy, to change you from a fair-to-middling Christian to a Paul or an Augustine, a Teresa of Avila or a Teresa of Calcutta.

As I near the biblical 70, there is one wish for you I cherish above all others. I wish you knew how special you are. I want you to experience a joy, a thrill, a satisfaction in God's presence within you that rivals what you feel when you fall in love, when you score a 4.0, when the Fighting Irish reach the N.I.T. finals, when you quaff for the first time "Molson madness." It will not dampen your natural ardor, put a lid on your native happiness; it will only intensify it. And it will inject a Christian sense into the sadness, the darkness, the tragedy that shadow human existence; for it will keep you from turning stoic or cynic, from sheer resignation to evil and adversity you can do little or nothing about. You won't spin helplessly between manic and depressive like a human Yo-yo.

My friends, only if the Spirit within you is a living force can you shape your lives along Christian lines, along the lines of a dying/rising Christ. Only in the power of the Spirit can you respond with a resounding "Yes!" to the question the Lord asked Ezekiel: "Son of man, can these [dry] bones live?" (Ezek 37:3). Only in pulsing consciousness of the Spirit will you learn and live the paschal mystery, its pith and marrow: *Life leaps from death*—from the death of the God-man and from your own ceaseless dying to sin and self. Only if you surrender to the Spirit without condition or reservation— "Lord of life, do with me what you will"—can you expect to exult "Death is dead, fear is no more." Only then will your laughter be Lazarus-like, full-throated, "a laugh so full of a complete acceptance of life, a profound assertion of joy in living, so devoid of all fear, that it [will be] infectious with love," so infectious that, despite themselves, those who hear it will be caught by it, swept away to the Lord who can spark such life, such laughter.

Hard to believe? I suppose so. But, as they say in the Big Apple, "Try it; you'll like it!"

Sacred Heart Church
University of Notre Dame
Notre Dame, Indiana
April 8, 1984

5

SIR, WE WOULD LIKE TO SEE JESUS
Fifth Sunday of Lent (B)

- ◆ Jeremiah 31:31–34
- ◆ Hebrews 5:7–9
- ◆ John 12:20–33

An exciting Gospel episode. At least it begins well. Some non-Jews have come up to Jerusalem for the Passover. They've heard about this controversial miracle-worker Jesus, heard that he's around. Like theater buffs at a stage door, they sidle up to Jesus' friend Philip: "Sir, we would like to see Jesus" (Jn 12:21). For some reason, Philip isn't sure they can; he checks it out with Andrew. Andrew doesn't know what to say, so he and Philip take it straight to the top: "Master, a group of Greeks are anxious to see you. No appointment. Not our kind, but good guys, up for the feast. What do we tell them?" At this point the reporter, John, seems to lose interest; he reports still another heavy speech of Jesus, this time about how it's better to die than to live. End of Gospel.

Exactly four weeks ago, I began mulling over that scene, with today's homily in mind. I was 33,000 feet above the earth, flying back from San Francisco. Suddenly, out of the blue above Nevada, an episode from the first century became a problem for the twentieth. I became Philip. Some visitors have come to Georgetown for Holy Week. They've heard from students that Jesus is around somewhere. They approach me, because they've been told I'm one of his disciples: "Sir, we would like to see Jesus." What do I say? Oh, I could pass the buck, hop over to campus ministry: "Hey, some folks from Philadelphia want to see Jesus. What shall I tell them?" Campus ministry isn't sure either, so we take it to the theology department. They're a bit puzzled, so we go to the top. What does Jesus tell me, and what do I tell the visitors? Three answers to three questions: (1) *Can* you see Jesus? (2) *How* do you see Jesus? (3) What will it *cost* you?

I

First, can you see Jesus? Indeed you can. I have it from the Master himself. Oh, you can't see him exactly as he was back then. Not the pudgy baby in a cradle of straw, clutching for his mother's breast. Not the pre-teen asking questions of teachers in the temple. Not the young adult leaving Nazareth to cry "The kingdom of God is at hand. Repent!" (Mk 1:15). Not the compassionate healer as he laid his hand on a leper, ate with sinners, bared his back to leather lashes, died in agony on a cross. Why not? Because that's history. You can *remember* him that way, but that is not the way he is now. He is risen, and though he still has his humanity, his body is such that even his closest friends did not recognize it when he rose.

And still you can see him—and see him now. Why do I say that? Because that is why the Son of God took flesh and nailed that flesh to crossed beams. He did not take your flesh only that you might see him *after* you die, in heaven. He did not sweat blood in a garden only that you might know *about* him, like a smart theologian. He did not bleed on wood merely that you might picture him in your imagination, hang a crucifix over your bed, say prayers to him. He lived and died that you might know him, love him, have direct experience of him, be aware of his presence, feel it, thrill to it—*now!* That God's Son might be as real to you right now as God was to Moses on Sinai, to His people as they crossed the Red Sea dry, to Isaiah and Hosea as they flung His word to the Jews, to Mary as she felt her infant stir inside her.

II

Yes, you *can* see Jesus. The question is, how? What does it mean to "see" Jesus . . . now? It's not a matter of 20-20 vision: You do not see Jesus with your eyes. It's more than imagination: conjuring up the way you think Jesus looks, or watching George Burns in *O God, You Devil.* No, to "see" Jesus here on earth is to experience Jesus, to encounter him, to come into contact with him. Not a vision, an image, voices. And still, actual contact with the real, risen, living Christ. Does that sound strange to you, "off the wall"? It should not—not to an intelligent Christian, not to anyone steeped in our rich tradition. Let me suggest two ways of encountering Christ. One way focuses on the people who touch your life day after day; the other way focuses on you.

First, focus on others. Even before you reached what we optimistically call "the age of reason," you were exhorted to see Jesus in your sisters and brothers. It was not pious twaddle, to keep you from "beating up" on one another. Jesus himself declared, in Matthew's striking passage, that when we feed the hungry and slake the thirsty, when we clothe the naked and house the stranger, when we visit the ailing and the jailed, we are doing this to him (Mt 25:31–46). Not just a favor to him; doing it to him.

Such is Mother Teresa's experience. When she cradles a skin-and-bones infant in the grime of Calcutta, she is cradling Christ. Such is Franciscan Father Ritter's experience. The 12,000 scarred and screwed-up youngsters who tramp through Covenant House in Times Square each year are the 12-year-old Jesus lost three days to Mary and Joseph in Jerusalem. Such should be your experience. When you dish out hot meals at SOME ("So Others Might Eat") or Bread for the City, when you house the homeless at Calvary or Deborah's Place, when you fill empty minds with beauty and truth in the inner city, when you move out to Appalachia or Peru to live with families that barely live, you should sense not simply the poverty of man but the presence of Christ. You should share a deep-seated Catholic conviction, a conviction set in startling syllables almost 1600 years ago by one of the most remarkable of Christian preachers, St. John Chrysostom. Preaching to his people in Antioch of Syria, Chrysostom called the poor in the public square an altar ready for sacrifice, and he proceeded to show that the poor are more venerable an altar than the altar of stone on which the Sacrifice was offered.

> This altar is composed of the very members of Christ, and the Lord's Body becomes an altar for you. This venerate: In the flesh you are offering the Lord's victim. This altar is more awesome than the altar in this church—not only more awesome than the altar of the Old Testament. Do not be troubled! You see, this altar [in the church] is a wondrous thing because of the Victim that has been placed thereon; but that altar, the altar of the compassionate man, is wondrous not simply for the same reason, but also because it is composed of the very Victim that makes this altar. Again, the former is a wondrous thing in that, though made of stone, it becomes holy because it receives the body of Christ; the

latter, because it *is* the Body of Christ. Therefore, it is more awesome than the altar near which you, a layman, are standing. . . .
This altar you can see set up everywhere, in the lane and in the
market, and at any hour you may sacrifice thereon; for here too
sacrifice is consummated.[1]

But it would be a mistake to identify Christ with the disadvan-
taged alone, to see his face only in the crucified. All of us reflect the
face of the Lord. The very first page of Scripture tells us that at the
birthday of our race God shaped us, man and woman, "in His own
image" (Gen 1:27). And the model on which God fashioned our humanity? An exciting early insight: What God had in mind when He
molded us in the first place was His own Son-to-be-made-flesh, the
Child of Bethlehem, the Christ who walked our ways and died our
death.[2] God made us the way He did because Christ was to be the
way he was. And in St. Paul's profound grasp of our new creation
in Christ, the Holy Spirit who lives in you transforms you day by
day into an ever more perfect Christ, because the very life of Christ
courses through you like another bloodstream. Even when sin dis-
torts the face of Christ we wear, our likeness to him never disappears altogether. His love is too strong to allow it.

Do you want to see Jesus? Look deeply into others—any other,
every other. But there is still another way of seeing him: by focusing
on yourself. Here we Catholics are terribly obtuse, nearsighted, myopic. Look at yourself. At this moment the living Christ, the Lord
who died for you and rose for you, the risen Christ is alive in you.
Don't take my word for it; listen to him the night before he died:
"If anyone loves me . . . my Father will love him [or her], and we will
come to him [or her] and make our home with him [or her]" (Jn
14:23). More than that: Within a half hour you will welcome the
same risen Christ into your very flesh—his body and blood, his human soul and his divineness. What does all this do to you—this gift
of God dwelling within you and this experience of Eucharist? Con-
cretely, do you encounter Christ? You should, you must; for encounter with Christ is the bone and marrow of Christian living. It
is the thrilling mystery of grace. Not some thing—simply persons
fused in love.

On the one hand, there is . . . you. You are not soul imprisoned
in body; you are a person. And what constitutes you as person is
intelligent love: the power you have to give yourself freely, profoundly, totally to another; the power to make an unreserved gift
of yourself, a gift expressed, translated, deepened in every thought

and word, every gesture and action, of each day. On the other hand, over against this person that is you, this person that is love, there is another person, the Christ who in loving you has made you lovable, Christ calling you, inviting you, drawing you, attracting you, urging you, not from outer space but from deep inside you, to a total self-giving in faith and hope and love. It is when you say yes, when like Mary you murmur "Let it happen to me according to your word" (Lk 1:38), it is then that encounter with Christ, close encounter, really begins. It is then that you see him somewhat as he sees you.

III

This raises my third question, a perilous question: What will it cost you to see Jesus? Here the rest of today's Gospel is suggestive, and it links encounter with Christ to experience of Lent. The clue? "I solemnly assure you, unless the grain of wheat falls into the earth and dies, it remains alone [just a grain of wheat]. But if it dies, it bears much fruit" (Jn 12:24).

Do you really want to see Jesus, encounter him person to person, touch him and thrill to him? Then you must follow him to Jerusalem. It is a journey that trudges to life through death. Not only when we breathe our last, but ceaselessly through our Christian existence.

You see, these 40 days are not an isolated episode in our lives, an annual replay of a past event. Lent is today. Lent is a paradigm, a model, a scenario for our living as Christians. We are journeying with Christ to Christ, and this means we must journey with him to Jerusalem, share his way of the cross, cry aloud with him constantly "Father, into your hands I commit my spirit" (Lk 23:46). That is why Lent is a caricature, a religious joke, if all it means is that I shift from steak to sole, give up Godivas, limit my malt and hops, tighten my waistline for Lauderdale. Lent is learning how to die—not when I'm 80 but now, today. Die to myself, to all that is less than human in me, less than Christlike.

Lent is learning through suffering. That is why today's reading from Hebrews is right on target: "Son though he was, [Jesus] learned obedience from what he suffered" (Heb 5:8). Oh yes, he had always been obedient, had spent his life doing his Father's will. But in Gethsemane, when in bloody sweat he begged his Father "Don't let me die," he learned what it means to get an answer different from what you asked. He learned what it means to take obedience to that point beyond which it can be taken no further: in St. Paul's words, "unto death, even death on a cross" (Phil 2:8). He learned to submit himself to the very conditions of human living from which he had prayed to be freed.[3]

What has this to do with seeing Jesus? Just about everything. You begin with a mystery-laden fact crucial to Christian existence: As with Jesus, so with you, it is in suffering that you learn obedience best. It is in dying to your own will that you learn to listen to God's will. It is in your Gethsemane, when your fragile humanity and your lust for life make you sweat blood, that you can hear at its most clear what the Lord wants of you. Once that happens, once you really hear Jesus, you will also *see* him. I promise.

Dahlgren Chapel
Georgetown University
and
Holy Trinity Church
Washington, D.C.
March 24, 1985

6

GOD SUFFERS WITH MAN
Passion/Palm Sunday (A)

- ◆ Isaiah 50:4–7
- ◆ Philippians 2:6–11
- ◆ Matthew 26:14—27:66

In one of his remarkable novels, the Jewish storyteller Elie Wiesel has one of his characters, Yehuda, gently reprove his troubled, reserved friend Gregor:

> It's inhuman to wall yourself up in pain and memories as if in a prison. Suffering must open us to others. It must not cause us to reject them. The Talmud tells us that God suffers with man. Why? In order to strengthen the bonds between creation and the creator; God chooses to suffer in order to better understand man and be better understood by him. But you, you insist upon suffering alone. Such suffering shrinks you, diminishes you. Friend, that is almost cruel.[1]

My brothers and sisters in Christ: You have listened once again to the passion, the suffering, of our Lord Jesus Christ. It calls for a minimum of preaching, a maximum of musing. Let me share with you three thoughts that struck me forcefully as I pondered the passage from Wiesel—Christian thoughts laid reverently upon the insights of the Jewish Talmud.

I

First, "God suffers with man." For us, that startling statement should be wonderfully and fearfully real. No exaggeration here, no fantasy run wild. What I have just read to you from the pen of Mat-

49

thew is literal truth. God's own divine Son borrowed our flesh—no, took it for ever. In that flesh he lived from dawn to dusk, from dusk to dawn, pretty much as we do. He ate and drank, spoke and slept, touched and healed, laughed and cried. Like us, he died; like us men and women, the God-man died. The way he died, we can say of him what the prophet Isaiah said of the Suffering Servant:

> He had no form or comeliness that we should look at him,
>   and no beauty that we should desire him.
> He was despised and rejected by men;
>   a man of sorrows, and acquainted with grief;
> and as one from whom men hide their faces
>   he was despised, and we esteemed him not. . . .
> All we like sheep have gone astray;
>   we have turned every one to his own way;
> and the Lord has laid on him the iniquity of us all.
> He was oppressed, and he was afflicted,
>   yet he opened not his mouth;
> like a lamb that is led to the slaughter,
>   and like a sheep that before its shearers is dumb,
>   so he opened not his mouth.
> By oppression and judgment he was taken away;
>   and as for his generation, who considered
> that he was cut off out of the land of the living,
>   stricken for the transgression of my people?
> And they made his grave with the wicked
>   and his tomb with evildoers,
> although he had done no violence,
>   and there was no deceit in his mouth.
>   (Isa 53:2b–3, 6–9)

On Calvary there is no need to exaggerate; the plain, unvarnished truth is staggering enough. It was difficult to believe that God could become man; it is more difficult still to believe that this God-man could die—and die as he did. But there it is: "Jesus cried again with a loud voice and yielded up his spirit" (Mt 27:50). Indeed, "God suffers with man."

II

But why? The Talmud says God suffers with man "to strengthen the bonds between creation and the creator . . . to better understand man and be better understood by him." "Yes, yes," I cry, as I glimpse Christ in Gethsemane, stand beneath his cross. Here is the same Son who, John's Gospel begins, "was in the beginning with God; all things were made through Him, and without Him was not anything made" (Jn 1:2–3). And now, in our flesh, the flesh he made, he sweats our blood and dies our death. Not that an all-loving God was not bonded to us from the first man's fashioning; but now this God of love shares our very sweat. Not that an all-knowing God did not *know* what it is like to be human; but now this God of all knowledge *experiences* how we feel, hurts the way you and I hurt. Nails tear his flesh, and loneliness breaks his heart. On the cross he feels our pain as he never could "in the beginning with God."

On the other side of the coin, you must admit that, seeing Jesus, you understand God better than if He had never left His heaven,[2] had never touched this earth with eyes and ears like ours, with hand and heart. Oh, I grant what Paul proclaimed to the people of Athens: God "is not far from each one of us, for 'in Him we live and move and have our being' " (Acts 17:27–28). But for all its glorious truth, that sort of understanding cannot compare with our grasp on God when we see the God-man helpless in a crib, helpless on a cross, hear him cry in anguish "My God, my God, why have you abandoned me?" (Mt 27:46), touch bloodstained hands imprisoned by nails. Here I can almost taste his love, smell it.

Love. . . . This is what, at bottom, strengthens the bonds that link us to God, deepens our understanding. For Calvary is not just another tragedy, the execution of one more innocent man. "God so loved the world that He gave His only Son, that whoever believes in him should not perish but have eternal life. For God sent the Son into the world . . . that the world might be saved through him" (Jn 3:16–17). This, in the last analysis, is why "God suffers with man." Not simply to be understood and to understand. The crucifixion of Christ is an act of love—a love that saves, that redeems. It is this that transforms suffering into sacrifice. The God-man not only suffered *with* us; he suffered *for* us. "The life I now live in the flesh," Paul exclaimed, "I live by faith in the Son of God, who loved me and gave himself for me" (Gal 2:20). It is not sheer crucifixion but crucified love that changed the world, changed you and me, reconciled us to God, made it possible for us to be one with Him through faith, with hope, in love.

III

This leads directly into my final musing: "Suffering must open us to others." Otherwise, as Yehuda warned Gregor, suffering can only shrink us, diminish us. History and our own memories are crammed with men and women imprisoned in their pain. Death of a dear one, disenchantment, depression; feelings of guilt or of utter worthlessness; acne or alcoholism or terminal cancer; the vast encyclopedia of illness and decay; simply growing old in a world that does not seem to care—a thousand and one afflictions we list under "suffering" wall us up "in pain and memories as if in a prison." Such turning in on myself may be understandable; at times it may be beyond my control; but it is always inhuman. At its worst, it is unchristian; for it keeps me from living the Christlife Paul trumpeted: "I rejoice in my sufferings for your sake, and in my flesh I complete what is lacking in Christ's afflictions for the sake of his body, that is, the Church . . ." (Col 1:24).

No more than my love of God is my suffering a private affair. As a Christian, as a member of Christ's own body, I dare not "insist on suffering alone." Suffering is my sharing in the passion of Christ; I suffer with him. The old Morning Offering is not impertinent here: "I offer you my prayers, works, joys, *and sufferings* of this day. . . ." United with his, my passion can touch my sisters and brothers with redeeming grace, can lend them the courage of Christ, the peace of Christ—yes, the joy of Christ. I suffer with them, and they with me.

This is not simply solid theology; I have experienced it time and time again. I saw it most intimately in the living *Pietà* that was my mother cradling the lifeless bodies of my father and brother, dead within three weeks of each other. Until her memory deserted her, a quarter century later, she lived and relived the agony of a husband and a son wasting away on hospital beds. And still she lived for others—this seemingly frail woman who shoveled 25 tons of coal to heat the flats she janitored for several months after my father died, this sensitive woman who must have been unbearably lonely and yet was a ceaseless source of strength to the heavy-burdened. She simply lived, lived simply, in God's presence. The Christ of Calvary was real to her—the abiding experience of a God-man ever shaping her, roughly and rudely at times, in the image of his dying/rising.

Dear friends, this Week of the Passion is not primarily a memory, a sad remembrance of a dying God. Christ is risen, to die no more. This is your week, your journey to Jerusalem. How will you journey? Alone with your pain, or in company with Christ? Clutching your cross to yourself, or arms outstretched like his, opening you to your crucified brothers and sisters? Choose! This week of *your* passion, choose!

Franciscan Renewal Center
Scottsdale, Arizona
April 15, 1984

7

DYING ON FRIDAY,
LIVING ON SUNDAY?
Passion/Palm Sunday (B)

> ♦ Isaiah 50:4–7
> ♦ Philippians 2:6–11
> ♦ Mark 14:1—15:47
> or
> 15:1–39

Today is a strange sort of day. Not only in Scottsdale but all through the Catholic world. From Hudson Bay to Cape Horn, from Bombay to Mozambique, we Catholics are weaving our way through a puzzling liturgy. We dance the liturgy in, wave palm branches in front of Jesus, cry a joy-packed "Hosanna!" to a triumphant king. Fifteen minutes later we are crushed with sadness, laid low in desolation. The king has been betrayed with a kiss, delivered to a Roman governor, lashed with whips, crowned with thorns, pinned to a cross till he breathes his last and is laid lifeless in a tomb. From triumph to tragedy in a quarter hour? What can such a liturgy mean? And what, if anything, might it say to our Christian living?

I

First, what meaning, what sense, does this Sunday have?[1] The meaning, the sense, lies in its very name: Passion/Palm Sunday. Passion and palms are not a contradiction here: sorrow over against joy, thorns versus palms, tragedy in conflict with triumph. Passion and palms are not enemies; they make up a single mystery. We call it the paschal mystery. And what is that? An inseparable twosome, an unbreakable two-in-one: the dying/rising of Jesus. Not sadness this Sunday, gladness next Sunday. Passion/Palm Sunday weds triumph to tragedy, kingship to shame, hosannas to curses, joy to sorrow. It suggests what Good Friday will trumpet to the far ends of the earth:

54

Our king triumphs not simply on Easter; he triumphs on Calvary. The tragedy *is* triumph; the sadness *is* gladness.

Does this sound like *non*sense? I'm not surprised. Every Christian mystery sounds like nonsense: a God who is One and Three; a Son of God who wears human flesh; a wafer that tastes like bread but is Christ's body and blood, soul and divinity. It collides with our experience, our way of viewing reality. So, too, for the paschal mystery—Lent, Holy Week, Easter; we must try to see it as God sees it, knowing all the while that we can never grasp it in our earth-bound existence, never make complete human sense of it. But eyes opened by faith can catch a glimpse of it, touch it without ever exhausting it.

What are we doing these 40 days? You answer: reproducing, re-presenting, living again the sufferings of Christ, his dying. Right. But why? You answer: So that on Easter we can celebrate his rising. Wrong. Lent is no more a preparation for the resurrection of Jesus than Advent was a preparation for the birth of Jesus. Jesus has risen, once and for all, and we dare not pretend that he has not. And we—we have risen with him, and so we live Lent as risen Christians, thrillingly aware that Christ is alive and we Christians are alive in him.

What, then, is the liturgy up to these 40 days? The Church is trying to initiate us gradually, progressively, ever more intensely into the paschal mystery, into the twin reality of Jesus dying and rising. Not the sheer history: dying on Friday, rising on Sunday. More the mystery: In Jesus' very dying there is rising; life comes *through* death, not simply after death.

To test this, recall the Sunday Gospels that have gone before. First Sunday: Jesus in the desert. The desert is indeed a place of wandering and confusion, of hungering and thirsting, of temptation and searching, yes of dying; but at the same time it is the place of discovery and covenant, of intimacy and love and new life, where God comes to meet His people. Second Sunday: the Transfiguration. On the death march to Jerusalem the disciples glimpse Jesus' glory; destined to die, he is revealed as the person of life. Third Sunday: the temple. The temple of Jesus' body, like the temple of stone, will indeed be destroyed; but in the very midst of destruction there will be resurrection. Fourth Sunday: light of the world. In the midst of darkness, Jesus is presented as the person of light, the light that brings life. Fifth Sunday: the grain of wheat. Falling into the earth and dying, the grain of wheat yields a rich harvest. And so today: passion and palms. Not palms *or* passion; both. Not triumph *or* tragedy; triumph *in* tragedy. Not a dying *or* a rising Christ; a dying/rising Christ. One mystery, one paschal mystery: life in and through death.

Put another way, the tragedy of Calvary is not a promise of triumph at Easter. The cross is itself a triumph. In Christ's death there is life. Lifted up in crucifixion, he draws men and women into his life. That is why the Church puts palms and thorns together. The King is triumphant not simply when he rises from the rock; he is triumphant when he is raised on the cross. Today I rejoice; on Good Friday I rejoice; for in Jesus' dying the world comes alive.

II

Heavy stuff? Perhaps. Dry bones? I think not. For, at its best, the liturgy ritualizes, symbolizes, sacramentalizes what goes on, or ought to go on, in the rest of our lives. At its best, liturgy gives expression to the faith experience of the Christian people, and liturgy helps mold that experience. And so my second question: What might Passion/Palm Sunday say to our Christian living?

Let me lock the answer into a single sentence: Like the life of Christ, your Christian life and mine is a journey to Jerusalem, and that journey is a dying/rising in his image. We dare not make the same mistake about our lives that we have made about our Lent. Just as Lent is not 40 days of mourning while we wait for Christ to burst the linen bands of his burial, so our life on earth is not a vale of tears while we wait for the final resurrection to wipe them away. To live as a Christian means to be ceaselessly shaped into Christ, and that means I am gradually, progressively, ever more intensely molded into the paschal mystery. My life, too, is a living/dying. Not swinging like a pendulum from one to the other; not manic in the morning and depressive in the evening. The two are wed together: In your dying is your living; in your dying is your rising.

This is not some vague mysticism. By "dying" I mean two concrete, down-to-earth realities. In journeying with Christ to Jerusalem, in trudging continually to life through death, you must die in two ways. You die to sin and you die to self.

You die to sin. This kind of dying you began at your baptism, when water washed you clean of Sin (with a capital S), the Sin that tyrannized humankind from Adam on. But this kind of dying is never done. Never done because it is not primarily negative, turning your back on evil. Dying to sin is turning to Christ, and this is like breathing: You stop it at peril to your life. But turning to Christ is not spinning like a top; that makes only for dizzy Christians. If sin is rejection, if sin is saying no to God and no to His creation, then dying to sin is an ever-increasing yes. You open yourself to God's presence wherever He is—and He is wherever you are. Open yourself to God not only at the Casa but on Camelback;[2] not merely at Mass but in the marketplace; not simply when Christ comes to you in Communion but when you meet him hungering for bread or justice, thirsting for water or affection, naked in body or vulnerable in spirit, a stranger to you or lost in your world, ailing in flesh or sick at heart, imprisoned behind bars of steel or sheer loneliness. In such dying to sin you will find life; for in such dying you find Christ . . . everywhere.

But dying to sin is not enough. To live fully, to live like Christ, you must die to self. And this can be more difficult than dying to sin. Why? Because, for the most part, you are dying to what is not forbidden, letting go of what is good. It means that you refuse to live in the past, are not detoured from living by the delusion that somewhere back there your life reached its peak or came to an end. It might be youth or middle age; it might be a moment of glory or years of fulfilment; it might be a home you inhabited, a possession you prized, a person you loved more than life; it might be your health or your job; it might be a Church that was once a rock, unmoved by the shifting sands of history and culture, sure guarantee of your peace and salvation. It might even be—I dare suggest it—an older Casa, familiar faces, ingrained ways of doing things.

Whatever the past, however rich and satisfying, you must move on. Don't forget the past; it is forever part of you. Simply refuse to live in the past. Like Jesus, leave Bethlehem and Nazareth, leave Bethany and the Sea of Galilee; turn your face to Jerusalem, your Jerusalem. You will, I suspect, find fresh crosses there; but for your consolation and strength, remember the paradoxical promise of our crucified and risen Redeemer: It is in losing your life that you find it; it is in dying that you come alive.

My friends: At this moment, in a small town in New Jersey, a lady I know is pinned to her last cross. Dear wife and devoted mother, she is still quite young. But the cancer is deep-seated, and very soon—within weeks, perhaps on Good Friday—God will ask her to let go of the last of her past: life itself. And with that life, the beloved who now surround her. Tough though it is, she has already murmured her yes. And with that yes has come a profound peace, the joy which Jesus vowed "no human being will take from you" (Jn

16:22). In her dying there is rising; in her dying there is living—not only for her but for so many who have been privileged to touch her cross. Please God, it will be so for you and for me.

Franciscan Renewal Center
Scottsdale, Arizona
March 31, 1985

8

WAS IT NOT NECESSARY . . .?
Good Friday 1

- ◆ Isaiah 52:13—53:12
- ◆ Hebrews 4:14–16; 5:7–9
- ◆ John 18:1—19:42

Two years ago Graham Greene published a delightful, insightful novel titled *Monsignor Quixote*. On a journey with a remarkable Communist mayor, the Spanish priest has a "terrible dream" that stays with him "like a cheap tune in the head."

> He had dreamt that Christ had been saved from the Cross by the legion of angels to which on an earlier occasion the Devil had told Him that He could appeal. So there was no final agony, no heavy stone which had to be rolled away, no discovery of an empty tomb. Father Quixote stood there watching on Golgotha as Christ stepped down from the Cross triumphant and acclaimed. The Roman soldiers, even the Centurion, knelt in His honor, and the people of Jerusalem poured up the hill to worship Him. The disciples clustered happily around. His mother smiled through her tears of joy. There was no ambiguity, no room for doubt and no room for faith at all. The whole world knew with certainty that Christ was the Son of God.
>
> It was only a dream, of course it was only a dream, but nonetheless Father Quixote had felt on waking the chill of despair felt by a man who realizes suddenly that he has taken up a profession which is of use to no one, who must continue to live in a kind of Saharan desert without doubt or faith, where everyone is certain that the same belief is true. He had found himself whispering, "God save me from such a belief."[1]

My friends, an ageless mystery haunts us on Good Friday: what might have been versus what actually happened. Let me muse a moment on each side of that mystery, then suggest what meaning it might have for our day-to-day Christian existence.

I

First, what might have been. Father Quixote's dream puts it dramatically. Jesus could have stepped down from the cross, to the amazement, the applause, the homage of the people who had screamed "Crucify him!" and the soldiers who had nailed him to the wood. But Quixote's dream is only one of many possibilities; for Jesus need not have come to Calvary at all. Let me dream a number of other dreams.

I dreamed that Jesus redeemed us in *Bethlehem*.[2] That first Christmas night the Son of God squeezed out of a woman's womb like any other infant, naked, helpless, frightened, squalling. Oh yes, angels were singing "Glory" to shepherds in the field, but the child did not hear them; he was lying in a feeding trough warmed by the breath of animals and by Mary's love. What redeemed us was that first baby cry—eyes closed, face wrinkled, fists clenched. It was enough—simply because the cry rose from the throat of the God-man. The Father was pleased, and His forgiving smile radiated through the world, from a crowded stable to the outposts of the earth, from that moment to the end of the age.

I dreamed that Jesus redeemed us at *Nazareth*. I watched him learning from Joseph how to shape a plow—the same One who had framed the universe out of nothing. I listened to him learning from Mary how to love God—the same One who was Himself the God of love. I marveled at his obedience to mother and father—the same One who could claim by right the obedience of all creation. What redeemed us was his first yes to a man and a woman. It was enough—simply because the yes was murmured to the Father by His only Son. The Father was pleased, and His forgiving smile radiated through the world.

I dreamed that Jesus redeemed us in the *wilderness*. There the Holy One of God fasted for 40 days and was hungry. There Satan tried to seduce Jesus from his Father's will, from his messianic mission. What redeemed us was a single pang of hunger. It was enough—simply because the hunger was the God-man's hunger for a people who had wandered from his love. The Father was pleased, and His forgiving smile radiated through the world.

I dreamed that Jesus redeemed us with a *word*—any one of the wondrous words of the Lord. "Father, I desire that where I am, they also whom you have given me may be with me" (Jn 17:24). "Take heart, son: Your sins are forgiven" (Mt 9:2). "Woman, where are they? Has no one condemned you? . . . Neither do I condemn you" (Jn 8:10–11). What redeemed us was a word—a word of welcome, of forgiveness—whispered not only over disciples or a paralytic or an adulteress, but over our sin-scarred world. It was enough—simply because it was God in flesh who breathed that word. The Father was pleased, and His forgiving smile radiated through the world.

I dreamed that Jesus redeemed us in the *garden,* where "his sweat became like great drops of blood falling down upon the ground" (Lk 22:44). I dreamed that when he prayed "Father, if you are willing, remove this cup from me" (v. 42), His Father was indeed willing, did remove the cup from him—all but one drop of blood, the symbol of his love. What redeemed us was that single drop of blood. It was enough—simply because it was the blood of the God-man, offered for every man and woman sprung from Adam. The Father was pleased, and His forgiving smile radiated through the world.

II

Stimulating, these dreams of what might have been. And without Father Quixote's "chill of despair"; for these dreams, unlike his, left room for faith, room for doubt. Still, they were only dreams, what might have been but actually was not. Oh yes, these things happened; but no one of them—birth or growth, hunger or word, bloody sweat—not all of them together were enough to redeem the world. They could have; they did not. Each played its part; nothing was for show. The crib was not created for artists, for Fra Filippo Lippi's "Adoration of the Virgin"; the three decades in Nazareth were not just carpentry school; the temptations were not play-acting. Each event in Jesus' life says something to us—about God and about ourselves. And each event did something; for it was a line, a scene, an act in that single drama we call salvation—our redemption from sin, from Satan, from ourselves.

And still, none of them was enough. Bethlehem was the beginning of a journey, a long journey into night, the journey to Jerusalem. Jesus himself made that clear: He "began to show his disciples that he must go to Jerusalem and suffer many things . . . and be killed . . ." (Mt 16:21). Remember his reminder to the discouraged disciples on the road to Emmaus: "Was it not necessary that the Christ should suffer these things . . .?" (Lk 24:26). Necessary not by some abstract theory, some law of nature. Necessary because this was the way God wanted it. No one compelled Christ to die: "For this reason the Father loves me, because I lay down my life, that I may take it again. No one takes it from me, but I lay it down of my own accord. I have power to lay it down, and I have power to take it again; this charge I have received from my Father" (Jn 10:17–18). This climax of free obedience is summed up in that lyrical Christological hymn we find in Paul's letter to the Christians of Philippi:

> Though of divine status,
> he did not treat like a miser's booty
> his right to be like God
> [his right to appear like Yahweh in glory],
> but emptied himself of it,
> to take up the status of a slave
> and become like men;
> having assumed human form,
> he still further humbled himself
> with an obedience that meant death—
> even death upon a cross!
>
> (Phil 2:6–8)[3]

Center stage in our salvation is Calvary. The victory of Christ over our fourfold slavery—over sin and the self, over death and the law—did not lie in his power to step down from the cross, embrace his mother, confound his enemies, and lay hold of his kingdom. His victory, even over death, was his dying.[4] "As Moses lifted up the serpent in the wilderness, so must the Son of Man be lifted up, that whoever believes in him may have eternal life" (Jn 3:14–15). That is why the taunt that must have torn his heart on Golgotha was the cry of the passers-by "If you are the Son of God, come down from the cross!" (Mt 27:40). No, the cross itself is triumph. It is not by a *descent* from the cross that man and woman dead in sin will come alive. "I, if I am lifted up from the earth, will draw all to myself" (Jn 12:32).

But why? Why a bloodsoaked death when other ways were open to an all-knowing, all-powerful God? Why a death so frightening even to Jesus that he begged his Father, if at all possible, to remove that cup from him: "Don't let me die!" (cf. Lk 22:42). In all honesty, we do not know. Even we strange characters called theologians, we who by profession beat our heads against the wall of God's mystery, even we have to confess with Job: "I have uttered what I did not understand, things too wonderful for me, which I did not know" (Job 42:3).

Oh yes, we can stammer a bit. We know that the cross is rooted in the mystery of God's love for us: "God so loved the world that He gave His only Son, that whoever believes in him should not perish but have eternal life" (Jn 3:16). We know from Jesus' own lips that love leaps to its dizziest height in the self-giving that is death: "Greater love than this no man has, that a man lay down his life for his friends" (Jn 15:13). We know that when the Son of God took our flesh as His very own, the God-man entered our human situation, where life reaches its fulfilment only by passing through death—a death which is the expression and revelation of sin in the world.[5] Sinless, he did not have to die the death of sin. For him, death was the expression of loving obedience, "the free transference of his entire created existence to God."[6] Out of love for his Father, out of love for you and me. In the mystery-laden designs of God, that total self-gift, "Father, into your hands I commit my spirit" (Lk 23:46), made our Lord's humanity and his grace for ever the heart of all human living.

III

Which brings me to my third point: What meaning might all this have for our day-to-day Christian existence? The possibilities are many; I focus on one facet. I mean . . . Christian discipleship. You see, to be a disciple, in the New Testament sense, is to be "called," to have a vocation that stems from Jesus: "Follow me." As a disciple, I can have but one master: Jesus. My response to him must be total: "Follow me, and leave the dead to bury their own dead" (Mt 8:22). Not just for today: "No one who puts his hand to the plow and looks back is fit for the kingdom of God" (Lk 9:62). To be a disciple is to pattern myself after the one master—and this master is a crucified master who turned savagely on Peter when he protested against the passion of his Lord.

To put it another way: For you and me, as well as for Jesus, human living is a journey to Jerusalem. The journey has varied lights and shadows: the miracle of our own Bethlehem, the growing pains of our Nazareth, the joy of our Cana, children in our arms as in the arms of Jesus, public life in its different dimensions, the wilderness and its temptations, Peter and John and Magdalene and even Judas intersecting our lives, the joy of communion with a living God, an occasional transfiguration—perhaps, as with Jesus, relatives and friends who think we are out of our minds (cf. Mk 3:21).

A fascinating journey, but it always leads to Jerusalem. To Calvary. If I realize deep within that death is inevitable, is sure to come, then, as Karl Rahner saw, "in this knowledge death is already present in human life and only by this does life assume its full gravity."[7] The crucial question is, how does this realization affect me, alter my life? Is death for me primarily a tragedy, something I dread as the end, refuse to think about? Is death like a dream, not real till I age or ail, a depressing event that will indeed come to pass, but no point in dwelling on it now, save to check my insurance policy?

I am not asking you to delight in your Jerusalem, to scoff at death. There is a darkness to death which even the Son of God cried out against. Death is cruel; death breaks the whole person; *I* will vanish from living reach and touch. And so I fear that, like Dylan Thomas, I may "not go gentle into that good night." I may well "burn and rave at close of day;/ Rage, rage against the dying of the light."[8]

Still, I trust that with God's grace I will increasingly see death for what Christ our Lord made it. Not a horribly painful event at the close of life, but that unique moment when the yes I have said to God all my life reaches its climax. Not something I endure, but something I do. Not a tragedy to be avoided at all costs, but the extraordinary experience when the Christ who *is* life, who has been my life, fashions me finally to his life, in his image. The moment when my journey reaches not its nadir but its high point. The day when, for all the human loss it entails, I can confidently cry with Christ "Father, into your hands I commit my spirit." The day when God will wipe away all tears from my eyes and murmur:

> All which I took from thee I did but take,
>   Not for thy harms,
> But just that thou might'st seek it in My arms.
>   All which thy child's mistake
> Fancies as lost, I have stored for thee at home:
>   Rise, clasp My hand, and come![9]

Franciscan Renewal Center
Scottsdale, Arizona
April 20, 1984

9

HE LOVED ME. . . .
Good Friday 2

- Isaiah 52:13—53:12
- Hebrews 4:14–16; 5:7–9
- John 18:1—19:42

Today, my friends, we have no choice. We who are alive have to talk about death. I do not like it. I would much rather hold your hand and tell you to cheer up, Easter is only a day and a half away. But two pieces of wood forbid it; two crossed beams tell me harshly that somebody died there. To save my life, I must discover (1) who died there, (2) why he died like that, and (3) what his dying means for my living. A word, a prayerful word, on each.

I

First, who died on the wood? A man, of course. Let me tell you how I remember him. Someone shaped very much like you and me: face, hands, feet; bone and blood; a brain and five senses. He began to live as you and I begin, cradled within a woman for nine mysterious months. He opened his eyes as we open ours, save that his opened in a cheerless stable miles from home. He grew up much as we do: a child among children; a small segment of relatives and friends; little startling to report, except three days in Jerusalem on his own. He never married, I am not quite sure why—perhaps because he had a mission from his Father that left no place whereon to rest his head. He made no waves till he was 30; then it was that he burst into Galilee like a storm at sea, proclaiming God's reigning, preaching repentance. For three years he trudged through a land holy in its history, simply doing good. If you were ill, he healed you. If you were hungry, he multiplied bread for you. If you were down on yourself, he lifted you up. If you were a sinner, you could count on him to share your supper. If you were a child, he gathered you in his arms and blessed you.

The trouble was, he made enemies. He was his own man, not particularly prudent. He turned tradition around, said the Sabbath was made for us, not we for the Sabbath. Unlike other Jewish disciples, his close followers did not fast, and he refused to force them. He censured the cities that would not believe in him, threatened a judgment on them more fearful than Sodom endured. He warned his own people that they might well be excluded from heaven's table, the Gentiles they despised take their place. He whipped traffickers from the temple, predicted that of this precious temple not a stone would be left upon a stone. He warned the rich against their riches, assailed the powerful for abusing their power. He even called Roman ruler Herod a fox, laughed at his threats.

His enemies did not lie down. They claimed he was possessed by Satan. They said he blasphemed. They called him a glutton and a drunkard. His own townspeople tried to throw him over a cliff. A high priest argued that, to keep the Romans from destroying the Jews, it was expedient that Jesus die.

When the end came, it was terribly sad. One of his own dear friends sold him for silver, betrayed him with a kiss. His enemies bound his gentle hands, flayed his naked back with whips, crowned his head with thorns, compelled him to carry his own cross, nailed him to it, and let him die in frightful, lonely agony. And his mother looked on.

Yes, it was a man who died on Calvary. And if that were all, we might still set a day apart—as we've done for Martin Luther King Jr.—to remember a man who made life more human for untold millions, and was murdered for it. But Calvary is more than Memphis; Calvary is unique. Unique because the man who died was more than man. The man who died on Calvary was the Son of God.

It baffles our minds, beggars our speech. Ever since the first Good Friday, theologians have struggled how to think it, stammered how to say it. For Christian mystery, it rivals the Blessed Trinity. We do not know how it can be, how to explain it. And still the fact cannot be denied, the central Christian reality: That figure writhing on the cross is the Second Person of the Trinity in human flesh. Man yes, but God-man. God's only Son took our flesh from a teen-age Jewish girl in Nazareth and died in that flesh outside Jerusalem. Mary's Son and God's Son is one and the same Son; and that Son-in-flesh "bowed his head and gave up his spirit" (Jn 19:30).

You and I can echo St. Paul's impassioned affirmation to the Christians of Corinth: "None of the rulers of this age understood this; for if they had, they would not have crucified the Lord of glory" (1 Cor 2:8). The man on the cross is the Lord of glory.

II

All of which raises urgently my second question: Why did the Lord of glory die like this? If he had been mere man, it would make sense: He couldn't avoid it; he was up against impossible odds; the cards were stacked against him. But it's different for the Lord of glory. He did not have to borrow our flesh, pass nine months imprisoned in a womb, grow up like any other Jewish youngster, get tired and thirsty and dusty and angry, take insults from his own creatures. He did not have to sweat blood in a garden, beg his Father "Don't let me die," be condemned like a common criminal. You remember how he chided Peter for drawing a sword in his defense: "Do you think that I cannot appeal to my Father, and He will at once send me more than 12 legions of angels?" (Mt 26:53). And you remember his words as Good Shepherd: "No one takes [my life] from me; I lay it down of my own accord" (Jn 10:18). He did not have to die.

Why, then, did he die? A clue comes from God's own Book, from the Gospel of John: "God so loved the world that He gave His only Son, that whoever believes in him should not perish but have eternal life" (Jn 3:16). It is St. Paul's amazed realization: He "loved me and gave himself for me" (Gal 2:20). The answer lies in love.

But the answer seems too facile. Yes, God saved us because He loved us. But could not divine imagination have discovered a different redemption, love-laden indeed but less difficult than death on Calvary? Couldn't God have simply forgiven us, asked only that we be "heartily sorry for having offended" Him? Or if this were not enough for divine justice, if God's Son had somehow to touch our earth in person, why didn't the God-man come clothed in majesty, King of kings and Lord of lords? Why frame his flesh of fears and tears, of meekness and weakness? And if his Father wanted him to die—good God, couldn't he have died in bed, died with dignity? Why ask him to breathe his last in bloody disgrace, mocked by the very world for which he was dying?

Frankly, I do not know. I suspect no one knows save the God who invented the Passion. But one fact rings loud and clear from

Calvary: Where God's love is concerned, we mortals are terribly dense, dreadfully uncomprehending. We experience, day after day, what men and women will endure for love's bittersweet sake. We know that when the chips are down, if we love wildly enough, we will fling life itself to the winds for one we love. But we find it strange to think this way of God. Perhaps because the God of our education sits up there like a Buddha, impassive, unmoving, hard as flint. Calvary cries more clearly than any theology textbook: We do not know our God. We have not grasped the thrilling truth in the first Letter of John: "In this is love, not that we loved God but that He loved us and sent His Son to be the expiation for our sins" (1 Jn 4:10). We cannot see that God was not content with some sort of legal redemption, a calm, cool, formal pardon for the sins of the world. He wanted to experience our earth-bound existence, live our human condition. He wanted to learn as we learn, with knowledge making a bloody entrance. He wanted to love as we love, surrounded by hate and lust. He wanted to experience at first hand what it feels like to grow and to hurt, to break out in laughter and to taste the salt of tears, to blacken with anger and whiten with fear. Sinless, he wanted to be where sin tyrannizes, sense what makes us the creatures of contradiction we are. He wanted not only to heal divinely but to lay hands of compassion on the scarred and the seared, on the lonely and the unloved. He wanted to feel what it's like to die.

In a word, God's Son wanted to be one of us, one with us. Even for God, especially for God, love is stronger than death. Greater love than this no one has. . . .

III

All of which raises urgently my third question: What does Jesus' dying mean for my living? It has to mean something highly important, if you recall Paul proclaiming to the Christians of Galatia: Christ "gave himself for me" (Gal 2:20). The Son of God did not visit this earth, share my flesh, the way I might spend a week on an Indian reservation: primarily to broaden my own experience of loneliness, joblessness, hopelessness, brokenness. Whatever Jesus did, whatever he experienced, whatever he suffered, all this was for me. To cap it all, he died for me.

You see, Jesus' dying did something for me and it says something to me. It did something for me. It freed me from a threefold slavery: to sin, to self, to death. Because Jesus died for me, I am no longer at odds with God, His enemy; with the grace that flows from Calvary, I can say no to Satan, no to sin. Because Jesus died for me, I am no no longer shackled in my small self, severed from my sisters and brothers by the mark of Cain; with the love that floods me from Calvary, I can reach out to others as he did, lay down life itself for my friends . . . or my enemies. Because Jesus died for me, death is no longer a door to darkness; with the life that leaps from Calvary, I too shall defeat death, rise to life with the risen Christ days without end.

In this context, Jesus' dying says something to me. It tells me that dying is not an isolated event, a disagreeable episode I endure once. As with Jesus, so with me, my entire life must be a journey to Jerusalem. As with him, so with me, I must ceaselessly let go . . . let go of yesterday. And to let go is to die a little. Jesus had to let go. Let go of the glory that was rightfully his as Son of God, to wear our inglorious flesh. Let go of secure little Nazareth, to trumpet a repentance many would resent. Let go of his mother, whose own deep hurt must have tormented him as she stood at a distance, as she heard his relatives murmur he was mad. Let go of Lazarus and Martha and Mary, all of whom "Jesus loved" (Jn 11:5). Let go of his beloved Twelve, who had still so much to learn. Let go of the hill of Transfiguration *and* the garden of Gethsemane. Let go, last and hardest of all, let go of the sheer miracle of being alive. He had to let go; otherwise he would never have set his face towards Jerusalem, and his dying would never have become our living.[1]

So, too, for you and me. For us, to live as Christians is to share in the dying/rising of Christ. Not in two stages: dying here, rising hereafter. One inseparable, continuous reality: In our dying is our rising—now. To journey with Jesus to Jerusalem, we have to let go of where we've been, so as to live more fully. It can be terribly painful, for the past may seem like the peak of human living: the sheer strength and lustiness of youth; a job in which I exulted; a wife or husband or child as close to me as I am to myself; ears that listened to me, hands that supported me, tongues that praised me; just the ability to walk tall and straight, to talk firm and fast; simply to be needed by somebody. Whoever you are, wherever you are, the past is real, is part of you. The peril is not in remembering the past; the peril lies in living therein. No, Christ is now. Only by a self-emptying similar to his can you grow into him, be shaped day after day in his likeness. In such dying is Christian living. By reaching out in faith and hope and love to whatever tomorrow may hold, you will discover, you will experience, what St. Paul found so exciting: "I have been crucified with Christ; it is no longer I who live, but Christ who lives in me; and the life I now live in the flesh I live by faith in the Son of God, who loved me and gave himself for me" (Gal 2:20).

Dear friends, Good Friday has an aura of sadness. How could it not? In the flesh he took, the Son of God died. But the sadness with which you entered this lovely temple of his should be transformed into a fresh joy with which you leave it—the joy which Jesus promised "no human being will take from you" (Jn 16:22). How could it not? Our good Lord did not simply die; he died *for you.* If he loves you that much, you must be quite extraordinary. The least—no, the best—you can do in return is: Don't simply live; live *for him.*

SS. Simon and Jude Cathedral
Phoenix, Arizona
April 5, 1985

EASTER

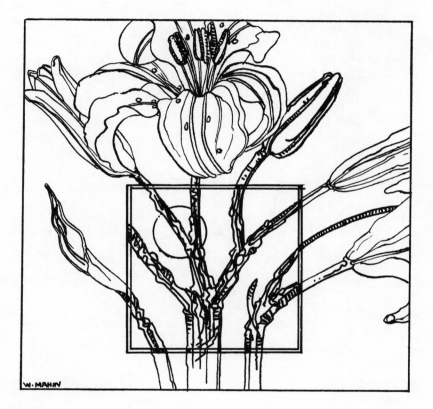

10

IF YOUR FAITH IS ALIVE. . . .
Second Sunday of Easter (A)

♦ Acts 2:42–47
♦ 1 Peter 1:3–9
♦ John 20:19–31

Some recent statistics disturb me. Most people believe that organized religion is the enemy of personal religion; experience of church does not lead to experience of God.[1] If you want to touch God, if you crave direct contact with divinity, you do not seek it, say, in Roman Catholicism. There you have the "forms and trappings" of real religion, not a one-to-one relationship with God. There you have laws that imprison, structures that suffocate, all sorts of intermediaries between you and God: dogma, priests, Mary, sacraments. To find God, follow the advice of Jesus: "When you pray, go into your room and shut the door . . ." (Mt 6:6).

Today's Liturgy of the Word suggests something quite different. Let me sketch it in three stages. First, a remarkable sentence from the Acts of the Apostles. Second, an unexpected exclamation from the apostle Thomas. Third, a modest word from your homilist.

I

First, a sentence from Acts. We are in Jerusalem. Jesus has risen from the dead. He has appeared to his mother[2] and to Magdalene, to disciples behind locked doors and on the shore of the open sea. He has returned to his Father and has sent his Spirit upon the disciples. And now the first Christians begin to live the Christlife, the life of oneness with the risen Lord.

How do they live it? Those who once walked and talked with

him, those who watched him die, those who repented and were baptized, those who were filled with the Holy Spirit—how do they carry
on their Christian existence? Each in his or her desert lean-to, each
undistracted by doctrine, each a private worshiper on a kneeler
made for one? Listen to the account in Acts: "They devoted themselves to (they persisted in) the apostles' teaching and the fellowship,
the breaking of the bread and the prayers" (Acts 2:42). Four facets
to their experience of God.

1) *The apostles' teaching.* Not some man-made set of propositions
nailed to a church door and threatening the unbeliever with hell-
fire. The apostles' teaching was everything Jesus had taught, all he
had said to them, all that the Holy Spirit brought back to their remembrance (cf. Jn 14:26). "Repent, and be baptized" (Acts 2:38).
"Unless you eat [my] flesh and drink [my] blood, you have no life
in you" (Jn 6:53). "Love one another as I have loved you" (Jn 15:12).
"As you did it to one of the least of these my brethren, you did it to
me" (Mt 25:40). "I live and [therefore] you shall live" (Jn 14:19). For
the first Christians, to listen to the apostles' teaching was to listen to
Jesus' teaching: "He who hears you hears me" (Lk 10:16). To listen
to Jesus was to listen to God. Not the forced feeding of a goose to
fashion a rich ecclesiastical *pâté;* to hear the word was to experience
God.

2) *The fellowship.* What did fellowship mean? Luke tells us a bit
later: "Now the company of those who believed were of one heart
and soul, and no one said that any of the things which he possessed
was his own, but they had everything in common" (Acts 4:32).
There was a splendid solidarity in the Jerusalem community. Luke
does not call his fellow Christians friends; he does not call them
brothers and sisters; he calls them simply "believers," because the
oneness among them was founded on faith—faith in the risen
Christ. And this spiritual oneness had a material component, was
expressed in the day-to-day life of the community: "There was not
a needy person among them; for as many as were possessors of
lands or houses sold them, and brought the proceeds of what was
sold and laid it at the apostles' feet; and distribution was made to
each as any had need" (Acts 4:34–35). They shared who they were,
and they shared what they had.[3] Not only because "the other" was
human; more importantly, because "the other" was Christ. To share
with the other was to experience the Other.

3) *The breaking of bread.* Not just ordinary table fellowship. Sup-
ping with one another was indeed significant, for it recalled the table fellowship Jesus had enjoyed with his followers. Still more

significant was the Supper of the Lord. I mean what St. Paul would write: "I received from the Lord what I delivered to you, that the Lord Jesus on the night when he was betrayed took bread . . . broke it and said: 'This is my body which is for you. Do this in remembrance of me' " (1 Cor 11:23–24). "The bread which we break," Paul asked, "is it not a communion in the body of Christ?" (1 Cor 10:16). Communion in the body of Christ! Here was an experience far exceeding the most luscious of lox and bagels. Little wonder that early communities sang at Communion the Psalmist's song: "O taste and see that the Lord is good!" (Ps 34:8). Taste! Communion was not a theological thesis; to break the bread was to "taste" the God-man. Here they experienced God's presence, as the disconsolate disciples had at Emmaus: "They recognized him in the breaking of the bread" (Lk 24:31, 35).[4]

4) *The prayers.* Not just prayers in closeted privacy. Over and above that, the first Christians prayed together, prayed even in the temple. They recalled the promise of Jesus: "Where two or three are gathered in my name, there am I in the midst of them" (Mt 18:20). To pray was not only to acknowledge sovereign Majesty; to pray was to enter the presence of God. To pray was to experience divine presence. As a lovable old laborer put it long years ago, "I say nothing to Him, and He says nothing to me; but I look at Him, and He looks at me."

What the Jerusalem Christians are telling us is where they experienced God, where they discovered Christ. Not by a me-and-Jesus spirituality. A personal relationship indeed, but through a community, with a community, in a community. The word of God, solidarity in soul and possessions, fellowship at their own table and the Lord's, awareness of God's presence everywhere—personal contact yes, but through the mystical body of Christ and his Eucharistic body.

II

All of which brings me to doubting Thomas. A fascinating fellow, with some hang-ups. Why wasn't he around on Easter Sunday, when Jesus first appeared, breathed his Spirit on the disciples, empowered them to forgive sin? What made him so skeptical, so mulish, when trusted friends like Peter, James, and John told him "We have seen the Lord" (Jn 20:25)? We do not know. What we do know is that the doubter uttered the most perfect affirmation of Christ's nature in all the Gospels. "Lord and God" translates the name of Israel's God (cf. Ps 35:23); "Lord and God" would become the common Christian confession of Christ, Son of God equal to the Father.

How did it happen? Easy, you will say; easy as falling off a log. After all, wasn't his Lord and God standing in front of Thomas? Was it not obvious he had risen from the dead? Only a fool would deny the evidence of his eyes.

Not so fast, my friends. Thomas did not "see" God; what he saw was a man. A unique man, I admit, a wonder man in risen flesh who appeared out of nowhere and walked through doors and still wore the wounds of his dying. Nevertheless, all Thomas could see with his eyes, all sheer reason could reveal to him, was a man. Remember when Jesus' friend Lazarus came forth from the tomb in Bethany? Not a single spectator shouted "My Lord and my God!" An infinite gulf separates "You are risen" from "You are God." The cry of Thomas went far beyond the evidence.

Because it exceeded the evidence, "My Lord and my God" was an act of faith; and faith for Thomas, as for us, was a gift, impossible without God's gracious giving. It was a response to God's self-revealing. Not simply the assent of his intellect to what God had certified: "I firmly believe that you are my Lord and my God." Faith is not a narrow head-trip. Faith in its fulness is a response of the whole person—not mind only, but heart and emotions and will as well. Thomas' cry was a doxology; I mean a paean of praise, of adoration. It was a yes to his Lord, a total gift of himself to his God.

Such faith is an experience. Personal, of course—a one-to-one experience of God. But notice: The experience took place in the midst of a community a-borning, disciples who had journeyed to Jerusalem with Jesus, had shared his Supper, had watched him die from near or afar.

III

Third, what do I hear the early Church and the apostle Thomas saying to you and me? They stress, I suggest, two profound realities: Christian life is life in community, and Christian faith is a religious experience. A word on each.

Christian life is life in community. Can you be saved, can you reach God, without membership in the Christian community? Obviously. You might as well get ready for it now: Your mansionmates in heaven will include Muslims and Moonies, Hindus and Buddhists, Jews and Confucianists, all manner of folk who would sooner drink strychnine than be baptized. But that is not the point. We begin with a fact: Here you are, baptized, like the Jerusalem Christians, into a community, a people. "You are the body of Christ," Paul proclaims to the Christians of Corinth, "and individually members of it" (1 Cor 12:27).

This is not an imposition; it is a privilege, a grace. Why you and not Khomeini or Qaddafi? I do not know. For some reason known to God alone, you are specially loved. Not because you are naturally lovable, irresistible even to the Trinity. Simply because God wants it so. As Teresa of Avila put it, "God loves everybody, but He has His friends."

But life in community demands love in community—in the very four areas the Jerusalem Christians prized. (1) Far from despising doctrine, you ought to cherish it; for the apostles' teaching is simply Jesus shaping a community mind, shaping it to his own mind. Difficult at times, distressing, disturbing, divisive, but well worth the struggle; for this, Jesus said, "is eternal life," to know the one true God and the Christ He sent (Jn 17:3). (2) Far from frowning on fellowship as somehow Protestant, you should see it as inescapably Christian; for fellowship is a sharing of who you are that reflects the unique oneness within the Trinity, a sharing of what you have that lightens the burden of those who experience so much of Christ's crucifixion, so little of his resurrection. (3) Far from making the table of the Lord your private party, in the breaking of the bread you too must be broken, to be given, as Jesus was given, to a broken world. (4) Far from imprisoning your prayer within your closet or even your heart, you must plunge into the prayers of the community, the people's prayerfulness, ceaseless awareness of God here present in your gathering together, here present in the preached word, here present in the broken bread.

A second profound reality: Christian faith is a religious experience. It will no longer do to apologize for your faith, to appeal to it uncomfortably when a clever debater has you over a barrel. Your faith is a thrilling thing not because it furnishes you a hatful of answers but because it makes for experience of the living God. You see, your faith is a living faith not when you are able to recite "I believe that you are one God in three divine Persons." Remember the Letter of James: "You believe that God is one. Even the demons believe—and shudder" (Jas 2:19). Your faith, like Thomas' faith, is a living faith when "My Lord and my God" is the flaming response of your whole being to the risen Jesus present before you, around you, within you; when it means "I love you, Lord, with every fiber of my flesh, every stirring of my spirit." And that, my friends, is an experience of God. Not a vision. Simply, you and God have touched.

A living faith within a community of faith. This brings me full circle, back to where I began: organized religion versus personal religion. To touch God, you need not rush helter-skelter from Dahlgren to Dumbarton Oaks or the Arboretum or Bethany Beach. If your faith is alive, you will touch the risen Christ as Jerusalem's first Christians touched him: in his word and in your fellowship, in his flesh and in the Our Father you raise to God hand-in-hand. If your faith is alive. . . .

Dahlgren Chapel
Georgetown University
Washington, D.C.
April 29, 1984

11

BY FAITH SHE GAVE HIM BIRTH
Fourth Sunday of Easter (A)

- ◆ Acts 2:14, 36–41
- ◆ 1 Peter 2:20–25
- ◆ John 10:1–10

A cute story used to circulate in Catholic circles. It told of an Italian peasant woman, touchingly simple in her piety. It seems that a clever Communist had proved to her, by all manner of rigorous argument, that there cannot possibly be a God. "All right," she responded. "There is no God. But we always have the mother of God."

We always have the mother of God. Despite today's Gospel of the Good Shepherd, Rome's rules for homilists allow us to focus on the shepherd's mother.[1] A good rule, for May is Mary's month—or used to be. And so my first point: the mother of Jesus. But this second Sunday of May calls for a word about all women who physically mother a Christ. And so my second point: other mothers. But the liturgy speaks to every Christian, everyone who gives birth to Christ. And so my third point: all of us.

I

First, the mother of Jesus. Devotion to Mary does not play the strong role in Catholic living that it did a generation ago. Several influences have been at work here. (1) We are trying to correct an old exaggeration, an imbalance: the feeling that Mary is more approachable than Jesus, that through her we can sneak into heaven past a God of strict justice, that if Jesus won't give you what you want, Mary will. (2) Many modern women do not find in Mary the role model their mothers did. Times have changed; people are different; her problems are not ours; even her Son was a cut above our children. (3) Mary and Joseph had a marriage our age won't buy: no sex, no passion, probably no arguments.

Heavy stuff indeed, and good material for lively discussion. But it would be tragic if such reasons kept us from seeing what it is that makes Mary the model she is—not only for mothers, not only for women, but for each Christian whatever the sex or stripe.

To begin with, Mary *was* a mother. Oh yes, her child was conceived of the Holy Spirit, but he grew in her and from her. She had to give him birth in a strange town, had to steal him away to Egypt to save him from a nervous king. He puzzled her, worried her, when at 12 he slipped away to argue theology in a temple. She had to stay at home, or stand apart with the crowd, not only when he multiplied bread and raised the dead, but when his townspeople cast him from a cliff, his enemies shouted he had a devil, his friends and relatives insisted he was mad. She felt as helpless as any mother when a disciple betrayed him with a kiss, when soldiers lashed his back and nailed him to the wood, when he cried out as if forsaken by his Father, when he breathed his last and she held him in her arms as not so long ago she had rocked him in Bethlehem.

And yet, believe it or not, mothering God-in-flesh is not our Lady's chief claim to fame. Not in God's eyes. More important than sheer motherhood was what St. Augustine realized when he wrote: "Mary was more blessed because she laid hold of faith in Christ than because she conceived the flesh of Christ. . . . Her motherly relationship to him would have been of no use to Mary, had she not carried Christ in her heart more happily even than she bore him in her body." She "conceived Christ in her mind before she conceived him in her womb." "It was by faith she gave him birth, it was by faith she conceived him."[2]

That is why the Second Vatican Council called the mother of Jesus "the Church's outstanding model in faith and love."[3] Model not in what she did, how she lived in Nazareth; few of us pass our day the way she did. Her endless legacy to all of us is her faith and her love. Not some vague "I believe," not some emotional "I love you." She lived what Jesus extolled: "Blessed are those who hear the word of God and keep it" (Lk 11:28; cf. 8:21). This is Mary preeminently: the woman who hears what God is saying and acts on it. She listened and she said yes—not only to the ecstasy of Bethlehem but to the sword of Calvary and beyond. Always and everywhere her response was the same: "Let it happen to me according to your word" (Lk 1:38). No human, short of Jesus, has listened more lovingly, responded more generously.

Role model? Yes—if you want to experience what loving faith is, if you want to touch what faithful love is.

II

Move now from the mother of Jesus to all women who physically mother a Christ. It is a good day to recall what a mother means. The trouble is, a celibate male does not carry much authority here. It would be so much easier, and so much wiser, were I simply to reproduce the remarkable Epilogue from Erma Bombeck's *Motherhood: The Second Oldest Profession.*[4] With uncommon sensitivity and singular humor, that gifted woman creates a dialogue between God and an angel as the Lord is putting the finishing touches on his fashioning of The Mother. In less than 500 words the dialogue recaptures a mother as heaven shaped her for earth: six pairs of hands and three pairs of eyes, softness wed to toughness, reason to compromise . . . and tears—tears of joy and pain, of disappointment and pride, of loneliness and compassion.

I cannot speak, as Bombeck does, from inside a mother. Still, there is something a son can say, a word fleshed out from half a century of loving experience with my own mother, seven decades of graced contact with other mothers. My mother lived much of her life when a woman's "place" was in the home. And so she lived, literally, for her family. Friends she had aplenty: Our block was filled with her friends—German and Jew, Italian and Irish. And yet, her focus was a special trinity; her whole being was centered on my father, my brother, and myself. We were her "career"; we were her life. The Mary who served us was as single-minded as the Mary who lived for Joseph and Jesus . . . and God.

I do not claim that my mother's manner of mothering must be imitated by all mothers. The second half of our century is radically different from the first half. The old German synthesis of woman, *Küche, Kinder, Kirche* ("kitchen, children, church"), is not God's call to all mothers in our land, perhaps not to most. Through profound pain and with genuine joy we men have just discovered what women have long sensed: that the world outside our kitchens and nurseries and sanctuaries is less human when more masculine, that every facet of earthly existence—social, economic, political—can reach its potential human richness, can "attain to the fulness of Christ" (Eph 4:13), only if it is salted as well with the wit and wisdom, the sensitivity and common sense, that God has given to woman, in a distinctive way to mothers.

No, I do not insist on a single way of mothering; the hungers of the human family are too many, too deep, to permit a narrow "This is the path every mother must take; every mother must mimic the Mary of Nazareth, the Mary whose life was bounded by four walls." But this I do say. Whether it's Mother Mary or my own mother, whether it's the mother of Cain and Abel or the countless mothers who have walked in her steps through the ages, each mother must be a model to her little ones, a model in faith and in love. In faith: I mean, at home and in the marketplace, always and everywhere, breathing the breathless response of Nazareth's Mary to each call of her Lord: "Let it happen to me according to your word. Let it be with me as you say." And this not coerced by fear; this out of love—love for God above all else, love for His human images, especially the images of God and of herself that grew to life from her flesh and blood.

Such is our expectation of mother; such, in large measure, has been our experience of her.

III

All of which leads to my third point. Even in Mary's month, even on Mothers' Day, the liturgy speaks to every Christian, everyone who gives birth to Christ.

Does that expression sound strange to you: "everyone who gives birth to Christ"? It has a long, venerable tradition, with roots in St. Paul's anguished address to the Christians of Galatia in their crisis: "My little children, with whom I am again in travail, in labor pains, until Christ be formed in you!" (Gal 4:19). It is a striking way of expressing what your Christian existence is all about. And it has two facets: (1) Christ's birth in you and (2) Christ's birth in others through you.

Christ's birth in you. When you were baptized, a miracle of grace took place. Most of you were too young, too new to life outside a mother, to sense anything save an unexpected splash of cold water from a stranger in black and white. In point of fact, a remarkable relationship sprang into being at that moment, a relationship between you and the risen Christ so intimate that we have not words that do justice to it, so intimate that we speak haltingly of it in terms of another incarnation, as if an angel sent from God were to address you as he addressed Mary: "Hail, O favored one, the Lord is with you! . . . The Holy Spirit will come upon you, and the power of the Most High will overshadow you; and therefore the child to be born of you will be called . . . Son of God" (Lk 1:28, 35). Oh, not born of you with bone and blood; and yet in mysterious wise the living Christ was beginning to be fashioned in you. At that instant you could have exulted with St. Paul: "It is no longer I who live, but Christ who lives in me" (Gal 2:20).

From that point on, Christian living is simply the gradual growth of Christ in you. Yes, we're still imprisoned by a metaphor, but the grace of Christ, your sharing in his divine life, is as real as the blood in your veins. "Apart from me," Jesus proclaimed, "you can do nothing" (Jn 15:5). One with him, your potential is all but boundless. Your faith becomes not a substitute for reason but a new way of seeing—seeing with the eyes of Christ. Hope is then not a gift you can get at Garfinckel's; it is your confidence that God will give you all you need to live a risen life. Love ceases to be sentimental slush, "never having to say you're sorry"; it is power in the Spirit to love God above all else, to love each sister and brother with the same love you lavish on yourself.

Christ's birth in others through you. You are indeed one with the risen Christ in a deeply personal love. But Christian existence is not just "you and Jesus." What did Mary do after the Son of God took flesh in her? Hug her little secret to herself? Wait for the women of Nazareth to send Hallmark cards? "In those days," Luke tells us, "Mary arose and went with haste into the hill country" (Lk 1:39) to help her relative Elizabeth, well on in years and six months with child. And at Mary's coming with Jesus, the child within Elizabeth "leaped for joy" (v. 44). A pithy statement of Christian living. Life with Christ is not a birthday party for two; it is a reaching out, to help Christ come to birth, come to life, in another.

God knows, there is a small world right around you peopled by men and women—children too—who may indeed have Christ within them, but he doesn't come alive. Some are faith-less: They do not see with the eyes of Christ, cannot see beyond the immediate hurt. Some are hopeless: They expect nothing from anyone—not from God, not from man or woman. Some are loveless: They feel unloved, find it hard to feel anything for anybody—save perhaps anger or envy.

It's a good day to touch your Christ to another—even if your whole future hangs on an A grade, and economics continues more mysterious than the Trinity. It doesn't take much, you know. Not a three-tiered homily; simply a small segment of your heart. Who knows, you just may trigger the response of an Elizabeth to a Mary: "When the voice of your greeting came to my ears," something within me "leaped for joy" (Lk 1:44).

Dahlgren Chapel
Georgetown University
and
Holy Trinity Church
Washington, D.C.
May 13, 1984

12

THE LOVE WE CELEBRATE
Sixth Sunday of Easter (B)

♦ Acts 10:25–26, 34–35, 44–48
♦ 1 John 4:7–10
♦ John 15:9–17

Three weeks ago I preached to you that a single monosyllable is the heart of Easter. It is, I insisted, a monosyllable that alone makes sense out of Calvary, a monosyllable that alone can explain why you gather here each Sunday, a monosyllable that alone gives point to the way we Christians think and act. That monosyllable is . . . life. "I came," Jesus told us, "that [you] might have life, and have it in abundance" (Jn 10:10).

Today the liturgy stresses another Easter monosyllable. This monosyllable does not *compete* with life for paschal importance; it puts flesh on life, makes life come alive, tells you more truly than a lie detector whether your life is Christ's life. This monosyllable is . . . love. "This is my commandment, that you love . . ." (Jn 15:12).

The problem is, how talk about love so that it makes human and Christian sense? It's not easy. Especially when the word "love" is built into every electronic guitar. Especially when "love" is used of everything from Christ's bloody sacrifice on Calvary to the unbuttoned promiscuity of Fire Island. Especially when the preacher has two strikes against him to begin with: I'm a celibate, I'm a Jesuit! Nevertheless, always more brash than the angels, I shall wrestle with Easter love, and you can decide, from your own experience, whether it makes human and Christian sense.

Three stages to my song of love: (1) What are we talking about when we talk of love? (2) How does such an understanding of love put flesh on Easter life? (3) What sort of challenge does this love fling out to you?

I

First, what are we talking about when we talk of love? The day-to-day notion of love is far too narrow. It's taken largely from TV. To love is to "make love," to go to bed. Dallas and Dynasty, Love Boat and Falcon Crest, Rituals and the "soaps," Mike Hammer—why, only Kojak is without love . . . so far. Our human and Christian tradition is much richer.

On the one hand, there is the *touch* of love. Touch, you know, is a wonderful and fearful thing. It says something. There is the touch that says "I care"—as when Jesus takes little children in his arms and blesses them. And there is the touch that says "I despise you"—as when Nazi animals throw little children into gas ovens. There is the intimate touch of husband and wife that says "You are dearer to me than all else on earth." And there is the rude touch of the rapist that says "I hate you." There is the touch of the surgeon that cuts only to heal, and the touch of the mugger that cuts only to hurt. There is the embrace that says "You are my friend," and the shove that says "You are my enemy." The contrasts are legion. The point is, love is part of touch when the "I" that God shaped in His image goes out to another, when my touch says, in different degrees, to spouse or stranger, to family or friend, to man or woman, to human or God, "You are part of me."

But there is love, too, without physical touch. At times more difficult, because when I love, my whole self bends to another—not just naked spirit. But quite possible. Jesus "loved Martha," John's Gospel tells us, "loved her sister and [their brother] Lazarus" (Jn 11:5). There can be love when I give bread to the hungry and water to the thirsty, when I clothe the shivering and house the stranger, when I visit the sick and the chained. There can be love when my eyes meet your eyes. There can be love between myself and a Jesus whose wounds I cannot touch, love between myself and a God who lives within me without my being able to put my arms around Him. There can be *if* . . . if the "I" that God shaped in His image goes out to them, if I am saying "You are part of me."

II

But how does such an understanding of love put flesh on Easter life? Easter life, remember, means to be alive in Christ, to share God's life. At this very moment Christ our Lord lives in you. You can cry with St. Paul "It is no longer I who live, but Christ who lives in me" (Gal 2:20). At this very moment Father, Son, and Holy Spirit live in you as in a sacred temple.

Now it is love that tells you what life means, Easter love that reveals what Easter life means. God's life in you is not a Jesuit's poetic fancy, Shelley's moonbeams kissing the sea. God's life in you is not something gauzelike and gossamer, cobwebs floating in air. God's life in you is God's love for you. Not a love that stays hidden in God's mind, a love we can talk about but never touch. God's love is wonderfully and fearfully concrete. Like your parents' love for you that gave you life, like the love of man and maid that transforms them, God's love for you changes you, makes you different. God's love is the creative word that brought you out of nothingness, made you some one. God's love for you is the writhing figure of His crucified Son that destroyed death in you. God's love for you is an empty tomb, the risen Christ who "always lives to make intercession" for you (Heb 7:25).

Put another way, God's life in you is a relationship. A relationship that graces you with powers beyond the sheerly human. Because God loves you, you can proclaim: "I believe. I believe what naked reason could never conceive. I believe in one God, Father, Son, and Spirit. I believe that God's only Son took my flesh, died for me, rose for me, lives for me. I believe in a church, a community of men and women linked as closely to Christ as a body to its head. I believe that I, this strange wedding of flesh and spirit, will live with God days without end." Because God loves you, you can hope. Hope for God from God. Hope in the midst of misery, from the hell of holocaust and the jaws of genocide, on the hungry sands of Ethiopia and in the thirsty desert of your own despair. Because God loves you, you can love as you could never have imagined: You can love God above all else in this world, love your sisters and brothers as a crucified Christ has loved you.

In a word, God's love for you means that God has gone out to you, has touched you. A touch that says: "I care for you. You are dearer to me than sea and sky, than bird or beast. If I cut you, it is only to heal you. You are my friend. You are part of me."

III

This summons up my third question: What sort of challenge does this love, this Easter love, fling out to you? It should indeed challenge you. After all, your Lord has told you bluntly: "This is my commandment, that you love. . . ." Not an invitation, R.S.V.P.; a command. True, he does not compel your love; and still he commands it. Why? Because the love that God has in mind, the love that makes you Christian, the love that puts flesh on your Easter life, is a relationship. If it takes two to tango, it takes two to love. Oh I know, God's love surrounds me whether I love Him or not. His love pursues me through all my infidelities, the love that proclaimed to the ancient people of Israel:

> Can a woman forget her sucking child,
>   that she should have no compassion on the son of her womb?
> Even these may forget,
>   yet I will not forget you.
> Behold, I have graven you on the palms of my hands. . . .
>   (Isa 49:14–16)

God's love can be one-sided. But that love will be fruitless, will not change me, unless I respond to it. In fact, my return of love *is* the change in me; the change in me *is* my loving.

Now this love God commands is not moonlight and roses, starry-eyed saints with lilies in hand. It's a tough love, and over the ages countless men and women have shrunk from it, found it impossible, unreasonable, absurd. It means that I can murmur: "Look, Lord, I don't pretend to understand you, but I still love you. Though you puzzle me day after day, I still love you. Though you tolerate wars, let a Hitler live and six million Jews die, I still love you. Though you do nothing about earthquakes in Guatemala, political prisons in the Gulag Peninsula, bloated bellies in flight from Cambodia, I still love you. Though you sit impassively in high heaven while innocents die in the womb and the nations brace for nuclear suicide, I still love you. Though one fourth of the people you claim to love go to sleep hungry each night, I still love you. Though my father and only brother died of cancer within three weeks of each other, and my mother turned senile, I still love you. Sometimes I'm not sure why I love you; but this I do know, that if you could give your own Son to a bloodsoaked death for me, you must care deeply—more deeply than my dull intellect can fathom."

Harsh though it seems, this is the type of love God demands of me. But even this is not enough. Jesus not only commanded: "You shall love the Lord your God with all your heart, and with all your soul, and with all your mind" (Mt 22:37). He added: "You shall love

your neighbor as yourself" (v. 39). In fact, "This is my command-
ment, that you love one another as I have loved you" (Jn 15:12).
Frankly, I don't know which is the more difficult: to love you as
Christ has loved me, or to love you as much as I love myself!

Fortunately, it's easy for me to love *you*. You are lovable people:
You applaud my preaching, appreciate my humor. The radical
Christian challenge is this: How can I love those I do not like? Americans love Iran's ayatollah? Irish Catholics love Iron Maiden
Thatcher? Tip O'Neill love Ronald Reagan? Is Jesus really asking
you to love the unlovable, the inhuman, the people who have done
you dirt, done you in? The rapist and the terrorist, butchers buried
in Bitburg[1] and neo-Nazis alive and well outside Chicago? Those
who hate you or hurt you, cheat you or scorn you? The enemy soldier who lusts for your blood? Seemingly yes—if you can credit the
Gospel, if you can believe your Lord and Master:

> You have heard that it was said, "You shall love your neighbor
> and hate your enemy." But I say to you, Love your enemies and
> pray for those who persecute you, so that you may be sons [and
> daughters] of your Father who is in heaven; for He makes His
> sun rise on the evil and on the good, and sends rain on the just
> and on the unjust. For if you love those who love you, what re-
> ward have you? Do not even the tax collectors do the same? And
> if you salute only your brethren, what more are you doing than
> others? Do not even the Gentiles do the same? You, therefore,
> must be perfect, as your heavenly Father is perfect.
>
> (Mt 5:43–48)

An impossible task? Unreal? Not really. Not if you have
grasped what Easter love means. Jesus is not asking you to go to bed
with the enemy, to like the detestable. He is commanding you to
care, to be concerned for every man, woman, or child who comes
into your ken, crosses your road. Unreal? Not if you ponder the
word you heard from the first Letter of John: "Beloved, if God so
loved us [loved us so dearly that He gave His own Son for our sins],
we also ought to love one another" (1 Jn 4:11). Unreal? Not if you
realize that what God commands He empowers us to do. We can
love as Jesus loved, not because we are supermen or wonder
women; only because he lives in us.

Here a highly practical point. Jesus is not asking you to begin
with Bitburg across the sea, do mental gymnastics on how your
heart can go out to a Castro or a Gorbachev. He is asking you to care
where you are: this community and this campus, where you work

and where you play, the home you take for granted and the streets you walk so lightly. Love begins in your personal cabbage patch. Here is love's challenge—enough challenges to stock a computer or a blue book. Here is where you must live the prayer that opened today's liturgy: "Ever-living God, help us . . . to express in our lives the love we celebrate."

The love we celebrate. A love that left heaven[2] to wear our flesh; a love that laughed with us and wept over us; a love that lived for the sinful and the hateful, for the despised and the despairing; a love that was crowned with thorns and consummated in crucifixion. Such is the love we celebrate. Is such the love we pray to express in our lives? If it is not, if we love only those who love us, what more are we doing than the good pagan?

A "hard saying" indeed (Jn 6:60). So hard that it helps to muse on it on Mothers' Day, in Mary's month. It helps to muse on the millions of Marys who express in their lives, express each day, the love of Christ we celebrate—mothers who live a crucified love and can still sing with Mary "My spirit delights in God my Savior" (Lk 1:47).

Dahlgren Chapel
Georgetown University
and
Holy Trinity Church
Washington, D.C.
May 12, 1985

ORDINARY TIME

13

IS CHRIST DIVIDED?
Third Sunday of the Year (A)

♦ Isaiah 8:23—9:3
♦ 1 Corinthians 1:10–13, 17
♦ Matthew 4:12–23

Today's readings should shake you. They report two historical facts, one consoling, the other distressing. The consoling fact? For a world groping in darkness, a brilliant light has broken; the messianic king has come to dispel the dark; henceforth God's people will live in the clear light of the Savior's day; "the kingdom of heaven is at hand" (Mt 4:17). The distressing fact? In the Christian community at Corinth there are "dissensions," there is "quarreling" (1 Cor 1:10, 11); whatever "light" there has been has apparently dimmed.

Here are two facts in conflict, and they raise three questions. First, what specifically was the problem *then,* the paradox of unprecedented light and community dissension? Second, what is our *present* problem, our Catholic community enlightened by Christ and disagreeing deep within? Third, how can we *live* with such a paradox, live not in hostility but in love? A word on each question.

I

First, what was the problem in Corinth, the problem in the spring of 57? Remember the context, the background. The Light of the world has come into the world, "the true Light that enlightens every human being" (Jn 1:9). This is the Christ who gives to all who believe "power to become children of God" (Jn 1:12), the Christ who brings "grace and truth" (Jn 1:17). Like Christians everywhere, the Christians of Corinth were walking not in darkness but in the light, in the light of Christ.

And yet, a generation after Christ was crucified, perhaps four rival factions had formed within the Corinthian community.[1] A better-educated minority was captivated by Apollos, a Jewish convert from Alexandria, "an eloquent man, well versed in the Scriptures" (Acts 18:24). A second group boasted a special attachment to Peter, prince of the apostles. A third group, the majority, poor freedmen and slaves, rocked and rolled for Paul, apostle of Corinth. A fourth group prided itself on a singular relationship to Christ, a relationship not shared by other Christians, even claimed a superior skill in practical morality.

Now these were not just academic differences: How many angels can sit on the head of a pin? They were not good-natured commercials: "This Bud's for you," Miller Lite for me. No, things had gotten nasty; Christians were exploding like enemies, like cats in a sack. Not only were they divided in mind; love itself was threatened.

All this upset Paul mightily; he waxed sarcastic. Factions founded on ministers of Christ? "I belong to Paul," "I belong to Apollos," "I belong to Peter" (1 Cor 1:12)? Absurd! Nonsense! And some Christians "belong to Christ"? "Is Christ divided?" (vv. 12–13). Some of you belong to him and others do not? Paul puts forth a solemn plea: "I appeal to you, brethren, by the name of our Lord Jesus Christ, that all of you say the same thing . . . that you be fully united in the same mind and in the same conviction" (v. 10).

II

My second question: What is our present problem, the paradox within the Catholic community today? Once again, recall the context, the background. The Light that is Christ has come not only into Bethlehem but into the world. The true Light enlightens not just his mother and the shepherds, not just the apostles and the people of Palestine, not just pope and priest; he enlightens all who believe in him. If we truly believe, if we welcome Christ as Lord and Savior, we are walking in his light. "Grace and truth" are God's gift to His people.

And yet, almost 20 centuries after the Light flooded the world, rival factions have formed within the Catholic community. Not so much "I belong to Hans Küng" or "I belong to William Buckley" or even (God save the mark!) "I belong to Walter Burghardt"—though there is a certain amount of "I belong to John Paul II (and you don't)." More critically, there is "quarreling" about who belongs to Christ.

I am not speaking of marginal Catholics, men and women living on the slippery edge of Catholicism: the Sunday Catholic, the Catholic content with externals, the Catholic whose religion is his or her private affair, Catholics who need no pope in board room or bedroom. I am speaking primarily of Catholics seriously committed to Christ within a community of faith, hope, and love. I am speaking of Catholics who recognize that the Church is not a democracy, not the rule of a majority, not "one person one vote." I am speaking of Catholics who love their Church despite its scars and wrinkles, who know that they too are sin-scarred and error-prone, who agonize over disunion and dissension.

Among such Catholics there is division and quarreling. The divisions touch the three most significant areas of Catholic existence: doctrine, liturgy, and morality. I mean what we believe, how we worship, and the way we live.

In doctrine, it seems that almost everything that once was accepted without question is being challenged, from the first apple to the Second Coming, from "one person" in Christ to "one true Church." In liturgy, the Mass that should be the unifying focus of the Catholic people is a divisive force: stately Latin or pedestrian English, hushed awe or rock-rolling decibels, Bach or the St. Louis Jesuits, missalettes or lay lector, celebrant respectfully solemn or celebrant smiling Brite, kiss of peace or me-and-Jesus, Communion in the hand or on the tongue, from consecrated fingers or extraordinary ministers? In morality, our people are rent asunder on nuclear destruction and premarital sex; divorce-and-remarriage is an increasing phenomenon for Catholics; and thousands upon thousands who love Christ and his Church dearly are among the 80 percent of married American Catholics who reject in practice the official position on artificial contraception.

Nor are these sheerly academic discussions, rollicking arguments over a Michelob. Many Catholics have a singular "gift" for moving from disagreement to dislike, to sarcasm, to something awfully close to hatred—often under the half-truth "Charity is truth." Real love is telling it as it is, and let the chips (and the bodies) fall where they may! Dissenters are traitors, liturgical dance is disco stuff, abortionists are murderers—and that's that! Besides, if a Catholic issue touches our personal lives intimately, it is difficult not

to cry out passionately against those who interfere with our freedom, our need to live humanly, the pressures from our conscience.
And so, members of the same body, we quarrel like Paul's Corinthians, like enemies; at times we excommunicate one another more
easily than any pope has ever dared.

III

Which brings me to my third question: How can we live with
such a paradox, live not in hostility but in love? Now a homily is not
a class in theology; it is an effort to help you to know Christ more
clearly, love him more dearly, follow him more nearly. Moreover,
the disagreements—doctrinal, liturgical, moral—are so vast and
complex that even a jabbering Jesuit cannot defuse them in five
minutes. Let me simply suggest a start, a springboard, a way to begin.

The Jewish philosopher Martin Buber declared that our highest human duty is to transform society into community.[2] Here, I
submit, lies our own critical need. The Catholic Church is a society;
Holy Trinity parish is a society; Dahlgren worshipers are a society.
Each is a group of men and women using common means to achieve
a common end. Each is a group of men and women working for
salvation, making its way to God, by believing in the Lord Jesus
Christ, by responding to his grace, by living a moral existence in
harmony with Church and conscience.

Now that is good . . . but not good enough—not Christian
enough, not Catholic enough. The Church, the parish, university
believers should be not simply a society but a community. What does
community add to society? In one word, intimacy. As Buber saw it,
you have a community where people reach out to one another in
mutual concern. Where the overriding relationship is not I-it but I-
thou. Where the indispensable ingredient, the glue that holds the
whole together, is love. Love not merely in personal relationships
but in working together for common values, the good of the community. We are a community to the extent that love binds us together, in the measure that love is what motivates us to work
together, to the degree that love drives us, despite our disagreements, to achieve intimacy with Christ and one another, now and
for ever.

This is, I admit, awfully abstract. Talking about love usually is—especially if a priest is doing the talking. Let me balance the abstract with the concrete: several facts and attitudes without which "Catholic love" is an empty phrase, sheer fantasy.

First, we are a pilgrim people. The ideal is indeed Paul's plea: "I appeal to you, by the name of our Lord Jesus Christ, that all of you say the same thing . . . that you be fully united in the same mind and in the same conviction" (1 Cor 1:10). That is the ideal; but the ideal will be realized only in heaven. Till then, we are pilgrims; we are on the way. We do not "have it made"—none of us, not even the pope. Not yet do we possess the truth in its fulness; not yet do we see with perfect clarity; our very sinfulness blurs our understanding. To know the risen Christ is a ceaseless struggle; it is agonizing struggle to be the community he had in mind when the Church was born of his blood and his Spirit.

Second, this means we must be humble. Not the false humility that whines "Step on me, I'm dirt." Humble rather in recognizing who I really am—my talents as well as my limitations. Humble in recognizing how relatively little I know of the God who revealed Himself in our flesh. Humble in recognizing that I too am swayed by passion and prejudice, by my likes and dislikes. Humble, therefore, in accepting direction from above, from those who, the New Testament tells us, have been placed over us to "tend the flock of God" (1 Pet 5:2).

Third, this does not imply that we accept direction blindly, shut our eyes to problems, still the voice of conscience. At times we cannot. But disagreement with pope or bishop should not come easily; it should shake us. Believe me, my friends, each time I dissent I bleed. And remember, there are different levels of disagreement. It is one thing to deny that Christ is God; it is quite another thing to say no to Communion in the hand. One no is a refusal to be a Christian; the other no is largely a matter of taste (or touch). We profess our belief that Christ "descended into hell"; but in the life of the Church this takes second place to "He descended from heaven." In day-to-day morality it is not simple to say just when dissent makes one less than Catholic. Here we should be slow to judge, reluctant to play prosecutor and jury. And even where the sin is crystal-clear, there is need to image the merciful Christ, whose heart went out especially to sinners.

Fourth, if my disagreement is to be Catholic, it must be impregnated with affection: a warm feeling for this sinful people of God, empathy with those who differ from me. Not an arrogant "No one can tell me what to do"; not a selfish "This is the way I feel about it, and that's that." No, this is my spiritual family, including the mighty men in miters. If I am soured on the Church, if I delight in its defects, if I am cynical about its so-called wealth, if I cannot stand Catholics who talk about Jesus as if he were alive, if I ridicule my peers who will not go to bed with me, if I operate on the naked edge of the faith, doing only what I have to do to escape a hell I do not really believe in—I much fear that I am not in love.

Fifth, another way of expressing it: What sacrifices have I made for the community, for Catholic unity? Oneness in Christ is not primarily a matter of the mind—your brilliant insights conquering my colossal stupidity. Paradoxically, our oneness rests in large measure on our willingness to suffer for it, to sacrifice for it, to say no to the pride in our very blood and bone. Our Lord was taken from the cross not to leave it empty; it is ours now to mount. Otherwise we are parasites on the community, looking only for what we can get from it, reluctant to give to it.

Sixth, a pungent question: Can I say to the Church, can I say to my parish, can I say to the community wherein I worship, what the Jewish exiles in Babylon said to their mother?

> If I forget you, O Jerusalem,
>   let my right hand wither!
> Let my tongue cleave to the roof of my mouth,
>   if I do not remember you,
> if I do not set Jerusalem
>   above my highest joy!
>
> (Ps 137:6)

My sisters and brothers in Christ: History and experience tell us that within our one Catholic body we will always have our differences. Differences large and differences small. For the most part, the differences are not in basic belief. But they can divide us and they do. Understandably; for the mystery of Christ is too vast to grasp, and we can be dreadfully petty. The crucial question is: Can we differ without disliking? Can we contradict without condemning? Can we debate without hate?

We had better—for our salvation's sake. You know, I spend most of my waking day playing theological detective, trying to unravel the mystery of God-with-us. But when I stand before the judgment seat of God, the judge who died for me will not ask me: Did you solve the mystery? He will simply ask: Did you love me above all else? And did you love your brothers and sisters as if they were your own self?

Dahlgren Chapel
Georgetown University
and
Holy Trinity Church
Washington, D.C.
January 22, 1984

14

EACH OF YOU IS JONAH
Third Sunday of the Year (B)

- Jonah 3:1–5, 10
- 1 Corinthians 7:29–31
- Mark 1:14–20

I think it's time we talked about Jonah. Let's begin with a bit of a bet. I'll wager that, when you hear the word "Jonah," one of two associations leaps into your head: three days in the belly of a whale, or a character who brings bad luck wherever he goes. The trouble is, this hardly does justice to a God-inspired book, a segment of Scripture. Jonah is not just the first occupant of an undersea condo without windows, not simply a symbol of misfortune like Calamity Jane. You will not appreciate Jonah if your knowledge is limited to Jonah-equals-whale-or-bad-luck; you will not sense his significance if the liturgy lends you only the six verses of our first reading. So then, three stages to my journey into Jonahland: (1) the man, (2) the meaning, (3) the message. Who was he? What was his importance for Israel? What might he say to you and me now?

I

First, the man. Who was Jonah and what was he about? For those of you who are skeptical about living conditions inside a big fish—lack of oxygen, raw seafood diet, toilet service—relax. The story is just that: a story. A short story: about 1300 English words. It's fiction, but fiction for a purpose, fiction with a message. A drama in two acts.

Act 1. The Lord orders Jonah to go to Nineveh, capital of Assyria: Preach repentance to the Ninevites, "for their wickedness has come up before me" (Jonah 1:2). But this vocation brings no joy to

100

Jonah. Preach penance to pagans, announce salvation to non-Jews? Uh-uh, not for Jonah. He flees as far from the Lord as he can, buys a ticket on a freighter bound for southern Spain. The Lord raises up a storm, and the ship threatens to break apart. The pagan sailors draw lots to discover who has brought them bad luck. Who else but Jonah? A good fellow at heart, he asks them to toss him overboard. They oblige; the sea settles; the sailors are converted to Israel's God. As for Jonah, a big fish, with instructions from above, swallows him whole. After three days, at the bidding of the Lord of the sea, the fish vomits him up. End of Act 1.

Act 2. The word of the Lord comes to Jonah a second time: Get thee to Nineveh! Jonah still dislikes the assignment, but this time he goes. How argue with a God who got you out of a "fishy" situation? He preaches; the people are converted; God spares the city. But Jonah is angry: Pagans the beneficiaries of God's pardon? He blows his stack, tells God to put him out of his misery: "It is better for me to die than to live" (4:3). He sulks outside the city, shaded from the sun by a plant God provides. Then God gets a worm to wither Jonah's sunscreen, and the sun beats down on his unprotected head. Jonah protests, is again angry enough to die. Now God lets him have it with both barrels: "You pity the plant, for which you did not labor, nor did you make it grow, which came into being in a night, and perished in a night" (4:10). And you resent my pitying 120,000 men and women "who do not know their right hand from their left" (4:11)? With that harsh question the Book of Jonah ends.

II

Second, the meaning. What was Jonah's importance for Israel? Why put Jonah among the prophets of the Old Testament? The prophets we know—Isaiah and Ezekiel, Jeremiah and Joel—had two impressive qualities: They were obedient to the Lord and they preached repentance. But look at Jonah: He disobeys the Lord and refuses to preach repentance. When finally he obeys and preaches, he gets angry when the Ninevites repent—angry enough to die. Why put a reluctant prophet in God's Book?

The point is, the Book of Jonah is not really centered on Jonah. Oh yes, it tells us much about Jonah, but it tells us much more about God. Yes, we discover once again how stupid a man sent by God can be; how difficult for him to grasp the goodness of his God; how narrow his outlook on those who are different, who worship other gods. More important still, we glimpse through Jonah how good God is, how loving; how His compassion embraces every creature in His universe, even (the last word in the book) the "cattle" (4:11). *All* men and women are the people of His caring. And so *all* are called to repent, for to repent simply means to turn to God.

Jonah could not see that. He could lose his cool, grow livid with wrath, when a castor-oil plant that was his sunblock withered; yet he could let thousands of humans perish in their unbelief without turning pale. Not a bad person. After all, Jonah was willing to drown for pagan sailors. Not bad; just myopic, shortsighted. Too wrapped up in his narrow nationalism. God was *his* God, the God of the Hebrews, imprisoned in one country, one temple, one ark of the covenant.

Whoever wrote this story, this satire, was using Jonah as an example, a warning to all narrow-minded Israelites. He was saying, in effect: "Each of you is Jonah—dreadfully nearsighted. Remember your mission, the universal vocation of Israel: to preach to the nations the endless breadth of God's mercy and forgiveness. Recall the calling of Abraham, representative of Israel: 'By you all the families of the earth shall be blessed' (Gen 12:3). Recollect God's word through Isaiah: 'I have given you as a covenant to the people, a light to the nations, to open the eyes that are blind' (Isa 42:6–7), 'that my salvation may reach to the end of the earth' (Isa 49:6)."

The meaning of Jonah? God's loving mercy waits for all who repent, whoever they are, wherever they live, whatever they've done.

III

Third, the message. What might Jonah say to you and me now? Two suggestions strike me, two messages above all. One is a matter of good Christian theology, the other a matter of good Christian living.

The theology is basically what Jonah's ghost writer was commending to ancient Israel: Think big about God! Through seven decades I've seen Christians shaping God in their own image—in each case, a dreadfully small God. Some of us still believe that only Roman Catholics will graze heaven's green pastures. Not only false but, as we sometimes chant at the Capital Center, "boring." Some Christians will let "outsiders" in, but on a selective basis: our kind, our color, a separate section for Jews (we'll be doing them a favor). There is the God who has a special affection for capitalist America, rewards the workaholic, and the God who loves only the poor and underprivileged. There is the God who marches with victorious armies, and the God who loves only the meek who turn the other cheek. Some, like the elder brother in Luke, sulk and pout when the Father rocks and rolls, serves turf-and-surf, for a prodigal son who has spent his last cent on whores. Some, tragically, refuse to believe that God can or will forgive *them:* My sin is too great.

Such, dear friends, such is not our God. Our God, the New Testament insists, "desires all men and women to be saved" (1 Tim 2:4). Our hope is the God-man Jesus Christ, who clothed himself in our flesh and carried it to a bloody cross not simply for the "nice guys"— his mother and most of the apostles, Teresa of Avila and Teresa of Calcutta, the Irish Republic and the Blue Army, Holy Trinity parishioners and holy Hoyas. God's compassion reaches out to sinners—and you know, that means everybody. Even a three-point homilist. Even those who stretch God's compassion to the breaking point—the proud, men and women who, like the Pharisee in the temple, thank God that they are "not like the rest of humankind" (Lk 18:11), who "have it made," have the world by the tail, don't need God after conception or implantation—even these God loves. There is a breaking point, yes; but it is not really God who reaches it. Only I—if and when I say a final no to God: "I know who you are, and I choose of my own free will to reject your love."

So much for good theology; what of good Christian living? Here we join Jonah fleeing God on a freighter. It brings to mind Francis Thompson's wondrous poem depicting God as "The Hound of Heaven," the poem that begins:

> I fled Him, down the nights and down the days;
> I fled Him, down the arches of the years;
> I fled Him, down the labyrinthine ways
>   Of my own mind; and in the mist of tears
> I hid from Him, and under running laughter.
>   Up vistaed hopes I sped;
>   And shot, precipitated,
> Adown Titanic glooms of chasmèd fears,
>   From those strong Feet that followed, followed after.
>   But with unhurrying chase,
>   And unperturbèd pace,
>   Deliberate speed, majestic instancy,
>   They beat—and a Voice beat
>   More instant than the Feet—
> 'All things betray thee, who betrayest Me.'[1]

Most of us, I fear, flee God in some way, at some time, to some extent. Oh, we're more sophisticated than Jonah: We know from our catechism days that God is everywhere, that a slow boat to China or a Qantas flight to Australia will not distance us from God. We flee God more effectively. Some of us limit God to one hour a week, resent it if God runs over into Redskins time. Or, full-time philosophers, we force God to prove that He exists, with arguments that convince not first-century fishermen but intellectuals of 2001. Or we blame our disinterest, our skepticism, on Sister Ignatius, who riddled our adolescent psyches beyond repair. Or our love stumbles on the tragedies that stalk human existence: a brain-damaged infant, starving skeletons in Ethiopia, war upon senseless war, "accidents" that shake our once-firm faith, sudden loss of all we held dear. Or we don't need God: Science is shaping a super-Adam, a super-Eve, with no rotten apples; technology is creating a brave new world beyond anything the Creator could have conceived. Or we simply don't have time for God right now: The struggle to make a decent living, to get ahead, the great grade rush—get me through this, dear God, and I'll make it up to you later, I promise!

I do not mock all this, belittle it, hold it inhuman. It's all touchingly human; that's precisely what makes it so dangerous. The human is so prominent, so overpowering, that the divine takes second place, turns unreal, is buried. God ceases to be God. And each of you can be Jonah.

I beg you, don't let that happen! The thrilling paradox is, the Love you may be fleeing is actually within you. Each of you is a temple of God, a shrine of the Spirit. To ignore Him is like ignoring your own flesh. To put Him off till Sunday is akin to holding your breath for a week. Challenge Him if you must, ask Him to show you His face, dump your anger and resentment on Him; but don't flee from Him. If you do, or if you have, I pray that, as with Francis Thompson in his life and in his poem, you will hear "That Voice round [you] like a bursting sea: . . . 'Lo, all things fly thee, for thou fliest Me.' "[2]

I do not say that if you keep fleeing, you will be miserable. I have never forgotten what a remarkable Jesuit, John Courtney Murray, told us in theology class 45 years ago: "Don't let anyone ever tell you that sinners are not happy." But this I do promise you. If you stop fleeing, if in response to Jesus you "repent and believe in the gospel" (Mk 1:15), if you turn to the God who lives and loves and leaps within you, if you listen to and live to the full the genuinely Good News Jesus proclaims to you, you will know a joy, a depth of delight, beyond your wildest imagining. But, dear Jonah, you have to stop running.

Dahlgren Chapel
Georgetown University
and
Holy Trinity Church
Washington, D.C.
January 27, 1985

15

ON THE JERICHO ROAD
Sixth Sunday of the Year (B)

- ◆ Leviticus 13:1–2, 44–46
- ◆ 1 Corinthians 10:30—11:1
- ◆ Mark 1:40–45

So what does a homilist do with leprosy? A learned lecture on skin diseases in the Old Testament? A spiritual application: psoriasis of the soul? Recall famous Father Damien of Molokai's leper colony, one day hale and hearty, the next day beginning his sermon with "We lepers . . ."? None of the above. It was a frustrating few days, till I was caught by the words of Mark after the leper begs for healing: "Moved with pity, [Jesus] stretched out his hand and touched him . . ." (Mk 1:41). Jesus was touched and he touched. Let's see this twin response then and now: in Jesus and in ourselves.

I

First, Jesus. If you consult your New Testament Greek dictionary, you will discover a thrilling word. The verb that is translated "moved with pity" is much more startling in the Greek.[1] Literally, it has to do with our bowels. Where we Westerners say "My heart goes out to you," the Hebrews often said "My bowels go out to you." It sounds strange, but it hints at a tremendous truth. Genuine feeling comes from deep inside us; the seat of our emotions is way down within. Love and hate, fears and tears, anger and delight—a score of emotions well up not from our hairline but from our deepest selves.

So it was with Jesus. That is why the Gospels time and again use that strong anatomical verb of him. His bowels "stirred with compassion" for a crowd of thousands that had stayed with him three

106

days and had nothing to eat: "I am unwilling to send them away
hungry, lest they faint on the way" (Mt 15:32). His bowels "stirred
with compassion" for all manner of sick people who had followed
him to a lonely place (Mt 14:14); for throngs that "were harassed
and helpless, like sheep without a shepherd" (Mt 9:36); for two
blind men on the roadside outside Jericho (Mt 20:34); for a mother
whose only son lay dead before her eyes (Lk 7:13). The father of an
epileptic boy appealed to the "bowels of [his] compassion" to help
his foaming, convulsing child (Mk 9:22). And here, in today's Gospel, Jesus' bowels "stirred with compassion" for a leper in the dust
crying "If you will, you can make me clean" (Mk 1:40–41).

Yes, time after time Jesus was touched—touched with pity, with
compassion, for all kinds of human infirmity. But that is only one
side of the coin. The other side: When touched, what did Jesus do?
When touched, he touched.[2] When the bowels of his compassion
stirred, he reached out. He touched—skin to skin. The hand of a
dead 12-year-old girl (Mk 5:41), of Peter's fevered mother-in-law
(Mt 8:15), of the epileptic boy (Mk 9:27); the eyes of the sightless
two outside Jericho (Mt 20:34); the ears and tongue of a deaf man
with a speech defect (Mk 7:33); the right ear of the high priest's
slave, cut off by swordsman Peter (Jn 18:10; Lk 22:51); a woman
bent over for 18 years (Lk 13:13). All these he touched. When Peter
was sinking in the sea, Jesus "reached out his hand and caught him"
(Mt 14:31). Children he not only blessed; he "took them in his arms"
(Mk 10:16). At the Last Supper he lovingly washed the feet of his
disciples (Jn 13:5).

I have pointed it out before, and I insist on it now: I am not
saying that Jesus was a hail-fellow-well-met, a backslapper, a
"gimme five" type, Dr. J after a spectacular dunk.[3] I *am* saying that
Jesus was more than a weaver of words. The Son of God took on
our total flesh: not only a mind and tongue but our sense life. When
Peter denied that he knew him, Jesus "looked at Peter" (Lk 22:61).
In the temple he listened to the teachers (Lk 2:46). He asked a Samaritan woman for a drink of water (Jn 4:7), ate with Pharisees and
sinners. He breathed the air of Galilee; the smells of Palestine were
his smells. He wept over Jerusalem and over Lazarus, over his city
and his friend. And just as humanly, he touched—not only the
lovely face of his mother but the lifeless skin of a leper. In fact, his
touch was as much part of his saving mission, as much part of his
redemptive task, as his words and his prayers. He touched to heal:
not only leprosy but the leper; not simply flesh but the lesion that
is sin and the hurt that scars the human heart.

I often wonder what it must have felt like—the hand of Jesus caressing my cheek, cupping my chin, just resting there on my head: "Your sins are forgiven. Be made clean. Open your eyes, your ears, your tongue. Stand up and walk." If no one ever spoke as this man spoke, surely no one ever touched the way he touched. How gentle, how strong, how loving!

II

So much for Jesus; but what of us? As for him, so for us, twin facets, two sides of a single coin: touched and touching. A word on each.

What touches me? What is it that breaks my skin, gets inside me, messes up my emotions, plays leapfrog with my passions? For some men and women, nothing does. They've been hurt, horribly hurt—in loving or trusting, in giving or sharing—and nothing, no one, is ever going to get to them again. They throw up a Berlin Wall between themselves and the other. From now on, it's strictly business. "Don't show me bare bones in Auschwitz, starving skeletons in Ethiopia, 10,000 homeless in D.C. I had nothing to do with any of that, and it's not my problem. Don't parade before my psyche the lonely and the loveless, the Hot Liners and the hate-full, those who can't hack it in today's jungle, can't cut it on a competitive campus. You need money for a good cause? I'll give it at the office; but don't ask me for anything more—compassion or love, indignation or anger, fear or a tear. You can touch my credit card; you can't touch me."

Sorry, friend, but it won't wash. To be touched is to be human; compassion is another word for Christian. The New Testament calls Jesus priest on two counts: He was appointed by God *and* he could "sympathize with our weaknesses" (Heb 4:15). Sympathize: literally, suffer with, feel with, com-passion. But priesthood is not limited to Jesus, is not a private preserve of the ordained. As the first Letter of Peter trumpeted to persecuted Christians of Asia Minor, "You are a chosen race, a royal priesthood . . ." (1 Pet 2:9). All of you share in the priesthood of Christ. But a priest without compassion, whose guts do not quiver before bloated bellies and empty eyes, who reddens not with anger over injustice, who does not hurt when I hurt, whose life is one steady blood pressure, an unvarying systole and diastole, this robot is not really a priest, does not walk in the footsteps of his Lord.

No, to be Christian is to "feel with." But that is simply one side of the coin. The other side: When I am moved, how do I respond? When touched, do I touch?

Four years ago I took part in the annual convocation of Ohio pastors. My most shivering experience? A black pastor from Texas preaching on the Good Samaritan. You remember that Gospel, I'm sure. How a Jew journeying from Jerusalem to Jericho was half killed by robbers. How first a priest, then a Levite, came upon him, looked, and "passed by on the other side" (Lk 10:31, 32). How a Samaritan happened upon him, "was moved with compassion . . . bound up his wounds . . . brought him to an inn and took care of him" (vv. 33–34). Commented the black pastor: The priest and the Levite were perfectly at home in Jerusalem. They could handle anything that had to do with the temple: circumcision and the Torah, the altar of incense and the table for the showbread, the animals to be sacrificed and the ark of the covenant. What they could not handle, he said in inimitable black accents, was "the é-vent on the Jericho road."

There you have the cutting edge of Christianity: "the é-vent on the Jericho road." The story of the Good Samaritan is not aimed exclusively at first-century Jews. The lawyer's question that triggered the story, "Who is my neighbor?" (Lk 10:29), echoes down the ages, across the globe. Each of us walks or rides or jogs a Jericho road every day. You don't have to search for it—in Lafayette Park, in D.C. General, in South Africa or the Middle East. Wherever your feet trod, that's your Jericho road. And on that road is a man, woman, or child less than fully alive, someone who needs to be touched.

But touch is a many-faceted thing. There is the touch of the Lebanese terrorist: cold, cruel, destructive. There is the touch of the Atlanta children's slayer: secret, lustful, pathological. There is the touch of the con artist: smooth, crafty, deceptive. And there is the lover's touch: at once strong and gentle, the kind of touch that brings healing and peace. The touch of Christ.

But to be effective, touch does not have to be physical. Skin on skin is powerful beyond compare *if* . . . if it is a symbol, if it says something: "I care" or "I'm sorry" or "I love you." But whether you make skin contact is not always important; what is important always is that you are reaching out. It is hearts that have to touch, even when hands do not. And so Mother Teresa can cradle a naked retarded child in the rubble of West Beirut, and Franciscan Father Ritter can simply welcome an 11-year-old prostitute to a refuge in

Times Square. The Good Samaritan can bandage a beat-up Jew, and a Washington lawyer can dish out Christmas dinner to the destitute. A priest can oil the senses of an ailing Christian or just listen with love to a problem he cannot solve. A pope can hold tenderly the hand that held a gun meant to kill him, or he can chant to young thousands in Madison Square Garden: "John Paul II, he loves you." A Georgetown student can skip hand in hand with a child of the slums or simply show him how to spell. A doctor can touch a growth to nothingness or just smile a tear away.

You know, there's something quite unusual about touching. To reach out, you don't need money in the bank, a razor-sharp mind, machine-fed muscles, a cover-girl personality. You don't even need hands. What you need is what you have, what you are: flesh and blood. You need only the bowels of compassion God gave you when He shaped you. The trouble is, this birthday gift of God we smother beneath all sorts of accumulated baggage, all those very human reasons that imprison us inside ourselves. I'm afraid of being rejected; I have enough problems of my own; I'm terribly shy; I've had a rough day; my postnasal drip is acting up; sorry, but it's Miller time. A thousand and one excuses, and some of them might well stand up in court.

What to do? Good friends, Lent is almost upon us. With it the recurring Catholic question: What shall I give up? Michelob or munchies, sex or bubble gum? The waistline penance—fast for the great spring break, the Lauderdale look? Not bad, but not particularly Christian, hardly in the image of Christ. Forget about giving up; simply give! Not some thing; some*one*. Give yourself! Copy the compassionate Christ. Walk the same old Jericho road, but now with eyes open, heart outstretched. Time and again you'll come upon someone—friend, enemy, stranger—someone who calls to you mutely for a little of your life, a touch of your heart.

If you hear that silent cry, try not to pass by on the other side. That silent cry . . . it just might be Christ.

Dahlgren Chapel
Georgetown University
and
Holy Trinity Church
Washington, D.C.
February 17, 1985

16

DO NOT BE ANXIOUS?
Eighth Sunday of the Year (A)

♦ Isaiah 49:14–15
♦ 1 Corinthians 4:1–5
♦ Matthew 6:24–34

In the movie version of Giuseppe di Lampedusa's historical novel *The Leopard,* there is a sharp piece of dialogue. The story opens in May 1860. The Bourbon kingdom of the Two Sicilies is about to fall; Palermo will soon be taken by Garibaldi. The Prince of Salina and Jesuit Father Pirrone are riding to Palermo in a carriage—the priest to visit a Jesuit house, the prince to visit his mistress. On the way the prince expresses his concern about the political and military situation. The priest consoles him: "Your Excellency, don't worry!" The prince turns on him angrily: "*You* dare to tell *me* not to worry? Christ promised you, promised the Church, immortality. He did not promise immortality to us, to our social class."[1]

I was reminded of that scene as I mulled over today's Gospel. "Do not be anxious about your life, what you shall eat or what you shall drink" (Mt 6:25)? Tell that to the starving in sub-Saharan Africa! "Do not be anxious about your body, what you shall put on" (ibid.)? Tell that to the shelter people in the District of Columbia! "Do not be anxious about tomorrow" (v. 34)? Tell that to the 15,436 U.S. Steel workers who lost their jobs with the new year!

We have a problem here—not artificial, terribly real. It is the problem of God's providence, His care for the human creatures He has fashioned in His own image. Let me confront the problem in three stages. First, a bit of background: the first reading, the snippet from Isaiah. Second, the Gospel text: What was it saying then? Third, a look at ourselves: What is today's Gospel saying now? So, from the Old Testament to the New Testament to the contemporary Christian.

I

First, the text from Isaiah. Our two verses are part of a dialogue between Yahweh and Jerusalem. In this section of Isaiah (chapters 40–55) you have what scholars call the Book of the Consolation of Israel.[2] In 587 B.C., Jerusalem had fallen to the Babylonians. City and temple were destroyed; the kingdom of Judah was reduced to a Babylonian province; thousands of Jews were deported to Babylonia. The most astonishing aspect of the Exile was the way Israel kept its faith alive, its law alive, its identity alive, its consciousness of continuity with the past—more alive than did their sisters and brothers back home in Palestine. Still, there were days of discouragement, of despair, days when the exiles could not help but ask: Has Yahweh failed His people? Are the gods of Babylonia superior to our God?

The depression of the exiles finds poignant expression in our first reading. "Zion [Jerusalem] said: 'The Lord has forsaken me, my Lord has forgotten me' " (Isa 49:14). That cry of despair from the people is countered by a strong affirmation from their Lord. Yahweh's union with His people has not been broken. Despite Israel's infidelities, He has not divorced her. Yahweh is faithful to His covenant and to His promises—a covenant and promises that make Jerusalem a particular object of His saving love. The figure Yahweh uses is striking. It is not the usual Old Testament figure, paternal love, the love of a father; it is a figure far more rare:

> Can a woman forget her sucking child,
> that she should have no compassion
> on the son of her womb?
> Even these may forget,
> yet I will not forget you.
>
> (Isa 49:15)

This love like a mother's, this love greater than any mother's, is followed by another striking image: "Behold, I have graven you on the palms of my hands" (v. 16)—like a tattoo, a symbol of permanent attachment. Jerusalem's walls will be rebuilt; the city will have more people than it can hold; the nations that enslaved her will be her slaves.

Yes, Yahweh does care. He never stops caring, even when His children have ceased to care.

II

Second, the Gospel text: What was it saying then? To understand it, you have to replace it in its context. You cannot rip a passage out of the Sermon on the Mount, shout it from a steeple or proclaim it from a pulpit, and claim its meaning is self-evident. Something has gone before it, verses that lend intelligence to it, verses without which our passage does not yield its full meaning. This section of Matthew 6 (vv. 19–34) is a collection of Jesus' sayings. All the sayings have a common theme: singleness of purpose. If you are a disciple of Jesus, you must fix your eyes only on God, on serving Him; you should not let yourself be distracted from that even by what people may consider legitimate concerns.[3]

The first saying (vv. 19–21): Lay up treasures not on earth but in heaven. "For where your treasure is, there will your heart be also" (v. 21). Where you see lasting value, there will your interests lie. The second saying (vv. 22–23): Your eye must be sound, healthy; that is, your intention must be simple. This is the clarity of vision by which you see true treasure and serve only one master. The third saying (v. 24): You cannot serve both God and material possessions. The fourth saying (vv. 25–34) is our passage: no anxious care about food, drink, clothing, about your most basic needs.

In this context, what kind of worry is Jesus castigating? Not, I assure you, planning for the future. You don't sit back on your haunches singing "thy kingdom come" and expecting Avignone Frères to cater your next meal. No, you sweat as profusely as the unbeliever, plan as shrewdly as the pagan. What Jesus is blasting is the kind of worry that leads to a divided loyalty, leads ultimately to an exclusive concentration on possessions—where God takes a back seat in your Seville.

But this does not solve the most perplexing problem in today's Gospel. Jesus seems to be saying that if his disciples focus on him, if they make him the center of their existence, they will not want for food or drink or clothes. Perhaps not Lobster Thermidor, Perrier water, Calvin Klein. But you'll fare better than the birds, look almost as lovely as the lilies. Seek first the kingdom of God, and God will provide the necessities of life. If you walk the way of life God requires of His subjects, "all these things shall be yours as well" (v. 33).

The trouble is, God does not seem to provide—not always. The thousands who starve or freeze to death each day across the world are hardly all heathens or lukewarm Christians. They include men and women who have fixed their gaze on Jesus, who love God above all else and love their fellows as much as they love themselves. They trust in God for a loaf of bread, a scoop of water, a warm jacket— and they do not get it; they die in agony.

III

This calls for a third point: What does today's Gospel say to you and me? The answer would be simple if Jesus had limited himself to the striking question "Which of you by being anxious can add one cubit [about 18 inches] to his stature [or: a single hour to his life]?" (v. 27).[4] If he had only said "Don't worry about your basic needs, about food and clothes. Why not? Because worrying about them won't do any good. It will merely irritate your colon, trigger your hiatal hernia, give you heartburn or a headache." Psychologists would nod sagely; unbelievers would see how sensible our Jesus is; and I could massage your tensions with the oil of positive thinking.

But Jesus says more: Trust in God, make me your only master, and you won't have to worry; you'll get everything you need. And our experience rebels: no, not true! Some get what they need and some don't; you cannot guarantee it. So where does that leave us? Did Jesus know what he was talking about?

There is much mystery here. How can there fail to be, when we are speaking of God, of His providence, of evil? I shall not dissipate all the clouds (even a theologian must bow before mystery); I shall rather suggest one way of looking at the Gospel that may prove of profit to you and me. It means leaving this liturgy for a moment and moving back 19 centuries, to the social situation of the early Christians.

You see, the Gospels were not written in a vacuum, in outer space; they often tell us what a Christian community was experiencing. In the early decades after the death of Jesus you had relatively small communities, and you had people who cared. Not that they never argued. Paul makes it clear that the Christians of Corinth were rent by "dissensions" and "quarreling" (1 Cor 1:10–11); Matthew "faced confusion, tension, conflict, and the destructive influence of false prophets within the community."[5] Even so, most were conscious of being a community, the body of the risen Christ. And those who lived the Christian life, those who put all their trust in God, did experience what Jesus promised. They had enough to eat, to drink; they had clothes on their backs. The community saw to that. Read the Acts of the Apostles about the Church in Jerusalem:

"There was not a needy person among them, for as many as were possessors of lands or houses sold them, and brought the proceeds of what was sold and laid it at the apostles' feet; and distribution was made to each as any had need" (Acts 4:34–35).

What I am suggesting is that Jesus was not laying the whole burden on his Father: You set your heart on God, and God will personally feed you. He will multiply loaves and fishes again, command drought in the Sahel to cease, raise the Dow Jones average and lower the unemployment rate. Not quite. In principle, the God who rained manna from heaven on the Israelites in the desert can ply the poor with sirloin strip and homogenized milk. But in practice, chances are He leaves that to His people, to the community, to us. Remember the strong section in the Epistle of James: "What does it profit, my brethren, if a man says he has faith but has not works? Can his faith save him? If a brother or sister is ill-clad and in lack of daily food, and one of you says to them, 'Go in peace, be warmed and filled,' without giving them the things needed for the body, what does it profit? So faith by itself, if it has no works, is dead" (Jas 2:14–17).

So then, when I look at the homeless in Thailand and our land, when I watch the soul-searing "Save the Children" programs on TV, when I see bloated bellies and staring eyes, might it not be time to stop asking questions about a God whose providence we fail to fathom, whose ways are not our ways, and turn my thoughts to the Christian community that is not really a community unless it cares? When so many Christians are crying out in despair "The Church has forsaken me, my Church has forgotten me," how honestly can we—we the Church—respond "Can a woman forget the child of her womb? Even these may forget, yet I will not forget you"? We may argue till doomsday about God and the problem of evil; but philosophy should not be a cop-out from the compassion that calls us to play Christ to our crucified sisters and brothers.

It's not just a question of food and clothes. All around us are well-fed folk who are empty of heart, wasting away deep within. All around us are finely-furred men and women who are cold in spirit, icebound in a thousand and one fears, shivering in a dark night of the soul. And where is the compassionate community, the caring Christian?

Do you remember the legend of St. Christopher? Here was a man who was taught Christianity by a hermit in a desert, was told that, if he wanted Christ to show himself, he must lodge by a river and, strong giant that he was, must carry over the river all who might wish to cross. One night a child asked to cross. But the water rose, and the child on his shoulders was heavy as lead, grew heavier and heavier, till the giant was afraid they would drown. On the other side he gasped: "Child, you have put me in great peril. Your weight was as if I had all the world on my shoulders. No greater burden could I bear." The child answered: "Christopher, do not be amazed. You have borne on your shoulders not only the world, but him who created the world. I am Jesus Christ, the King whom you serve in this work."[6]

Almost three decades ago, in a remarkable poem, Anne Morrow Lindbergh captured the meaning of St. Christopher ("Christ-bearer") for our age. The poem is entitled "Saint for Our Time" and it runs as follows:

> Christopher, come back to earth again.
> There is no age in history when men
> So cried for you, Saint of a midnight wild,
> Who stood beside a stream and heard a child.
> Not even Francis, brother to the poor,
> Who, barefoot, begged for alms from door to door,
> And pity-tortured kissed the leper's brow—
> Not even Francis is so needed now
> As you, Christ-bearer.

> Christopher, we die
> Not for lack of charity; we lie
> Imprisoned in our sepulchers of stone,
> Wanting your gift, O Saint, your gift alone.
> No one will take the burden of the whole
> Upon his shoulders; each man in his soul
> Thinks his particular grief too great to bear
> Without demanding still another's share.

> But you—you chose to bear a brother's load
> And every man who travelled down your road
> You ferried on your back across the flood
> Until one night beside the stream there stood,
> Wrapped in a cloak of storm, a child who cried
> And begged safe passage to the other side—
> A child who weighed upon your back like lead,
> Like earth upon the shoulders of the dead—
> And, struggling to the bank while torrents whirled,
> You found that on your shoulders leaned a world.

No wonder that the burden was so great:
You carried in your arms the monstrous weight
Of all men's happiness and all men's pain,
And all men's sorrows on your back had lain.
Even their sins you carried as your own—
Even their sins, you, Christopher, alone!

But who today will take the risk or blame
For someone else? Everyone is the same,
Dreading his neighbor's tongue or pen or deed.
Imprisoned in fear we stand and do not heed
The cry that you once heard across the stream.
"There is no cry," we say, "it is a dream."

Christopher, the waters rise again,
As on that night, the waters rise; the rain
Bites like a whip across a prisoner's back;
The lightning strikes like fighters in attack;
And thunder, like a time-bomb, detonates
The starless sky no searchlight penetrates.

The child is crying on the further shore:
Christopher, come back to earth once more.[7]

Dahlgren Chapel
Georgetown University
and
Holy Trinity Church
Washington, D.C.
February 26, 1984

17

A BROTHER WHOM I HAVE PARDONED
Twenty-fourth Sunday of the Year (A)

- Sirach 27:30—28:7
- Romans 14:7–9
- Matthew 18:21–35

During the Christmas season of '83, a photo from Rome flashed across the world. The scene: the corner of a prison cell. The actors: two men close together on molded-plastic chairs. One in a white cassock, white cape, white skullcap. The other in a blue crew-neck sweater, jeans, blue-and-white running shoes from which the laces had been removed. *Time* told it touchingly:

> . . . last week, in an extraordinary moment of grace, the violence
> in St. Peter's Square was transformed. In a bare, white-walled cell
> in Rome's Rebibbia prison, John Paul tenderly held the hand that
> had held the gun that was meant to kill him. For 21 minutes, the
> Pope sat with his would-be assassin, Mehmet Ali Agca. The two
> talked softly. Once or twice Agca laughed. The Pope forgave him
> for the shooting. At the end of the meeting, Agca either kissed
> the Pope's ring or pressed the Pope's hand to his forehead in a
> Muslim gesture of respect. . . . [1]

What did they talk about? That, said the Pope as he left the cell, "will have to remain a secret between him and me. I spoke to him as a brother whom I have pardoned, and who has my complete trust."[2]

That picture more expressive than a thousand words, that simple phrase "a brother whom I have pardoned," challenge us mightily this 24th Sunday of the Church's year. They give life to the liturgy of the word you have just heard. To the Wisdom of Sirach: "Forgive your neighbor the wrong he has done, and then your sins will be pardoned when you pray" (Sir 28:2). To the responsorial psalm: "Bless the Lord . . . who forgives all your iniquity" (Ps 103:2–3). To the Gospel parable of the Unforgiving Debtor and the anger of his king: "I canceled your ten-million-dollar debt out of compassion for you. Shouldn't you have done the same for 20 dollars?" (cf. Mt 18:32–33).[3] Rome's Rebibbia gives life to these readings, challenges us, not because the Pope provides a simple, coin-machine solution to the world's problems of hurt and hate, of injury and forgiveness, of retaliation versus reconciliation. Quite the contrary. The Pope's "I pardoned him" raises all sorts of agonizing issues, global as well as personal. It forces me to confront problems more perilous than the latest pinprick to my inflated ego. It compels me to ask what being a Christian demands of me in a hate-saturated society. Let me unfold this thesis in three stages, three questions. (1) Why is there a particular problem here? (2) Is there a practicable Christian response to the problem? (3) How do you and I fit into the problem and the response?

I

First, why is there a particular problem here? Doesn't any problem of forgiveness turn academic for a committed Christian in the face of two Gospel sentences? On the level of principle, you have the Lord's Prayer: "Forgive us . . . as we also have forgiven" (Mt 6:12). On the level of example, you have the Crucified's prayer: "Father, forgive them; for they know not what they do" (Lk 23:34). Beneath the cross, the problem is not what we *ought* to do; the problem is, are we Christian enough to do it?

Softly now; not so fast! Are there no conditions that affect forgiveness? A rabbi tells us that Jewish tradition links forgiveness to change—change in behavior, change in human action; links forgiveness to evidence of real contrition, genuine sorrow for the sin. Israel, therefore, will not reconcile with the PLO as long as the PLO takes responsibility for destroying a bus, for bombing women and children, as long as the PLO is bent on the destruction of Israel. How can Israel do otherwise in good conscience? And do not we Catholics expect absolution, God's forgiveness, in the sacrament of penance only if we are sorry for what we have done and promise to change our lives, not to commit the same sin again?

Time magazine itself asks: "If it had been 6 million Catholics who were exterminated in the Nazi death camps, would the Pope have forgiven Adolf Eichmann? Or would he have had Eichmann hunted down, taken to Rome for trial and executed, as the Jews brought Eichmann to Jerusalem for judgment and hanging?"[4]

More than that. As *Time* read it, the Pope's dramatic act was not simply a private, one-on-one affair; it was meant to blazon a message to the world. If we really want peace, our hearts must be changed; we must offer to the enemy the bread of love. But this too, Christian though it is, stirs up problems. (1) Does forgiveness mean we waive punishment, return the rapist to the scene of his crime, Agca to Turkey? If it does, what happens to justice, to the moral order? How can society survive? (2) Is forgiveness another way of saying "Forget it"? Then what of Elie Wiesel's reminder that, for Jews, to forget is a crime against justice and memory, that if you forget, you become the executioner's accomplice? (3) Does forgiveness mean that a nation simply forgives its foes, a people no longer holds anything against its age-old enemies? But in the Middle East, in the Balkans, in the north of Ireland, to forgive my enemy is to betray my father, my grandfather, my great grandfather; to forgive is treason. "So, between Armenians and Turks, Northern Irish Catholics and Protestants, between South Moluccans and Dutch, between Lebanese Maronites and Druse, between Hatfields and McCoys, between Montagues and Capulets, the ancient fury persists. The enemy is timeless. His very existence is unforgivable, but also indispensable."[5]

Forgiveness and contrition . . . forgiveness and punishment . . . forgiveness and justice . . . forgiveness and the very existence of a people—Pope John Paul did get a huge pot boiling, didn't he?

II

This leads logically into my second question: Is there a practicable Christian response to these problems? The Christian moral tradition has much of value to say to such issues, many rich insights; but, as Jesus said to his disciples the eve of his death, "you cannot bear them now" (Jn 16:12). A sermon is not a seminar. I shall therefore play not the professor but the preacher. I shall simply suggest one way of approaching forgiveness, an approach that does not pretend to settle all the problems I've raised, an approach that may open you to hear what the God of forgiveness might be saying to you—not to Agca, not to Elie Wiesel, not to your best friend, but to you.

This approach begins with God, because forgiveness begins

with God. Today's responsorial psalm is eloquent testimony from the heart of the Hebrew tradition:

> The Lord is merciful and gracious,
>> slow to anger and abounding in steadfast love. . . .
> He does not deal with us according to our sins,
>> nor requite us according to our iniquities. . . .
> As far as the east is from the west,
>> so far does He remove our transgressions from us.
>> (Ps 103:8, 10, 12)

What comes through with blinding clarity from the Old Testament is that God is a God of forgiveness because He is a God of love.[6] Sin was a Jew's refusal of love, the refusal of men and women to let themselves be loved by a God who "suffers" from not being loved. "My people . . . have forsaken me, the fountain of living waters, and hewed out cisterns for themselves, broken cisterns, that can hold no water" (Jer 2:13). The striking feature of divine love is this: If woman or man turns unfaithful, God stays ceaselessly faithful. His people might, often did, refuse God's love; but God never stopped offering love. He would pardon lovelessness, but only on condition that the Jew agreed to love anew. Call it contrition, confession, conversion—the basic condition for forgiveness was that sinners renounce the very basis of their sinning, permit themselves to love. But even this was beyond the sinner's native power; God had to give the sinner "a new heart, a new spirit" (Ezek 36:26). This He does, for to pardon is characteristic of God: "Thou sparest all things, for they are thine, O Lord who lovest the living" (Wis 11:26).

For Christians, this message of love comes incarnate in Jesus. "God so loved the world that He gave His only Son . . . sent the Son into the world, not to condemn the world, but that the world might be saved through him" (Jn 3:16–17). It was for sinners he took flesh; for sinners he lived and loved; for sinners he was nailed to bloody wood and died in frightful agony; for sinners he defied death, defeated death, ascended in deathless glory to his Father. His living, dying, rising had one end in view: "Father, forgive them. . . ."

But what does it mean for God to forgive? What sense should we draw from Jesus' proclamation to the paralytic, "Man, your sins are forgiven you" (Lk 5:20)? It does not mean that God forgets our foolishness; to forget is beyond God's power. It does not mean that my sin is no longer a fact; every infidelity of mine is indelibly inscribed in history. What, then, does it mean?

For God, to forgive me is to change me. The Catholic tradition will not tolerate the thesis that, when God forgives, He simply slides His crucified Son between my sin and His own wrath, that I stay the same as before but the Father sees only Christ, not sinful me. No, I have been changed. Not skin-deep; at the very roots of my being. I have a new relationship to God: I am no longer at enmity with Him, I am His friend. This is not just a manner of speaking. My whole person is alive with the life of God. Father, Son, and Holy Spirit live within me. Their love courses through me, and I—I am in love again. Not just in word; I am one with God. I am St. Paul's "new creature," a "new creation" (2 Cor 5:17).

Now this kind of forgiveness is indeed divine. Only God can forgive like this—where the very forgiveness *is* a change in the other, where the words "I forgive you" tell the offender that he or she is different, has been changed, transformed from enemy to friend.

III

But if only God can forgive like this, what is left for man and woman? This brings me to my third question: How do you and I fit into this? When John Paul murmured to Agca "I forgive you," we cannot say that Agca was changed deep within, became a "new creature." Oh yes, he laughed once or twice; at the end he "either kissed the Pope's ring or pressed the Pope's hand to his forehead in a Muslim gesture of respect."[7] But transformed? Perhaps he was; but if he was, it was God who changed him.

Ah, here we may be touching the heart of the matter. It is God who changes hearts, but men and women can be His instruments. How? By shouting "I forgive you" no matter what is happening out there? No, that would be unrealistic, counterproductive. Forgiveness has no meaning, in heaven or on earth, if the sinner persists in his sin, if he still blasts babies to bits with his bombs. We dare not say "I no longer hold this against you." Too much else is at stake: the life of a child, the life of a nation, the whole moral order, the City of Man.

What, then, can I do? I can, like John the Baptist, "go before the Lord to prepare His ways" (Lk 1:76). This is what John Paul did. Agca had not called out to him: "Come to Rebibbia; come to me in prison." The Pope took the first step. He offered to the enemy the bread of love. Not that papal presence was itself sufficient to change a Turkish heart. Rather that God might well use John Paul's gesture like the "matter" of a sacrament, like the water of baptism or the bread of Eucharist, infuse it with His own power, make it an instrument of His grace. Water and bread are (at least for you and me) everyday stuff; we take them for granted—soak our skin in one, slap peanut butter and jelly on the other. What an incredible difference when God turns them into effective signs of His presence, makes a child of God through the water, feeds that child with Christ's flesh through the bread!

Similarly for you and me. Even when sheer earthly realism, the demands of justice, survival itself forbid a simplistic "forgive and forget," we are not helpless; we have a Christian task no one of us may ever forswear, ever neglect. I have to make every feasible effort to be present in love to those who hate, ready to reconcile, to offer friendship. Not to "let bygones be bygones"; rather to be an instrument of change in all-powerful hands. An instrument God can use, like bread and water, to soften a heart hardened by hate, raw with resentment.

How you do it, what gesture you make in a concrete situation, no homilist can tell you. A reader wrote to *Time:* The Pope can afford to forgive; that's his job. But don't ask the survivors of the death camps to do so. "The victims' ashes and bones . . . would be desecrated by such a gesture."[8] Most of us are not asked to do the impossible, the unforgivable. Most of us have only to swallow pride, show ourselves a little more loving than the other, make some gesture God can use to change a human heart, the same God who, as Jesus reminded us, "makes His sun rise on the evil and on the good, and sends rain on the just and on the unjust" (Mt 5:45).

While readying this homily, I was struck more forcefully than ever before by an injunction of Jesus I use frequently at our rite of Eucharistic reconciliation: "If you are offering your gift at the altar, and there remember that your brother [or sister] has something against you, leave your gift there before the altar and go, first be reconciled to your brother [or sister], and then come and offer your gift" (Mt 5:23–24). You know, in 70 years I've never done that. Have you?[9]

Sacred Heart Church
University of Notre Dame
Notre Dame, Indiana
September 16, 1984

18

ARE YOU ENVIOUS BECAUSE
I AM GOOD?
Twenty-fifth Sunday of the Year (A)

- ◆ Isaiah 55:6–9
- ◆ Philippians 1:20–24, 27
- ◆ Matthew 20:1–16

Today's parable should raise your eyebrows. Especially these days, when justice and human rights are headlines. An employer pays all his laborers the same salary, whether they began work at six or nine or twelve or three or five. And he justifies his salary system with a questionable principle: "Am I not allowed to do what I choose with what belongs to me?" (Mt 20:15). Don't tell me what to do with my money! Isn't this a neat lesson to take home, to the office, to your roommates? No wonder the parable ends with "the last will be first, and the first last" (v. 16). Come the revolution. . . .

To lower your eyebrows, you ought to pose three questions. First, what is the Gospel actually about? Second, what does the parable have to do with "the kingdom of heaven" (v. 1)? Third, what possible significance can the parable have for the 80's, for you and me?

I

First, what is the Gospel actually about? Not economics; not a just wage; not labor-management relationships. This is a parable, a story Jesus made up to make a point, to leave a lesson, to impress a religious truth indelibly on his disciples.[1] But to understand the point, the lesson, the religious truth, you dare not misunderstand the story.[2]

You see, the employer is not uncaring, unfeeling, arbitrary; quite the contrary. The parable is set in a period when unemployment is a fearful threat. The vineyard owner contracts with the 6 a.m. crowd: a full day's work, a full day's pay. A laboring man's ordinary pay—bare subsistence at the time, enough to stay alive. To those who start work at nine or noon or three: "I'll give you whatever is fair" (v. 4)—which to them means a certain fraction of the full day's pay. Evening comes, time to pay up . . . and everybody gets exactly the same amount, a full day's pay. Even those who had worked only from five to six!

The early birds are furious. What is this, a pilot version of *Falcon Crest*?[3] "We've worked twelve full hours, these last lazy louts a single hour. We slaved under the burning midday sun; these fellows enjoyed the cool of evening" (cf. v. 12). How arbitrary can you get? Lucky there wasn't a grape pickers' union then; Cesar Chavez would never have stood for that!

If, my friends, you agree with the outburst, your heart may be in the right place, but your head is not. The main stress of the story is not on the industrious sunrise crowd; they got what they merited, a just wage. The stress is on the latecomers—all of them, but especially those who had gossiped the day away in the marketplace. More accurately, the stress is on the owner, the employer. He knows that the five-to-six crew did not beat a path to his vineyard, are not gung ho for hard work, would rather drink the Manischewitz than make it. And still they touch his heart. If he pays them what they deserve, one twelfth of a day's pay, "they will have practically nothing to take home; the pay for an hour's work will not keep a family; their children will go hungry if the father comes home empty-handed."[4] Out of pity for their poverty, he pays them a full day's wages.

The owner is not being arbitrary, only compassionate to the poor. That is why he can say to one of the disgruntled: "My dear fellow, I am doing you no wrong" (v. 13). He is not being cheated; he is getting all he deserves; there is no injustice here. Even when the owner asks, "Am I not allowed to do what I choose with what belongs to me?" (v. 15), he is not claiming he can pay *less* than a fair wage; he is saying he can pay *more*. "Are you envious," he asks the grumbler, "because I am good? Do you begrudge my generosity?" (v. 15).

II

Which brings me to my second question, the point of the story, its lesson, its religious truth: What does the parable have to do with "the kingdom of heaven"? (v. 1). Very simply: This, Jesus says, is how God deals with men and women, with you and me. The way the vineyard owner acted towards his employees, this is the way the Lord of the kingdom acts towards His subjects. This is what our God is like: He is merciful, He is good.

The point is, no one earns the kingdom of heaven. No one. Not even the Christian who has never grieved God gravely. Not Antony the Hermit, who served God faithfully for 105 years; not Agnes of Rome, martyred at thirteen. Not Francis of Assisi or Mother Teresa. The kingdom is a gift, because the kingdom is won by grace, and grace is God's free giving. That is why even the saints, for all their trust in God, for all their love of God, have to work out their salvation in fear and trembling; their very trust, their very love, is a gift. That is why, no matter how faithful we are day after day through a lifetime, we must still pray for what we call "final perseverance": the grace to die in God's arms, in God's love. No one, however holy, can demand this from God as a strict right, in strict justice. Not even those who labor in the vineyard from the sun's rising, from their baptism into Christ.

And what of those who come in at the last hour? What of the deathbed convert who for decades had his cake and ate it, broke every law of God and man, wallowed in lust and raped the earth, killed thousands wantonly and starved the poor? What if Adolf Hitler's last words were an utterly sincere "My God, I'm sorry; I love you"? Will you too murmur against God's mercy? Will you too grumble: "These last worked only one hour, and you have made them equal to us who have borne the burden of the day and the scorching heat"? Will you too complain with the elder brother of the prodigal son: "Lo, these many years I have served you and never have I disobeyed a command of yours; yet you never gave me a young goat, that I might make merry with my friends. But when this son of yours came, who has devoured your livelihood with harlots, you killed for him the fatted calf" (Lk 15:29–30)? Will you too begrudge God's generosity, claim He is unfair?

If you do, you will be quite unhappy with Jesus himself. He saw "more joy in heaven over one sinner who repents than over 99 righteous persons who need no repentance" (Lk 15:7). When a criminal on his own cross of death begged to be remembered at the coming of the kingdom, Jesus did not respond: "Tough, man. You're too late. It's almost 3 p.m. You should have come around at nine." No, sir! "Truly, I say to you, today you will be with me in paradise" (Lk 23:43).

Unjust? Yes, thank God! I, for one, am wonderfully content with a God who refuses to be just. If He dealt with me just as my deeds deserve, I'm afraid I would not merit to enjoy Him ecstatically for eternity, gaze on the face of Christ and his mother days without end, live the fulness of life for ever without tears, without fears. If one day Christ summons me, "Come, blessed of my Father" (Mt 25:34), it will not be because his Father is just, but because He is good . . . a God whose name is Mercy.

III

Which brings me to my third question: What possible significance can the parable of the Good Employer[5] have for the 80's, for you and me? Over and above, of course, the brilliant theology you've just been privileged to hear!

Let me focus on a widespread American axiom. It runs along these lines: You get what you deserve. Nothing comes free. You want money? Work for it. You want love? Earn it. You want mercy? Show you deserve it. For the rest, do unto others before they do it unto you. Watch out for the lazies on the Mall, welfare lines, free hot dogs at school, affluent Hoyas with federal loans; it's a con game. By all means, give others what they deserve—but not one penny more.

Now this is not a lecture on economics; it's a homily. I dare not tell you how to run a business; theology is tough enough. I shall not downgrade justice; I shall simply look at justice through God's eyes.[6]

Do you remember how God rejected Israel's burnt offerings and blood sacrifices, her incense and her feasts, her prayers and the melody of her harps, even her first-born? "What does the Lord require of you?" we read in Micah. God's answer: "To do justice . . ." (Mic 6:8). But the justice God asked of Israel was not merely the justice in a textbook of ethics: Give to each man, woman, and child what is due to each, what each has a rigorous right to demand, because he or she is a human being, has rights that can be proven by philosophy or have been written into law. Justice was a whole web of relationships that stemmed from Israel's covenant with God. The

Israelites were to father the fatherless and befriend the stranger, not because the orphan and the outsider deserved it, but because this was the way *God* had acted with *them*. In freeing the oppressed, they were mirroring the compassionate God who had delivered *them* from oppression, had freed them from Pharaoh. In loving the loveless, the unloved, the unlovable, they were imaging the God who kept lavishing His love on Israel, no matter how often she rejected it.

And we? Our Christian justice is not satisfied when we give to another what that other *deserves*. You and I have a covenant with God that ties us for ever to every child of God. A whole web of relationships stems from our commitment to Christ, a Christ who wore our flesh and bled for us, not because we had earned Bethlehem and Calvary, but because left to ourselves we are helpless, hopeless. We are to act towards others as Christ our Lord has acted towards us—and precisely because Christ has acted this way.

Basic to Christian living is an awesome fact: All that is good in you is yours not by right but by gift. Oh yes, there is much you have earned: your degree and your salary, your house and garden, your friends and perhaps your enemies, a Miller Lite and a good night's sleep. But all this is possible only because so much has been given to you: life itself . . . eyes to see and hands to touch . . . a mind to shape ideas and a heart to beat with love . . . God in your soul and Christ in your flesh . . . the power to believe where others deny, to hope where others despair, to love where others hate. This, and so much more, is sheer gift, not reward for your Brite smile, your winsome wit, your fidelity from early morn. Why, even your fidelity is a gift. "If we but turn to God," Augustine insisted, "that itself is a gift of God." Each of you is incredibly dear to the Lord, but none of you could have done a thing to earn it, to demand it.

The godlike response? Do unto others as God has done unto you. As Jesus told the Twelve on sending them out, "You received without paying for it; give without being paid for it" (Mt 10:8). Many do. Three weeks ago ten GU grads flew to Peru, to give a year to the poor. At least 500 GU students give care and love to the District's underprivileged. Holy Trinity parishioners feed the hungry, shelter the homeless, give holistic health care without cost—save to themselves. You rarely ask whether the outstretched hands have earned your love. You simply do to them as God has done to you— from the first day of creation through God's Good Friday on Calvary to this wonderfully gracious Day of the Lord.

One final thought. Suppose you don't have all that much to

give, what then? For your consolation, I've never run across anyone like that. You are to give as God has given to you. Now God's most remarkable gift to you is Himself. So, "Go and do likewise" (Lk 11:37). The bread you give can be lifesaving; more life-giving still is the gift of yourself. Never forget the admonition of the 17th-century apostle of charity St. Vincent de Paul: Unless you love, the poor will not forgive you for the bread they have to take from you. Unless you love. . . . Fortunately, the love you need is the love you have: I mean the Holy Spirit within you, the very Spirit of love. Let the Spirit loose and you need not envy Mother Teresa. All she does, like Mary of Nazareth, is let the Holy Spirit overshadow her. Try it and you won't be tempted to grumble about the Lord of the vineyard, to complain because His ways are not our ways. You'll be too lost in wonder at how good He is. You may even experience how through your love some latecomer will throw himself at the last moment into God's merciful arms. It will make your day . . . or your life.

Dahlgren Chapel
Georgetown University
and
Holy Trinity Church
Washington, D.C.
September 23, 1984

19

FROM SACRIFICE TO MERCY
Twenty-sixth Sunday of the Year (A)

♦ Ezekiel 18:25–28
♦ Philippians 2:1–11
♦ Matthew 21:28–32

On the face of it, today's Gospel is simplicity itself. A father and two sons. Each son is asked to work in the father's vineyard. One refuses, then goes. The other says "I go, sir" (Mt 21:30), but never does. Which of them was obedient? Hardly a puzzle. The application? The really obedient among the Jews were not the religious rulers but the ungodly toll collectors and harlots. These will enter God's kingdom; the high and mighty will not.

The trouble is, this is a snippet, a paragraph cut out of the Gospels and pasted up for the 26th Sunday of the Church's year. There is no context—nothing before, nothing after. It only makes Gospel sense, only regains its richness, if you replace it within the Gospel. Let's do that first, then see what it might say to all Christians, and end with a word on St. Mary's.

I

First, put the parable back into the Gospels.[1] The parable of the Two Sons belongs to a special group, parables that tell us not only that salvation has dawned, that the Redeemer has appeared, but that salvation has come to the poor, that Jesus has come to save sinners. It belongs to the parables of mercy. You remember them, I'm sure. The shepherd who loses one sheep, leaves the other 99 in the wilderness, goes after the one that has strayed: "There will be more joy in heaven over one sinner who repents than over 99 righteous persons who need no repentance" (Lk 15:7). The woman who loses

130

one silver coin (perhaps 20 cents), forgets about the rest of her money, lights a lamp, sweeps the house frantically till she finds it: "Just so . . . there is joy before the angels of God over one sinner who repents" (Lk 15:10). The two men whose debts are forgiven—about 90 dollars and nine: "Which will love [the creditor] more? The one . . . to whom he forgave more" (Lk 7:42–43). The Pharisee and the toll collector in the temple: "I tell you, this man [the despised toll collector] went down to his house justified [right with God] rather than [the Pharisee]" (Lk 18:14). And now the two sons: "Truly, I say to you, the toll collectors and the harlots go into the kingdom of God before you" (Mt 21:31).

Now there is a fascinating facet to these parables of mercy. Each of them was addressed to opponents of Jesus: murmuring scribes, grumbling Pharisees, critical theologians, and here today, members of the Sanhedrin. These are enemies of the gospel, indignant that Jesus should assert that God cares about sinners, incensed that he would eat with people they despised. What does he tell them? These sinners, these people you despise, are nearer to God than you. They may have disobeyed God's call; their professions have debased them; but they have shown sorrow and repentance. More than that, these are the people who can appreciate God's goodness; they have what Jesus' critics lack: a deep gratitude to God for His goodness.

It's a strong lesson, strongly phrased. Those who should have been the leading candidates for entry into God's kingdom are precisely those who are in danger of not getting in at all. Pharisees, models of observance, whose lifeblood was the law of Moses, who knew the law thoroughly and followed it exactly: Sabbath and feast days, ritual purity, tithing, dietary rules—all 613 imperatives. The scribes, lawyers and teachers of the law, devoted to its study and exposition. Members of the Sanhedrin, the supreme council and tribunal of the Jews. These fine fellows will watch the lowliest of the low parading into the kingdom, and they will be standing outside scratching their heads, wondering what went wrong.

II

What did go wrong? Precisely here is the parable's pertinence for all Christians. The men with power, the men with knowledge, were sure they were upright, righteous, right with God. Why? Because they knew the law and they kept it—to the last jot and tittle. If anything was prescribed, they knew it and they did it.

Everything—save one thing. Everything—save the most significant thing. I mean what Jesus said to the Pharisees: "Go, and learn
what this means: 'I desire mercy, and not sacrifice' " (Mt 9:13; cf.
Hos 6:6). Of course the sacrifices in the temple were important;
God Himself had prescribed them. But when the Jews' burnt offerings took precedence over burning injustice, when temple observance kept them from fathering the fatherless and succoring the
stranger, from defending the downtrodden and protecting the
poor, then their sacrifices became an "abomination" to the Lord.
Yes, an abomination (cf. Isa 1:11–17).

I shall never forget a sermon I heard several years ago in Co-
lumbus, Ohio. The preacher was a black Baptist from Texas. The
sermon dealt with Jesus' story of the poor fellow on his way from
Jerusalem to Jericho (cf. Lk 10:30–37). You remember how he fell
among robbers, who stripped him, beat him, left him half-dead.
How a priest, traveling the same route, saw the stricken Jew and
"passed by on the other side" (v. 32). The Baptist preacher, with
moving eloquence, described how competent and comfortable the
priest was in the Jerusalem temple. He could handle it all with prac-
ticed ease: the altar and the sacrifices, the vestments and the incense, the wood and the ashes—anything that had to do with the
temple. No trouble there, no sweat. "What he could not handle was
the é-vent on the Jericho road."

And so for us Christians. Of course our faith is precious to us;
it is our response to God's disclosure of Himself. But, to echo the
Letter of James, "What does it profit, my brothers and sisters, if a
man says he has faith but has not works? Can his faith save him? If
a brother or sister is ill-clad and in lack of daily food, and one of you
says to them, 'Go in peace, be warmed and filled,' without giving
them the things needed for the body, what does it profit?" (Jas 2:14–
16). Of course our love of God takes priority over all else; unless we
love God, we lose God, now and for ever. But the first commandment of the law makes no Jewish or Christian sense without the second commandment: "You shall love your neighbor as you love
yourself" (Lev 19:18; Mt 22:39). Of course the Sacrifice of the Mass
is the focus, the center, the heart of our worship. But even this
unique memorial of Jesus' passion makes no Christian sense if we
cannot handle "the é-vent on the Jericho road," if we are Sunday
Christians unfailingly on time for Mass, while all about us are men,
women, and children half-dead for want of our bread or our love.

Christ our Savior is not a respecter of persons. At the Last
Judgment he will not say to me: "Ah yes, you're a priest. Enter into

the joy of your Lord!" If we can believe the Gospel of Matthew, Christ will want to know what I did when his belly was bloated with hunger, his tongue tortured with thirst; when he had no pillow for his head, no clothes for his nakedness; when he was alone with his sickness or a faceless number in a jail (cf. Mt 25:31–46).

III

Good friends in Christ: This year St. Mary's celebrates 150 years. There is indeed much to celebrate: the first High Mass in 1834, the new church in 1858, the new school building in 1873, the new rectory in 1905, the bell tower in 1940, the new stained-glass windows in 1947, the new organ in 1953, the new altar of sacrifice in 1966, and so on and so forth. Splendid indeed, for all of this is an expression of the deep love for God that has distinguished St. Mary's for a century and a half. But do you know what impresses me even more in your history? Listen to it:

1856: Sisters of the Irish Order of St. Bridget begin . . . working with the poor.

1858–59: Sister Mary dePazzi founds St. Mary's soup kitchen and cares for over 40 families during the hard winter. Father Daniel Moore delivers a fiery sermon against slavery. . . . St. Mary's opens a House of Mercy "for the protection of distressed women of good character."

1859: St. Mary's Saint Vincent de Paul Men's Society raises money for the poor regardless of religious belief.

1861: Sacred concerts are given to raise money for widows and orphans of the Civil War.

1864: Sisters of St. Joseph of Carondolet open a home for orphaned boys. . . .

1870's: St. Mary's Industrial School for orphaned girls opens.

1881: Day care center for small children is opened.

1918: Influenza rages in Rochester. Sisters from St. Mary's work among the black community of Rochester, and minister to the many victims of the epidemic.[2]

The list could go on and on; you know it far better than I. The point is, you are not only *in* but *at* "the heart of downtown Rochester." Which is another way of saying that your love of God is not, never has been, imprisoned within these lovely walls. Your "Jericho road" begins at the steps of this church, stretches in every direction, wherever life is threatened, wherever a child of God lies helpless, longing for the healing "oil and wine" (Lk 10:34) of your love. From Sacrifice to mercy. . . .

With your history, with your spirit, I am not afraid that "the toll collectors and the harlots," the unfortunates of this world, will "go into the kingdom of God before you." I suspect you will all go in together!

St. Mary's Church
Rochester, New York
September 29–30, 1984

20

I HAVE LEARNED TO BE CONTENT
Twenty-eighth Sunday of the Year (A)

+ Isaiah 25:6–10
+ Philippians 4:12–14, 19–20
+ Matthew 22:1–14

For a homilist, today's three readings are all rich in promise. I was tempted to take off from Isaiah—his banquet-image of messianic happiness, when Yahweh will "swallow up death for ever, wipe away tears from all faces" (Isa 25:8). But I felt that this might be too remote from the Golden Dome,[1] where death is not a threat and laughter drowns out your tears. I would love to involve you in the Gospel parable of the marriage feast for a king's son. But my favorite sermon on that parable has been published,[2] and it would be jesuitical to foist a canned homily on you. Which leaves me with Paul to the Philippians. An extraordinary passage, something of a sleeper, more to it than meets the eye—with a strong Christian message for the young. Two stages to my development: (1) What did the passage from Philippians mean for Paul? (2) What might it say to you and me?

I

What was Paul telling the Christians at Philippi in Macedonia? Here I submit three items: some realities of Paul's life, his reaction to these realities, and the secret behind his reaction.

First, some realities about Paul, some facts from his life.[3] That life was a remarkable wedding of good times and bad, of joy and sorrow, a thriller heaven-sent for a TV special. He *may* have been short and bald, beard thick and nose unmistakable, eyebrows touching, legs bowed; still, he was in fact impressive, forceful, fiery. With

135

the Christians of Corinth he found himself weak, "in much fear and trembling" (1 Cor 2:3), in Asia Minor "so utterly, unbearably crushed" that he "despaired of life itself" (2 Cor 1:8). On the other hand, he was caught up in ecstasy, "caught up into paradise"—such ecstasy that he "heard things that cannot be told, which a human may not utter" (2 Cor 12:2–4). He was stoned and left for dead; riots rose up against him, plots to kill him; he was shipwrecked three times, imprisoned in Jerusalem, Caesarea, and Rome. In his own moving confession, he was countlessly beaten, often near death, in danger from rivers and robbers, in danger from Jews and Gentiles, in danger in the city and the wilderness and at sea, in danger from false brethren, in danger from hunger and thirst and cold, daily anxious for all the churches (cf. 2 Cor 11:23–28). And yet, all through his letters, the words "joyful," "happy," "delighted," "cheerful," "glad" run like a ceaseless refrain. Joy was a profound reality in Paul's life, as profound as sorrow.

Second, Paul's reaction to these realities. Very simply, "I have learned, whatever my circumstances, to be content" (Phil 4:11). Content. Not like a cow chewing its cud. Not indifferent, uninterested, neutral, unconcerned, apathetic: "I couldn't care less." Not masochistic: "Hit me again, I like it." It's an interesting Greek word Paul uses. It speaks of someone who is independent, not enslaved to external events or other people, has whatever he needs for peace and balance, is not the prey of each passing wind, is not a Yo-yo manipulated by all sorts of jerks. Paul is his own man.

Third, the secret behind Paul's reaction. Listen to him: "I know how to be abased, and I know how to abound. In any and all circumstances I have learned the secret of facing fulness and hunger, abundance and want" (v. 12). He has "learned the secret." Another remarkable Greek word. As in the great mystery religions, Paul has been initiated, he possesses the secret. And what is that? "I can do all things in him who gives me strength" (v. 13). This is not the proud independence, the utter self-sufficiency, of the Stoics. Paul relies totally on, is intimately one with, one other, an unseen power. His independence he acquires not by isolation but by incorporation. All things are his, but only in so far as he is Christ's, and because Christ is God's.[4] The Lord has initiated him into what Karl Barth translated as "the mystery of life with its ups and downs of having and being without."[5]

II

My second question: What might the passage from Philippians say to you and me? Perhaps to you even more importantly than to me, if only because there are hundreds of you at the dawning of adult life, and a solitary I in its twilight. What do I find in Paul that, from my experience, should speak to you as Christian men and women? The same three items Paul put to the Philippians.

First, some facts from your life. I do not know you, and I have no crystal ball in which to watch your years evolve. But this much I can say: Your life will be, perhaps already is, a wedding of good and evil, of joy and sorrow, of satisfaction and frustration, of rapture and despair. In varied ways it will crisscross Paul's "fulness and hunger, abundance and want." How do I know this? From seven decades of people-watching—on the streets and TV, in class and the confessional, between book covers and on hospital beds, through two World Wars and in the silent ferment of my own soul. It simply means that your life will be very human, that you will experience, with the poet Gerard Manley Hopkins, how, on the one hand, "all is seared with trade; bleared, smeared with toil;/ And wears man's smudge and shares man's smell"; and on the other, "The world is charged with the grandeur of God./ . . . There lives the dearest freshness deep down things . . . / Because the Holy Ghost over the bent/ World broods with warm breast and with ah! bright wings."[6]

Put another way, you may well experience the profound insight of the dominant force in Jewish Orthodoxy, the rabbi philosopher Joseph B. Soloveitchik. In a powerful 1965 essay, "The Lonely Man of Faith," he contrasted the first Adam of the creation (Genesis 1) and the second Adam (Genesis 2).

> The first Adam boldly subdues the earth, while the second Adam humbly quests for God. Both Adams exist within each person and are mandated by God, Soloveitchik holds, but in modern times the first Adam threatens to overwhelm the second, and has even become "demonic." When the second Adam begins to speak the language of faith, writes the Rav, he "finds himself lonely, forsaken, misunderstood, at times even ridiculed by Adam the first, by himself."[7]

Second, your reaction to these realities. Will you be enslaved to the circumstances in which you find yourself, or your own master? Some of you will be quite wealthy, some politically powerful, some top-rank in medicine or law, physical science or computer science, possibly even church hierarchy. Others will just about make it, scratch and claw to break even, cry to heaven against the injustice of the system. Still others will move from want to abundance, from abundance to want. All of you will experience the human comedy, the human tragedy, will wrestle with faith and doubt, hope and despair, love and lovelessness. Will you be able to say with Paul "I have learned, whatever my circumstances, to be content"? Not because you are settled into a rut; not because you haven't the energy to change who and what and where you are. While toiling to transform your circumstances, your acre of God's world, how will you live the actual moment, the moment of having or the moment of being without? How do you live it now?

Frankly, I don't know. But this I do know: You cannot live St. Paul's "I know how to be abased, and I know how to abound" without Paul's secret: "I can do all things in him who gives me strength." *All* things. Not only how to take the rough and the rude, the bloody and the bizarre—the stroke or growth, the aortic aneurism or auto accident, the Beirut terrorism or the breakup of a marriage, the thousand and one ills that plague human existence, turn individual and family life topsy-turvy, transform ecstasy into agony, life into death. Only with strength that is God-given will you be able to say with Paul: "For the sake of Christ I am content with weaknesses, insults, hardships, persecutions, and calamities; for when I am weak, then I am strong" (2 Cor 12:10).

At the moment, the other side of the coin intrigues me more: Will you "know how to abound"? Barring nuclear war, most of you will soon live the good life: high-paying job with a future, family that adores you (understandably), friends of your own kind, gracious surroundings. No problem—save one: How will you live with it? Easy, you answer. Not at all easy, I retort. The secret St. Paul learned was how to face not only his hunger but his plenty; God's strength was necessary not only for indigence but for abundance.

But why? When you have everything you need for the good life, why do you need God's empowering grace? Empowering you, enabling you, to do what? To realize that Paul was addressing *all* Christians when he told the Christians of Philippi they must "work out [their] salvation with fear and trembling" (Phil 2:12). Rich or poor, powerful or impotent, hale or infirm, delighted with life or desperate for death, whoever you are, you can lose your God—will lose Him unless you love Him, unless you live the startling assertion of Jesus, "Apart from me you can do nothing" (Jn 15:5). It is God who enables you to see that your abundance—success and wealth, intelligence and health, life itself—is given you not to clutch but to share. You need God to open not only your eyes but your hearts and your hands to a world where 40,000 children starve to death each day, teen-agers kill themselves by the thousands each year, grown men disappear at the whim of dictators, and the aged rummage for food in garbage cans; where all too often women are chattel, blacks are cattle, and the poor live in squalor and die in the streets; where war is a constant and whole nations are enslaved to the Russian Bear. You need God to persuade you that you are less than Christian, less than human, if this world's crosses do not crucify you, if you do not lift the cross, like Simon of Cyrene, from the shoulders of some struggling Christ.

My friends, it will be a high point in your Christian growth when you are able to say with sincerity "I have learned Paul's secret: how to live with little, how to live with much." Not because you are natively shrewd, but because you are divinely graced. Very simply, because like Paul you are "in Christ."

Flanner Hall
University of Notre Dame
Notre Dame, Indiana
October 14, 1984

21

EXPERIENCE OF GOD,
EXPERIENCE OF EVIL
Thirtieth Sunday of the Year (A)

- ◆ Exodus 22:20–26
- ◆ 1 Thessalonians 5:5–10
- ◆ Matthew 22:34–40

The best of quotations have a built-in problem. Years and use turn them stale; they lose their flavor. "A bird in the hand is worth two in the bush." "A stitch in time saves nine." Or the Irish "A soft word never yet broke a tooth." Even, one day, "This Bud's for you." So for today's Gospel. It's old hat, flat beer. Love God above all else? Love your neighbor as you love yourself? We've heard it all too often, imbibed it with the Church's milk. It has lost its bite. If we could only give it TV life, commercialize it, sit Jesus down at a Jerusalem bar, have the Twelve jostling him, show them hoisting a Manischewitz and harmonizing a jingle, "This God's for you." Perhaps we can come close. Three scenes: (1) Jesus surrounded by Pharisees; (2) Jesus surrounded by disciples; (3) Jesus surrounded by you and me.

I

First, picture Jesus surrounded by Pharisees. Somewhat like hostile reporters hustling a political candidate, everyone shouting his or her rude question. A clever lawyer tries to trip Jesus up, outsmart him: "Teacher, which is the great commandment in the law?" (Mt 22:36). A tricky question. Why? Because the law had 613 commandments: 248 do's and 365 don't's. Pick the wrong one and over the very first commandment. Many a Pharisee would have nodded sagely, had Jesus stopped after a single sentence, his excerpt from the great prayer in Deuteronomy:

> Hear, O Israel! The Lord is our God, the Lord alone! Therefore, you shall love the Lord, your God, with all your heart, and with all your soul, and with all your strength. Take to heart these words which I enjoin on you today. Drill them into your children. Speak of them at home and abroad, whether you are busy or at rest. Bind them at your wrist as a sign and let them be as a pendant on your forehead. Write them on the doorposts of your houses and on your gates.
>
> (Deut 6:4–9)

This prayer devout Jews recited long before Bethlehem; here was their exultant proclamation of faith. A book of law expressed the relation of man and woman to God in terms of love: Israel's love for God and God's love for Israel. At no moment might the Israelite forget that love; it had to be transmitted to the next generation. A total love, for "heart" included mind and will and emotions; "soul" was the whole, vital human person.[1]

No, it is not with this response that Jesus surprises the Pharisees. What startles them is a "second" commandment: "You shall love your neighbor as yourself." (Mt 22:39). It startles them because to find it they would have to rummage through all sorts of rules in Leviticus (Lev 19:1–37; see v. 18). It startles them because Jesus proclaims that this second commandment is "like" the first. Loving your neighbor is like loving God? Wow! It startles them because for them the neighbor is only a fellow Israelite or a resident alien; for Jesus, the neighbor is the despised Samaritan, the idolatrous Gentile, the enemy. It startles them because Jesus weds this commandment to the first, to fashion one twin commandment, "greater" than all the rest (Mk 12:31). It startles them because on these "depend all the law and the prophets" (Mt 22:40), all of Scripture; in these two all 613 regulations are comprised. Live these two and you live them all. Live these two and you are doing God's will, His total will.[2]

A fascinating footnote: At least one of Jesus' hearers was *not* startled. In Mark's version, the very lawyer who had put the question reacted like this: "Well said, teacher! . . . To love [God] with all the heart, and with all the understanding, and with all the strength, and to love one's neighbor as oneself, is much more than all whole burnt offerings and sacrifices" (Mk 12:33). And Jesus replied pithily: "You are not far from the kingdom of God" (v. 34).[3]

II

Second, picture Jesus surrounded by his disciples. You see, the twin commandment is so all-embracing, so ingenious, so liberating that we might think it takes care of Christian existence as well. But note what the question was: "Which is the great commandment in the law?" In the law . . . in the Jewish law. This is the question Jesus answers. Oh yes, the answer lays a burden on Christians as well as Jews. We too have to love God above all else, love others as we love ourselves. Do that and the God of Abraham, Isaac, and Jacob will be happy with you.

Happy, but not satisfied. The God of Abraham, Isaac, and Jacob is also the God of Jesus. So, steal into the Last Supper. Focus your audiovisual on Jesus and the Eleven (Judas has slunk out into the dark). "A new commandment I give to you: Love one another as I have loved you" (Jn 13:34). Not just "Love one another." Not simply "Love one another as you love yourselves." No, "Love one another as I have loved you."

Over that short sentence Scripture scholars have spilled scads of ink and blood.[4] What precisely is it that is "new" in this commandment? You may argue that what is new is the model of love: Our love for one another must mirror Jesus' love for us.[5] How did he love us? You can scarcely count the ways. For love of us, he shed the glory that was his with the Father, was born of a teen-age Jewish girl, wore not only our clothes but our flesh, grew up in a small village where everyone knew his every secret save the one big secret—that he was not Joseph's son but God's. For love of us, he walked the dusty ways of Palestine, healing the sick and raising the dead, comforting the afflicted and afflicting the comfortable, hungry at times and thirsty, with no set place to rest his head. Each syllable, each gesture, was shaped of love, all of it crowned by love's last spasm on a cross. No greater love than this, to lay down your life for a friend (Jn 15:13)—or for an enemy.

This indeed is the way we ought to love. But you will not grasp how new the commandment is unless you situate it within the Supper that gave it to us. The context of the "new commandment" is the "new covenant": "This cup which is poured out for you is the new covenant in my blood" (Lk 22:20). Both expressions, "new covenant" and "new commandment," reflect an early Christian conviction: In Jesus and his followers is fulfilled the dream of the prophet Jeremiah:

"Behold, the days are coming," says the Lord, "when I will make a new covenant with the house of Israel and the house of Judah, not like the covenant which I made with their fathers when I took them by the hand to bring them out of the land of Egypt, my covenant which they broke, though I was their husband," says the Lord. "But this is the covenant which I will make with the house of Israel after those days," says the Lord: "I will put my law within them, and I will write it upon their hearts; and I will be their God, and they shall be my people. And no longer shall each man teach his neighbor and each his brother, saying, 'Know the Lord,' for they shall all know me, from the least of them to the greatest," says the Lord; "for I will forgive their iniquity, and I will remember their sin no more."

(Jer 31:31–34)

What is it that distinguishes God's covenant love from the noblest forms of human love? It is so splendidly spontaneous. Love is not forced from God by some power outside, not seduced from God by our lovable personalities. Quite the opposite. God's love goes out to men and women who are sinners, who are utterly unworthy of love divine, cannot demand that love, become God's beloved simply because He wants it so, can love God only because He loves them. This kind of love we Christians find "new," discover in its most radical form, when God gives us His only Son—to reveal that love and to live it in very death.

Such should be our own new love. It is the prayer of Jesus to his Father after the Supper: "I in them and you in me, that they may become perfectly one, so that the world may know that you have sent me and have loved them even as you have loved me" (Jn 17:23).

III

Which brings me to my third commercial: Picture Jesus surrounded by you and me. It's a larger crowd than the Pharisees, larger than the original disciples. As we jostle him, push him off dry land and into a boat, what question should we ask him? Not "the great commandment"; we know that. Not who our model is in loving; that is still Jesus. Today's question is a how: How ought we to live the love commandment in the eighties?

There is no single answer for all; God speaks to us in varied ways. We have to keep asking with St. Paul "What shall *I* do, Lord?"

(Acts 22:10). The danger is, I may sit on well-cushioned haunches waiting for Jesus to knock me over and spell it out. Knocking Christians over is not the Lord's standard operational procedure; he works more subtly, through his grace in our hearts. Let me simply turn your thinking into one channel.

On both levels, love of God and love of others, there is a basic problem: my experience. Better, my inexperience. It is dreadfully difficult to love God above all else, especially in crisis, if I have not touched God, if God is an abstraction. Prime Mover, Creator of the universe, Lord of the living and the dead, author of the Ten Commandments—there is no pulsing, throbbing, one-to-one relationship here. I am not speaking of a vision, an ecstasy, an experience "out of this world." I mean the experience theologian Karl Rahner put with good reason on the pen of St. Ignatius Loyola:

> All I say is I knew God, nameless and unfathomable, silent and yet near, bestowing Himself upon me in His Trinity. I knew God beyond all concrete imaginings. I knew Him clearly in such nearness and grace as is impossible to confound or mistake. . . . I knew God Himself, not simply human words describing Him. . . . I mean God really and truly . . . the ineffable mystery, the darkness which only becomes eternal light for the man who allows himself to be swallowed up by it unconditionally. It is precisely this God, He and none other, whom I personally experienced as the God who comes down to us, who comes close to us, the God in whose incomprehensible fire we are not, in fact, burnt away but become ourselves and of eternal value. . . . Through Him, if we allow ourselves to be taken up by Him, we are not destroyed but given to ourselves truly for the first time. . . . This experience is grace indeed and basically there is no one to whom it is refused.[6]

Have I experienced God in some such way? If I have not, it will be extraordinarily hard for me to love God more than I love myself, more than I love another whose eyes I can meet, whose flesh I can caress.

So, too, for the second commandment, the commandment "like" love of God. If a former Vice President of the United States sounded callous when he remarked "If you've seen one slum, you've seen them all,"[7] I can prove still more callous if I haven't experienced even one. I mean an experience such as black social worker Roger Wilkins had in Cleveland a quarter century ago:

If you went into that house it was like going into a coffin. The people were white and they were pale, and they had blue numbers on their arms. That house smelled like death because the people were scared to go out, and they wouldn't let anybody come in. They only let me come in because I was the man with the money. The woman had been in Auschwitz; the man had been in some other, less well-known camp; and somehow they had survived; somehow they had married; somehow they'd come to Cleveland; somehow I was the government, and I was a kid. Of course, I'd known about the war. I'd had friends at school in Harlem who had been refugees from Germany. But I had never seen this evil in its face that way before. After a while, I gained their confidence. One day I heard—I swear to you this is true—a scratching inside a closet, and I asked, what is that in that closet? And then I opened the door and there was a kid in the closet. The worst-looking, most malnourished kid I ever saw. It was their child, and they were afraid to bring that child out of the closet because they thought Hitler would come from the grave and burn that child.

I said, you can't do this. You can't inflict the pain of history on this child. I will help you find a school for this child. I did. . . . [8]

Experience of God, experience of evil. I may have been wrong a few moments ago. Maybe, like Paul, I do need to be knocked to the ground . . . if I am to get up as a Christian.

> Dahlgren Chapel
> Georgetown University
> Washington, D.C.
> October 28, 1984

22

WELL DONE, FAITHFUL SERVANT!
Thirty-third Sunday of the Year (A)

- Proverbs 31:10–13, 19–20, 30–31
- 2 Thessalonians 5:1–6
- Matthew 25:14–30

Today's three readings may leave you with a large question mark: So what? From the Old Testament we have a detailed portrait of the ideal wife—a portrait many American women today will not buy. From Paul we have a passionate exhortation to stay awake, not be caught by surprise when Christ comes—an exhortation that makes sense only if you are convinced Armageddon is right around the corner. From Jesus we have a puzzling parable of three servants entrusted with their master's money; two are rewarded for investing bullishly; the third is flayed for not investing at all. Anyone want to give a homily?

In point of fact, one powerful word links Proverbs to Jesus, and both to Paul. Today you heard the word in the parable alone; yet it is a key word for the "ideal wife" as well, and for the wide-awake Christian. That key word is "faithful." To grasp this, you have to get behind the details, behind the externals of the portrait, the exhortation, the parable. Not overlook them; simply get behind them. Move from what is secondary to what is primary, from what is time-conditioned to what transcends time, from what was said to this or that people to what is said to all of us. So then, two stages to my movement this afternoon, both focused on the word "faithful." Very simply: faithful then and faithful now.

I

First, faithful then. I mean, specifically, faithful in the biblical sense.[1] It is God above all who is faithful. However unfaithful herself, Israel could confidently count on God's word, depend without doubting on His promises. That divine fidelity finds its human perfection in Jesus. He fulfils his Father's will even unto crucifixion, makes it possible for us to be faithful, "remains faithful even if we are faithless" (2 Tim 2:13). And the New Testament "faithful"? Not only are they reliable, dependable, trustworthy. They are faith-full, full of faith. They can be trusted completely because they have entrusted themselves completely: to God and His Christ, to God's people, to God's creation.

Such is the ideal wife of Proverbs. Don't be distracted by details: the distaff under her left arm, her household chores, her rising at night (presumably her husband needs his sleep), even "*she* does *him* good" (Prov 31:12). The soul of the portrait is a single syllable: "The heart of her husband *trusts* in her" (v. 11). She is faithful. Everyone in the picture can depend on her: husband, children, servants, merchants, even the poor. To all of these she has pledged herself, and she keeps her word. And not only these: She "fears the Lord" (v. 30). Oh, not fright, not terror, not panic; simply, reverential awe in the presence of the living God, a God who never goes back on His own promises.

So, too, for the servants in Matthew's parable.[2] You can, like Matthew and other early Christians, make an allegory of it. The merchant is Christ; his journey is his ascension to heaven; his return "after a long time" (Mt 25:19) is his second coming; he ushers his own into the Messianic banquet; the rest he casts "into the outer darkness" (v. 30). But Jesus himself had a simpler message. He was addressing the religious leaders of the Jews, especially the scribes. Much had been entrusted to them—in particular, the Word of God. Soon they would have to render a reckoning: How had they used what had been committed to them? Had they been "faithful" (vv. 21, 23), like the first and second servants? Or had they been "slothful" (v. 26), idle, lazy, indolent, like the third? Had they used God's Word in harmony with God's will, traded on their trust, made it pay off? Or had they frustrated God's Word by worrying about themselves, neglecting to use the trust, refusing to risk, renouncing responsibility for the money by burying it according to rabbinical law?

Similarly for Paul's Thessalonians. Like him, they were waiting for the Lord to return—and quite soon. Paul is not about to pass out a timetable of the Second Coming; he doesn't have one. All he knows is that, whenever the Lord comes, it will be sudden, "like a thief in the night" (1 Thess 5:2). The conclusion? "Keep awake and be sober" (v. 6). Awake. Not only eyes open so that they could see Christ coming on a pink cloud. Wide-awake in every way, watching for Christ in every circumstance. Sober. Not merely masters of their Manischewitz but masters of themselves, free of all excess, enslaved only to Christ. In a word, faithful: full of faith and keeping faith.

II

Such was fidelity then: for a Jewish wife, for an Old Testament religious leader, for an early Christian. My second question: What does it mean to be faithful now?[3] Not an easy question, if only because the word "faithful" is no longer a parlor word. Dogs are faithful; Federal Express is faithful; Marines are "always faithful"; but much of America is uncomfortable with it, from coaches to spouses.

But this is not a philippic against infidelity; I want to be positive, even upbeat. You see, it is a distinguished title you and I bear: We are the Christian faithful. The faithful. Like many another hackneyed expression, this too rolls off our tongues without a second thought. And yet, this perhaps more than any other single word sums up who we are as Christians. We are men and women who are full of faith and who keep faith. It tells who we are, because it tells whom we love. Let me explain.

We are Christian faithful, first, because we are committed to Christ. No commitment may take precedence over that. In baptism God "put His seal upon us" (2 Cor 1:22), the seal of the Spirit. Somewhat as a Roman soldier was branded with the seal of the emperor, somewhat as animals have been branded with their owner's mark, so Christians are stamped with the seal of the Spirit: We belong to Christ, and through him to the Father. Renounce it we can, with our lips or our lives, but the seal is ceaselessly there. From here to eternity we belong to Christ.

The problem is, how live the logic of this relationship? How be faithful to the Christ who owns us? A twin response: filled with faith and keeping faith. Filled with faith. Not only an intellectual confession: "I believe in Jesus Christ, God's only Son, our Lord, born of the Virgin Mary. . . ." Important indeed, but not enough. My whole self must leap out to him—mind and heart, will and emotions. Such faith alone is alive, alive with love. Such faith alone is a Christian response to the love that was crucified for me, the loving person "apart from" whom I "can do nothing" (Jn 15:5). Mother Teresa phrased it in her simple, direct fashion:

> I do not think anyone needs God's grace as much as I. There are times when I feel so helpless and so hopeless. And I think that is why God makes use of me. In my work I can do nothing of myself, and so I need him 24 hours a day. And if a day had more than 24 hours, I would have even more need of him.[4]

Such faith makes it possible for me to keep faith. Because I have entrusted myself completely to Christ, he can trust me completely. Because I love him, I will be like him. And the more like him I am, the more likely I am to keep faith with him even unto crucifixion: "Not my will but thine be done" (Lk 22:42).

Second, we are Christian faithful because we are faithful to the Body of Christ, committed to the community of Christ. Precisely here lies the agonizing heart of our contemporary Catholic concern; here is the crisis of fidelity at its most crucial. What does it *mean* to be faithful to the community, to the Church? It would be fairly simple if all 700 million of us were of a single mind. But we are not; we are dreadfully divided. From contraception to the kiss of peace, from nuclear first-strike to Communion in the hand, from capital punishment to American capitalism, from remarriage after divorce to religion in politics, from priestly celibacy to women's ordination, from human rights to funding for abortion—on these and a host of other issues we Catholics are not only at odds; at times we claw one another like cats in a sack.

It is not that our wills are evil, our intentions bad. Oh yes, there are indifferent Catholics, Sunday Catholics, foxhole Catholics, social Catholics, birth-and-burial Catholics, way-out Catholics, Catholics who couldn't care less whether the pope lives or dies. But most of the faithful I have known through seven decades are precisely that: Christians who are trying desperately to be faithful. But it's a struggle: between the clear call from Rome and the crucifying confusion at home; between a Mass they drank in with their mothers' milk and a Mass that leaves them angry or just cold; between a liberty-loving culture that fashions them from the womb and a hard-nosed Church that refuses to move with their times; between commandments presumably from God and a conscience equally from God; between choices that baffle their minds and buffet their hearts.

How, then, be faithful—full of faith and keeping faith? A homily is not a computer: Press the right button and out pops the right response. I do not come to you with a hatful of answers, Georgetown telling you what Notre Dame cannot. Still, I submit, today's readings suggest how today's faithful can work out their faithfulness. Three suggestions, from contemplation on Proverbs, on Matthew, on Paul.

1) The word from Proverbs: Fidelity is where you are; faithfulness is here and now. The wife of Proverbs was not peering over the hills at distant Syria, not planning how to be faithful in her senility. Fidelity was right there; fidelity was husband and children, servants and merchants, the poor and God. To each of these she had pledged herself, and she was a woman of her word.

And so for you. Fidelity is here and now; faithfulness is fall 1984. You have pledged yourself. To whom? To the Christian community: to live this day in holiness of heart, in sinlessness, somewhat as Christ our Lord lived. Your baptism may have been "forced," amid wails of protest. Your presence here is a free, fresh commitment. From your humble "I confess to you, my brothers and sisters" to the "Amen" you murmur to "The body of Christ," you are saying to one another: I am part of you, I belong to you, you can trust me. Who can trust you, rely on you? Not only the Lord. Your roommate, the student whose hand you're holding, the parents whose sweat and blood and tears sent you here, an honorable lady called Notre Dame, your wife or husband. And not because your genes make you nice guys and dolls. Rather because the grace of our Lord Jesus Christ courses through you like another bloodstream.

Allow a visiting Jesuit to intrude on your recent gridiron grief. I share it, believe me. But do you know what moves me most about your situation? A short sentence from your administration, a sentence that surprises a world that worships success: "We have made a contract."[5]

2) The word from Matthew: Christian fidelity calls for risk. Which of the servants were called "faithful"? Not the servant who played it safe, hid the thousand dollars in the ground. Only the servants who took a chance, traded with the money their master had entrusted to them.

And so for you. It is one thing to be faithful when the issues are stark and clear, when you know the way to go and what will end well, when it doesn't cost anything, doesn't threaten your way of life. It is quite another thing to grope in darkness, when you are not sure, when you're afraid, when discipleship costs, when you must lose your life in order to find it, when the Lord simply says: "You have your gifts: my Church and your conscience, my grace and your good sense. Trade with them till I come." You may indeed trade badly, choose poorly, decide wrongly; but when the Master comes he will not ask how often you were right but how honestly you tried, not how brilliant you were but how loving, not how close to the vest you played it but how ready you were to risk all for him. Very simply, did you always kick on fourth-and-one?[6]

3) The word from Paul: Fidelity is a Christ who comes in surprising ways. If you want to hear "Well done, good and faithful servant" from a Christ riding clouds of glory, then welcome him when he comes hungry and thirsty, lonely and unloved, in rags or in pain, imprisoned by all sorts of fears. To be faithful, all you have to do is touch each hand that stretches out to you. That's all. That's all?

Sacred Heart Church
University of Notre Dame
Notre Dame, Indiana
November 17, 1984

MEDLEY

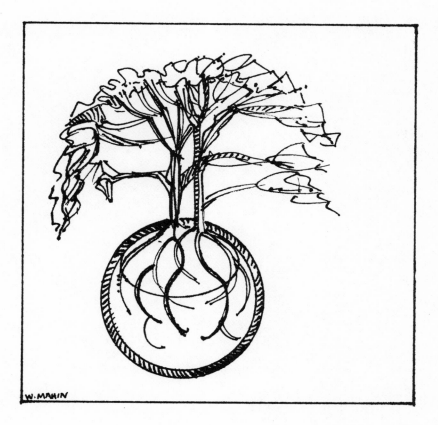

23

SALT OF THE EARTH,
LIGHT OF THE WORLD
Wedding Homily 1

◆ Tobit 8:4–9
◆ 1 John 3:18–24
◆ Matthew 5:13–16

Today's Gospel tells us more than your ears may have heard. You see, not too long ago Cathy and Sam would have had nothing to say about the scriptural readings at their wedding. That had all been decided in Rome, and more likely than not Cathy would have wriggled some wrinkles into her wedding gown as I proclaimed from St. Paul, "Wives, be subject to your husbands, as to the Lord" (Eph 5:22). And Sam's sweat might have unstarched his collar as I seemingly addressed to him Christ's dire warning, "What God has joined together, let not man put asunder" (Mk 10:9).

Today bride and groom may choose their liturgical readings. Within limits, of course: Gibran's *Prophet* should not unseat a Hebrew prophet. What Sam and Cathy have chosen tells us a good deal about them, more perhaps than they realize; for they have chosen with care. Not to delay the maitre d' at the Governor Morris, I shall pass over Tobias' lovely prayer to "find mercy and grow old together with" Sarah (Tob 8:7), pass over John's pertinent reminder, "God is greater than our hearts" (1 Jn 3:20). I shall focus on the striking words of Jesus borrowed from the Sermon on the Mount: "You are the salt of the earth. . . . You are the light of the world" (Mt 5:13–14). What did they mean on the Mount,[1] and what might they suggest in Basking Ridge?

I

What did the words of Jesus mean on the Mount? Here I burden you with a bit of learning.[2] To describe his disciples, to characterize those who have said yes to his "Follow me," Jesus uses two metaphors: salt and light. In Palestine each item was a must. Salt was irreplaceable. Not yet for Margaritas, but to improve the taste, say, of meat and fish; more importantly, to preserve them. A small thing indeed, a pinch of salt, compared to the meat and fish, yet incomparably important. It changed what it touched, kept it from spoiling, from rotting. That is why, in Old Testament times, salt was used to season every sacrifice. It was a sign, sign of a permanent covenant between the Lord and His people, a covenant that would not corrupt, that would last for ever.

What Jesus is telling us is that this world of ours depends for its moral well-being on the Christian disciple, on the faithful, on you and me. Small and insignificant as we may seem, it is our task to improve the quality of human living, change what we touch, preserve our sin-scarred, tear-stained earth from destruction. If the disciple turns flat, lifeless, tasteless, if like salt from the Dead Sea we give off a stale and alkaline taste, our brothers and sisters will suffer, will spoil, will corrupt. And we? We will be worthless, fit only for the rubbish heap, deserve to be thrown into the street with the rest of the refuse.

And what of the light? In the one-room cottage of the Oriental peasant, the small dish-like devices in which oil was burned were indispensable. Not a very bright light; hardly our 3-way Sylvania; but without it life would have been dark indeed. I could not have seen you once the sun went down, could not have read the Torah, could not have walked with sure foot and light heart. So much of life would have stopped—like the evening in New York City in the 60's, when I saw all the lights go out, and a city of millions sat in darkness, afraid to move.

What Jesus is telling us is that we who believe in him are not allowed to hide our gifts in a sort of flour bin, keep them to ourselves or for our groupies. They should attract all manner of people: our faith give pause to the skeptic, our hope lend heart to the disheartened, our love cool the anger of those who hate. Not attract them simply to ourselves, but that they may "give praise to [our] heavenly Father" (Mt 5:16).

II

All well and good. All of us are bound by our baptism to be salt of the earth and light of the world. Even a Jesuit! But why this Gospel today, in Basking Ridge, at a wedding? Because, dear Cathy and Sam, you will from this hour forward bear an uncommon burden. You are to be salt and light in a manner impossible to you before: You are to be salt and light *together*.

One early Christian writer called the family "a little church." You and your children will be the Church in miniature. Here, in the family, is where God's people is born, grows, comes to flower. Without such as you, one in flesh and spirit, without the living fruit of your love, there would soon be no people of God—or only a faithful remnant.

Your task is to salt and light family life. Fifty percent of American marriages end in disaster; they corrupt. Your marriage should be a sign to others that love unto death is not an unreal ideal, that no manner of human obstacle need triumph over divine grace. And such a sign it can indeed be; for your love, St. Paul proclaims, your two-in-oneness has been raised by God to an incredible level. It represents, signifies, symbolizes the love that obtains between God-in-flesh and the Church he created from his blood. No other love can rival that profound symbolism.

But if such is to be your love, what in the concrete does it ask of you? Three demands above all else. Like the love of God-made-man, it demands, first, that your love take flesh. You will live your love not in heaven but on earth, not with angels but among men and women. On a paradoxical planet where children of God die for one another and kill one another; where vows are held sacred and vows are sold for silver; where children are accepted and aborted, adored and abused, hugged to life and choked to death. It is this flesh-and-blood world that your love must salt and light. By the way you live your love, you can give your acre of God's world reason to hope once more that two can be one; that a family can pray together, play together, stay together; that the human family may yet survive our inhuman folly.

Second, your love, like the love of God-made-man, has to be a crucified love. Not that you are fated to be "sad sacks," enduring each other because you have not the energy to do aught else. Rather because all earthly love walks a rocky road, bounces its head and heart against frustration—from a messy bathtub to the illness that devastates a personality. The Christian approach, like the way of Christ's cross, is not sheer endurance. You give light to your world when the Calvaries that haunt and daunt wedded love are seen precisely as that: Calvaries. I mean, you live them as your share in the sufferings of Christ, experiences that are not lost hopes but your role in redemption—your own redemption and the world's. With each crisis, you die a little; but only that you may give richer life, to each other and to those who taste your salt, glimpse your light.

Third, your love, like the love of Christ for his people, will salt the earth if you can flavor it with joy. Despite our foolishness and our sinfulness, Christ takes delight in his people. He smiles gently on our foolishness, forgives our sinfulness, always makes the first gesture to restore a tattered love, welcomes the prodigal home with a fatted calf—or today, with a dozen roses and a Pizza Peperone.

And so for you. There will surely be some ecstatic moments of wedded grace, but for the most part your joy will be a soft, quiet joy. But none the less profound and delightful. I mean a deep delight in each other, a delight that may ebb and flow as you discover how wonderfully and fearfully human the other is, but still a delight that will grow . . . *if*. If you never take each other for granted, but are ceaselessly lost in wonder that a Cathy or a Sam can love you as you are, love you totally, literally love you to death. If you can sustain the delightful, if somewhat bizarre, sense of humor you now possess. If you refuse to take yourself too seriously, make the world revolve around your schedule or your cereal, your hiatal hernia or your wounded pride. If each of you admits that it is not only the other who rubs the wrong way, who wears a fallen nature, whose character is flawed. If no sun sets before your anger cools, before you murmur "I love you." If you are as open to fresh ideas as to fresh vegetables. If you move out together to the downtrodden and the underprivileged, to those who have tasted more of Jesus' crucifixion than of his resurrection, those who have never experienced love such as yours. If you realize that earthly love does not really conquer all, that only the Holy Spirit can deepen the selflessness you share this day, make it triumph over our native smallness. If, in a word, you never forget that you are in this together—together with Christ your Love.

Love that takes flesh in the midst of frail humanity, love that lives in the shadow of a cross, love that is charged with joy and delight—this is the love that recaptures the love of our Lord for his people. Such love will surely salt your earth and light your world: lend fresh flavor to others' love, preserve love that threatens to corrupt, inspire your sisters and brothers to praise not you but the God who fathers the love of man and maid and pervades it with His presence.

One final word. If Cathy and Sam are to live the Gospel of salt and light, it will not be by themselves, on some "Fantasy Island."[3]

They will need support—God's and yours. God's help they will infallibly have, as long as they hunger and thirst for it. It is your help they seek. Not fondue forks or a chafing dish, welcome as these may be. Rather the powerful example of so many of you who, a year ago or 50, pledged yourselves to a love that would put all other loves to shame. Today's young love should spark not nostalgic envy but fresh commitment.

What do I mean? In a few moments I shall ask Sam and Cathy to join their hands as symbol of their ceaseless oneness. At that moment, if it's not uncommonly uncomfortable, I would ask the wedded among you to link your hands and silently repeat to each other the awesome words that will bind Cathy and Sam for ever, words that for you have already taken on flesh, may well have been bruised by the wood of the cross, have surely been seasoned by a measure of joy and delight: "I take you . . . to have and to hold . . . for better, for worse . . . for richer, for poorer . . . in sickness and in health . . . until death do us part."

Do that, with experience of wedded life already yours, and a remarkable little miracle will transpire today. The first marriage Cathy and Sam will salt is yours; the first acre of earth their love will light is you.

St. James Church
Basking Ridge, New Jersey
September 22, 1984

24

ABOVE ALL THESE PUT ON LOVE
Wedding Homily 2

♦ Genesis 2:18–24
♦ Colossians 3:12–17
♦ John 17:20–26

Annie and Michael: On a wedding day two problems plague a preacher. On the one hand, everything worth saying has seemingly been said—perhaps best by poets. On the other hand, no one but you two can actually say what should be said—if only because you say it not with naked syllables but with your eyes, your touch, your life.

Still, you have eased my "mission impossible." The readings you have chosen from God's own Book suggest, share with us, what this day means to you. All three texts focus on oneness, on love, but in different ways. Genesis tells us how love began; Paul tells us how love grows; Jesus tells us how love peaks. A word on each.

I

Genesis tells us how love began.[1] Not God's love, but ours. After the Lord has fashioned the first man, He declares: "It is not good for the man to be alone; I will make him a helper fit for him" (Gen 2:18). Now be careful not to read too much into that sentence. Do not conclude that it would be good for a *woman* to be alone. God's statement has for springboard a fact: Adam is there. If Eve had been created first, I doubt not that God would have said: "It is not good for the woman to be alone."

The point is, both man and woman need a counterpart, someone who "corresponds to" him or her. Genesis 2 develops that idea with incomparable imagery. After declaring that the man should

160

not be alone, God brings to Adam the beasts and birds He has just created. Why? To have Adam "name" them, "to see what he would call them" (v. 19). Oh, not a bare description, like road runner or robin redbreast. In the Hebrew mentality, for Adam to "name" something was for Adam to recognize its nature, see it for what it is, give it the meaning it had for Adam in his world. And what the first man saw was this: Not one of these creatures of field or sky—however swift or lovely, however gentle and affectionate—was "fit for him," suitable for him, could complement him, complete his being. For all their likeness to him, they were not like enough to him.

So the man remains alone; but the Lord God is not yet done. He shapes a creature at once different from him and strikingly similar. So similar, so kin to him, that Scripture imagines God fashioning this other out of the man's very body. But don't be distracted by poetic detail: Adam is not really losing a rib, he is gaining a woman.

Now note Adam's reaction. When God brings the first woman to the first man, as before He had brought bird and beast, the effect is electric. When first he sets eyes on her, he exclaims in ecstasy: "This one, at last, is bone of my bones and flesh of my flesh!" (v. 23). "This one"—three times he shouts it—here is man's joyful surprise as he welcomes his one equal on earth, his peer and companion. Now, and for ever, we have two; neither man nor woman is alone. Here, the author adds, is a kinship, an attraction, so strong that it will loosen the strongest bonds in early life, the bonds that bind to parents and home: "That is why a man leaves his father and his mother and cleaves to his wife, and they become one flesh" (v. 24).

So, in Scripture's symbolic description, so did love begin, the love of man and woman. It began with God. A God of high imagination. A God so imaginative that He invented not one image of Himself but two. Similar in shape and spirit, yet not the same. Two divinely designed to become one, while remaining two. Made, therefore, for love, where there is indeed "I and thou," but never "mine and thine."

II

If Genesis tells us how love began, Paul tells us how love grows. What he says should be true of all Christians, married or not, even a Jesuit! But Paul's advice to the Christians of an insignificant town in Asia Minor has special pertinence for those who wed in Christ.

For if marriage was made in Paradise, it has to be lived on earth. An imperfect earth, where love and hate wrestle in daily and deadly duel, where men and women find it increasingly hard to say "for ever," where two-in-one has a 50% mortality rate. This frightening figure suggests that good will is not enough, sexual attraction is not enough, nice guys and dolls are not enough. Not enough to overcome our bad will, the ravages of age and illness, personalities that change. If the family, which early Christians called "a little church," is to grow, it needs what "the big Church" needs to grow. It needs Christ our Lord. Paul spells it out to the Colossians.

First, forgive one another (Col 3:13). It sounds so easy this evening, when all you see is the love light in each other's eyes. Forgive those blue and brown orbs? No sweat! The test, as your dear parents can attest, is the passage of years. I mean, when you take each other for granted, forget the miracle that is Annie and Michael, the miracle that leaves you breathless today; when your frail humanity breaks out; when only one of you shows up weak. Paul's answer is not: Summon up your reserves of natural goodness; be true to the Compton chromosomes, the O'Leary genes. No. For Paul, the motive and the model and the means is Christ our Lord. Forgive one another "as the Lord has forgiven you" (v. 13). Forgive *because* Christ has forgiven you; forgive *the way* Christ has forgiven you; forgive *through* the grace of Christ within you. Not pompously, in the grand manner. Forgiveness is another word for compassion, another word for love.

Second, "let the peace of Christ rule in your hearts" (v. 15). The peace of Christ is not just a gracious greeting before Communion. The peace of Christ is the peace *brought by* Christ. And that peace, the peace the angels sang the first Christmas, is not some mixture of bubbly good cheer. It is a harmony inside you, between you, with God, a harmony that stems from the presence of Christ in you. For, as Paul put it so pithily, "[Christ] is our peace" (Eph 2:14). It does not mean that, from here on in, you will live placid, unruffled lives, free of the anxieties that assault the unbeliever. Your lives, too, will be a tissue of gladness and sadness, of rapture and pain. What the peace of Christ promises is that Christ will always be there, will always be yours. And because he is there, because he is yours, disagreement need not destroy you, failure frustrate you, living together lose its excitement. Only remember, the Christ within you is not a panic button, a last resort, a God of foxholes and catastrophes. To enjoy his peace, you have to love him—love him as passionately as you love each other.

Third, "be thankful" (v. 15). Not only now, when everything around you conspires to swell your hearts with gratitude. Even more so when your hours return to routine; when life-together is second nature; when even your healing hands have grown bored with bone and blood, with fever and fear. Thank God each day for the wonder of your being, the wonder of your love: for eyes that meet so tenderly, for ears that drink in the music of each other's voice, for a touch that cannot lie. Thank God for parents who have watered this day with their tears and anointed it with their laughter. Thank God for your vocations of mercy that mirror the Christ who not only preached a kingdom of love but "laid his hands" on the sick "and healed them" (Lk 4:40). Thank God . . . for God. Paul's Greek word for "thankful" translates literally as "eucharists": "Be eucharists." In a unique way, this very Eucharist that solemnizes your self-giving is a thanksgiving: your prayer of thanks to a God who brought you together, a God who joins you together, a God who in a few short moments will rest in your flesh.

III

If Genesis tells us how love began, if Paul tells us how love grows, Jesus tells us how love peaks: "I, Father, in them and thou in me, that they may become perfectly one . . . even as we are one" (Jn 17:23, 22). Your love, Michael and Annie, is a touching thing because it is so wonderfully human. All that the word "love" conjures up is here: tenderness and thoughtfulness, affection and ardor, self-giving and self-sacrifice—all that is here. But there is more, far more. Within you is the one gift that can make you "perfectly one," so utterly one that your oneness, your love, will reflect the oneness, the love, that exists between God the Father and God the Son.

You see, a tremendous truth about the Trinity, a truth that makes God's life meaningful for your life, is that the Trinity is the total realization, the consummate model, of perfect love. God's secret is this: There is "I and thou" without "mine and thine"—what St. Augustine called "those ice-cold words." The Father gives to the Son literally all that He Himself has—all that makes Him God, all that makes Him Love. And the Son, who receives from the Father literally all that He has, is a perfect Son, because He is the perfect image of His Father. And, incredibly, this love of Father and Son, this love is itself a person: This love *is* the Holy Spirit.

A mystery indeed, the mystery of mysteries. Don't try to solve it; simply live in its shadow. I mean, it is quite possible for your love to peak, to reach heights where human love resembles divine. Why possible? Because the gift that makes it possible rests within you; you are temples of God. "If anyone loves me," Jesus promised, "my Father will love him/her, and we will come to him/her and make our home with him/her" (Jn 14:23). You can love each other as Father and Son love each other, because Father and Son live in you. Not in poetry but in reality. Right now. If God is alive in you, there will always be "I and thou"; there need never be "mine and thine."

A final word. Today's readings were indeed selected by one couple, but they have a wider resonance. Annie and Michael will live their love not on an isolated island or on some romantic "Love Boat."[2] They will live their love in community, a community of living men and women, a community especially of couples who, a year ago or 50, swore the selfsame love we celebrate this evening. To grow in love, Michael and Annie need a gift you alone can give. Not food processors or chafing pans, welcome as these may be. More importantly, the exciting example of your own love, the compassion and peace and gratitude that mark your life together—proof positive that it can be done, that wedded love can grow with the years, can peak even on a cross.

Today's celebration, my friends, is not a spectator sport; you are intimately involved. And so, when Annie and Michael join hands to express their total yes, I would ask the wedded among you to link your own hands once again, to echo softly their promise and yours, ever ancient, ever new: "I take you . . . to have and to hold . . . for better, for worse . . . for richer, for poorer . . . in sickness and in health . . . until death do us part."

Do that, and a small miracle may come to pass. At that moment, just as the wedded love of Michael and Annie begins, your own love may peak. No gift more precious can you give.

Sacred Heart Church
Hartsdale, New York
November 24, 1984

25

HUMOR, WONDER, AND THE OTHER
Wedding Homily 3

♦ Ecclesiastes 3:1–8
♦ Colossians 3:12–17
♦ John 15:9–12

Every Catholic wedding has a built-in paradox. The paradox is not the bride and groom; the paradox is the preacher. On the one hand, a confirmed bachelor is not your prime choice for marriage counselor. I play Ann Landers without firsthand experience; I am a coach who never got into the game. On the other hand, I've been a wedlock watcher for seven decades, from the wedded life of my mother and father to the marriages of the 80's with their 50% casualty rate. It is from this lengthy, if limited, experience that three sets of ideas have just recently gelled, three qualities a man and woman must share if they are to live in love for life as man and wife. These I presume to lay before you, Mary Beth and Bill, in a kind of first edition.

What three gifts do you need, next year and the next fifty? First, a sense of humor; second, a sense of wonder; third, a sense of the other. A word on each.

I

To begin with, you need a sense of humor. I don't mean you can recognize a raunchy joke. More profoundly, you can discover, appreciate, express what is comical or incongruous, absurd or ridiculous, in an idea, an event, a situation—even a person. That is why M*A*S*H is so enjoyable; it is good humor.[1] Hawkeye has a keen eye for what does not fit, what doesn't quite make sense, what is absurd—in himself and his colleagues, in military brass and war

165

itself. He sees all this for what it is, mocks it boisterously or gently, but always, I think, with compassion and love. He acts out what the English novelist Thackeray put so well: Humor is "a mixture of love and wit."

So then, my first medicine for the married is laughter. Not always, of course. You do not laugh at cancer or a coronary, make merry over famine in Ethiopia. It means that you take yourself seriously, but not too seriously. You see and smile at or roar over the little and large absurdities in your make-up: the strange creature who believes and doubts, hopes and fears, loves and hates—afraid of your joy, feeling bad if you feel good. You see and smile at the faults and foibles in the other half—from the way he slurps his Sanka to the time she takes to put on her face. And you can look at the world together with light laughter, amused at the absurd all around you. Oh, not arrogant or supercilious or haughty or proud. Simply aware that life out there, if at times grim, can only be lived humanly if you see it for the contradiction it is: a world where men and women kill one another and die for one another, where the angel and the devil in all of us vie for supremacy, where so much of our time is taken up with the superficial, where men don't weep because it's weak and womanly, where people work themselves into ulcers to have fun, play games to get ahead, to be liked, to be admired, where to be in fashion is to re-create yourself from head to foot in line with the gospel according to TV.

If laughter can sometimes save a life, as it did Norman Cousins,[2] it can save a marriage. In a recent editorial in the *Journal of the American Medical Association,* humorist Art Buchwald admitted that there are "many unanswered questions": Can you laugh yourself to death? If laughter is such good medicine, why will not Medicare or Medicaid pay for it? Can you transplant a sense of humor? And much scientific work remains to be done "before the Food and Drug Administration will permit [laughter] to be used in large doses."[3] Nevertheless, a fascinating fact remains; I've seen it time and time again. Prescription number 1 for a healthy marriage is a sense of humor: to see the incongruous in yourself, in the other, in the world, talk wittily about it, laugh lovingly over it. A mixture of love and wit.

II

Second, you need a sense of wonder. I don't mean curiosity, perplexity, doubt. I mean that, even after a quarter century on this paradoxical planet, you two can still be surprised, delighted, amazed. Amazed at what? Amazed at being alive.

Alive, first, to your world—a world outside and inside. Amazed that with a flicker of eyelids you can span a universe, from an amoeba to outer space; you can open your ears to a skylark or Michael Jackson, smell the scents of Chicago, feast your taste buds with Lasagna or ice cream, touch a face or a flower. Amazed that your mind can shape an idea, roam from Connecticut to Connemara, know yourself, a friend, God. Amazed that you can play and pray, dance and weep, like and love. Rarely bored, blasé, unfeeling—even hovering over an impacted molar or a cancerous growth.[4] Lifeless only if you are touching merely a tooth or a lump; alive if you are in touch with a person, a man or woman or child whose ache you realize is part of them, intimate to their growing or their shrinking.

Alive, second, to your God. *Your* God. This is not pretty poetry; it is unvarnished truth. The Son of God declared that if you love him, his Father loves you, and they make their home in you (Jn 14:23). Amazing, isn't it? A God of eternal mystery, a God who could easily get along without you, has not only fashioned a world for you, but has chosen to live in you, to enliven you with His life, to make you more human by making you more divine. Your task together is to be *aware* of God within you, excited by His closeness, thrill to His touch.

Alive to your world, alive to your God: With such life you can be alive to each other. I mean, ceaselessly surprised, delighted, amazed by the other. Amazed at the miracle that is your love. Amazed that your eyes could ever have met (Jimmy the Greek would have taken that bet off the board). Amazed that this first exchange should have blossomed into a lasting exchange. Amazed that in a few moments you will stand before God and the community and declare: "All we are we give to each other, to treasure together, to share as one." Ready to be surprised for life by the other, as a Christian is ever ready to be surprised by the Spirit. Not knowing what shape the surprise will take, knowing only that you will be surprised. All lost in wonder at the gift of God, the gift of the other.

III

Which leads naturally into my third point. If you are to be lost in wonder at the wonder that is the other, you have to develop a sense of the other. Rather than get lost in gossamer abstractions, let me share with you a simple, yet extraordinary, experience.

Several years ago a dear friend of mine died. Perry had been married almost 60 years. The first anniversary of his marriage he was flat broke. So he went into a florist shop, asked the florist to trust him for a single rose. The florist did; Perry brought the rose to Bess—together with a love letter. Each anniversary till he died, that lovely ritual was re-enacted: two roses, three, ten, 25, 40—always with a love letter. And one moving afternoon in a New York restaurant, with children and grandchildren all about, before the cake was cut, in came 50 roses—with a love letter. After 50 years he still greeted his wife with an affectionate kiss after each separation, no matter how short. Wherever they walked, he offered his arm, though she needed it not. Each meal he seated her at table, even when there was no one to see. And whenever this amateur bartender (from whom I learned so much) mixed drinks for friends before dinner, no one ever drank before Perry called Bess from the kitchen—Bess who never drank—called her in for the first toast: "To the queen!"

This is not a commercial for cocktails. That marriage lasted through good times and bad, through sickness and health, because Bess and Perry had a ceaseless sense of the other. A businessman, he never put business before Bess. A homemaker who had friends beyond counting, her priority was Perry. And together, why, the paradox was that their very concern for each other impelled them to all others—any and every person who needed their love and their care. This is how they were able to live the commandment of Jesus that Mary Beth and Bill have selected as their special Gospel: "This is my commandment, that you love one another as I have loved you" (Jn 15:12). Love one another as Jesus loved you—from a stall in Bethlehem to a cross on Calvary.

A final word, good friends. A word to all of you. You are not just an audience, spectators at a spectacle, spellbound at a sacred ceremony that involves only Bill and Mary Beth. You are intimate to their life together, incredibly important. Married life, you know, is not lived on a fantasy island, in idyllic isolation. It calls for a community, men and women who, for all their very human differences, cherish much the same ideals. It will not be easy for Mary Beth and

Bill to sustain their sense of humor, their sense of wonder, their sense of the other, if their closest friends, especially their wedded friends, are humorless, wonderless, self-centered.

That is why, when Bill and Mary Beth join hands and hearts and voices in total self-giving, I shall ask the wedded among you to link your own hands. I ask you to renew silently your own wedding vows. Not a prosaic sort of fidelity; rather, a fresh, imaginative promise on three levels. You will try, first, to recapture a laughter you may have lost, your ability to look at yourselves and your world with humor, with a loving wit. You will try, second, to recover a sense of wonder at the miracle of being alive: alive to the people around you, alive to the God within you, alive to the love tingling in the hand you hold. You will try, third, to revive your sense of the other, a ceaseless tender awareness of one who shares your life as no other can, as no other will.

Do that, promise that, and your gift to Mary Beth and Bill will prove more precious than silver, more lasting than Irish linen. For you will share with them what is most dear to you, most private and personal and profound. You will share not only your individual love; you will share with them the love you share with each other. No greater gift can you give this day.

St. Catherine of Siena Church
Trumbull, Connecticut
December 29, 1984

26

NOT ON SAND BUT ON ROCK
Wedding Homily 4

◆ Tobit 8:4–7
◆ Romans 8:31b–35, 37–39
◆ Matthew 7:21, 24–29

Philosophers say we are what we choose. Do you want to know what manner of man or woman you are? Check your choices, the decisions you've made: about work and play, friends and enemies, religion and possessions, values and disvalues, the times you've said yes to this, no to that. Theologians say the same thing in different language: We are what we love.

And so this morning. We can tell much about Marguerite and Jim from their choices. I am not thinking, at this moment, of their most fascinating choice, their choice of each other. That choice is a tribute to their high intelligence! I am thinking rather of the readings they have chosen, the excerpts they have selected from Tobit, from Paul, from Jesus. At some risk, let me sketch what these three choices tell me about Marguerite and Jim, about the way they seem to see their life together.

I

First, Tobit. Some good Christians might be embarrassed by that selection, read aloud in church. Tobias rises from bed and says to Sarah: "Get up, and let us pray . . ." (Tob 8:4). Pray? On their wedding night? Gross! There's a time and place for everything, even for prayer. Pray in church or on retreat, in a foxhole or on a mountain top, before meals and during exams, for sun over Lauderdale and for Hoyas in Lexington.[1] But pray on your wedding night? Terribly gauche, isn't it?

170

Not really. Through Tobias and Sarah, Jim and Marguerite are telling us that for them the divine hovers over all that is human, the unseen God is intimate to every facet of His creation. It reflects a favorite prayer of mine that goes back a long way: "Direct, O Lord, our actions by your holy inspiration, and carry them on by your gracious assistance, that every prayer and work of ours may always begin from you, and through you be happily ended." Every work of theirs: Mass *and* medicine,[2] a sirloin *and* a sigmoidoscopy, love for the ailing *and* love for each other.

More than that: Recall what Sarah and Tobias were praying *about*. They recognized what their tradition trumpets and our tradition echoes. It is God who stands at the very beginning of marriage. It is God who played the overture to marriage when He shaped man and woman in such wise that each is incomplete without the other. It is God who made marriage "not because of lust" (Tob 8:7) but to mirror His love and to enrich our love, to people the earth with human images of God. And it is God's "mercy" that will grant to Jim and Marguerite, as to Tobias and Sarah, the grace to "grow old together" (v. 7).

That, my friends, is why we celebrate today not in a field of lilies but in a house of God. Marriage was indeed made in heaven. "Blessed are you, O God of our fathers . . ." (v. 5).

II

But if marriage was made in heaven, marriage must be lived on earth. That is why the passage from Matthew is so pertinent, the words of Jesus powerfully appropriate. The God who invented marriage did indeed intend it to be a thing of beauty, a joy for ever; but He did not promise it would be paradise. Marguerite and Jim know they are building a house, not atop pink clouds but amid the grit of human living, the gore of human dying. And so the rain will fall, the floods will come, the winds will blow and beat upon their house.

To marry is to risk—as to stay single is to risk. I do not know precisely what perils will beat against your house. With Yogi Berra, "I never make predictions, especially about the future." But it does not take a prophet to suggest that, given your twin professions, life-together-for-life will challenge you two in uncommon ways, may test your love to the breaking point. After decades of experience, the venerated physician Sir William Osler put it pungently in 1904:

". . . medicine is an exacting mistress."[3] Medicine can hound you, enslave you, claim every waking hour. And not because you are selfish. Quite the contrary: because you have vowed to serve, to save, to cheat death, to bring life. Medicine has saved lives and killed marriages. And I'm not sure whether a husband-and-wife team doubles the risk or shaves it in half! When you are captured by two loves, it takes more than love to cut the Gordian knot. Love must be wed to understanding, to courage, to self-sacrifice. Which means, love must be wed to grace, wed to God.

Other winds will blow, beat upon the house you have built, imperil your oneness. If the healing art lends you a "high," day-to-day reality can lay you low. For all your skills, patients will abandon you for more appealing placebos. For all the lives you save, some of us will be so unco-operative as to die on you. And then, like a doctor friend in Phoenix, a thoracic surgeon whose patient died unexpectedly last Monday after an operation, you will be distressed, depressed, wonder what you might have done differently, done better. A significant segment of your wedded love must be the support you supply to each other when the dark clouds gather—especially the growing realization that you are fearfully finite, that you are not the savior of the world, that you are not God.

The possible perils are legion, but this is not the place to detail them. More important at this point than any peril is the strength you find in the affirmation of Jesus: "Everyone . . . who hears these words of mine and does them will be like a wise man who built his house upon the rock; and the rain fell, and the floods came, and the winds blew and beat upon that house, but it did not fall, because it had been founded on the rock" (Mt 8:24–25). You have founded your marriage not on sand but on a rock. Which leads me to your selection from St. Paul, his impassioned cry of confidence from the depths of danger.

III

When Paul wrote his letter to the Christians of Rome, somewhere in the 50's of the first century, it was extraordinarily difficult to be a Christian—difficult and dangerous. Listen to what Paul says he himself endured:

> . . . imprisonments, with countless beatings, and often near death. Five times I have received at the hands of the Jews the

forty lashes less one. Three times I have been beaten with rods
[by the Romans]; once I was stoned. Three times I have been
shipwrecked; a night and a day I have been adrift at sea; on fre-
quent journeys, in danger from rivers, danger from robbers,
danger from my own people, danger from Gentiles, danger in
the city, danger in the wilderness, danger at sea, danger from
false brethren; in toil and hardship, through many a sleepless
night, in hunger and thirst, often without food, in cold and ex-
posure. And, apart from other things, there is the daily pressure
upon me of my anxiety for all the churches.

(2 Cor 11:23–28)[4]

In the midst of all this he could cry boldly that nothing "in all creation" could "separate [him] from God's love in Christ Jesus our
Lord" (Rom 8:38). Nothing in all creation. . . .

So too, Marguerite and Jim, so too for you. The rock foundation of the house you are building, the reason why you can hope to
"grow old together" in limitless love, is not your high IQs, your spar-
kling personalities, your native thoughtfulness—not even the wonderfully human love that links your hands and hearts today. These
are powerful forces indeed, priceless components of your wedded
oneness, to be cherished and deepened. But in the Christian vision
of living and loving, these are not enough. "Apart from me," Jesus
said solemnly the night before he died, "apart from me you can do
nothing" (Jn 15:5). St. Paul clothed this skeleton with flesh and
blood when he focused our Christian confidence on God's love for
us. Not a wispy, gossamer love floating about in the heavens. No,
the bone-and-gristle love that broke into our world with Christ. "He
who did not spare His own Son but gave him up for us all, will He
not also give us all things with him?" (Rom 8:32).

Of course He will! It does not mean that your perils will disappear, that your garden will always be Eden and never Gethsemane. It simply means what you two have grasped, the secret of
Christian success, the secret Paul professed: "I can do all things in
him who gives me strength" (Phil 4:13). The rain will still fall, the
floods will still come, the winds will still blow and beat upon your
house; but the house will stand, because the rock on which you have
built is God's very own love for you, a love consummated in crucifixion.

One swift warning, hardly necessary in your case: God's love
makes demands on you. You may not take your risen Christ for
granted, closet him with the Waterford crystal, shelve him with your
wedding pictures. Love calls for loving. You know that from your

experience with each other: Your love is continuing to grow because you are continually responding to love. It is no different with Christ your Lord. His love will always be there, wherever you are; but it will fill you and thrill you, warm you and vivify you, only if your living is a return of loving—loving with a consuming passion the Christ who loved you in his own consuming passion. Not only in bad times but in good; not only in poverty but in wealth; not only in sickness but in health. In a word, don't simply die with Christ; live for him, as you live for each other.

Live like that, love like that, and even when the winds blow you will experience the joy which Jesus promised "no one will take from you" (Jn 16:22). Your house will stand, for it is built on rock; it is built on Christ, crucified and risen.

Dahlgren Chapel
Georgetown University
Washington, D.C.
April 13, 1985

27

LOVE NEVER ENDS?
Wedding Homily 5

♦ 1 Corinthians 12:31—13:8a
♦ Matthew 5:1–9

In the stormy 60's, when everything traditionally sacred seemed "up for grabs," some theologians surprised us with a seductive theory. To decide what is moral, to act in ethical fashion, to live as a Christian, you don't need the thousand and one principles of the past; you can dispense with all that paraphernalia, all that baggage, of right and justice and so on. All you need is love. Why? Because love has an inbuilt compass that "homes" it unerringly on to the essence of an issue, the pith of a problem. Love and you've got it made.

In response to the compass theory, an Anglican canon with wisdom and wit told a touching story, the story of an elephant, a loving elephant. It seems that this particular elephant noticed an ostrich leave her nest to get a drink of water. The elephant rumbled over to the nest and, out of pure love, sat on the ostrich eggs to keep them warm. "Love," observed the canon, "can be a fuddy-duddy elephantine thing."[1]

My sermon will not play down St. Paul's paean to love. I intend simply to uncover two profound truths that lie hidden in that matchless song of praise. First, love—specifically, wedded love—is tough. Second, such love is possible only if you are not two but three.

I

First then: Love—specifically, wedded love—is tough. I mean a dictionary definition of "tough": Love makes heavy demands on you; love is extremely difficult to cope with. Read Paul's ode to love again, but this time listen to what Castaneda called the space between the sounds.

Of course "love is patient and kind"; but lovers are dreadfully impatient and can be terribly unkind. I chafe and fret if you keep me waiting—for breakfast or the bathroom, for a theatre curtain or a Redskins kickoff. I know you so intimately that, if I'm not careful, I dissect you the way Tom Shales cuts up a pitiful film for the *Post*. Naturally, it's for your own good, so you can be as perfect as I am.

Of course "love is not jealous"; but lovers can and do grow green-eyed with jealousy. I grudge you your job, its fascination for you, the hours it tears you from me. I envy you your friends; they seem so much more interesting than mine. I am suspicious of the way you smile at someone attractive—a smile that should be reserved for me.

Of course "love is not rude"; but lovers can be barbarously boorish. Familiarity, the ages tell us, breeds contempt. I see so much of you that I neglect you in a group without a gram of guilt. Your anniversaries, once sheer delight to me, now burden my memory. My touch and my kiss have turned routine; I get awfully good at play-acting.

Of course "love does not insist on its own way"; but lovers get rigidly set in their ways. Age plays tricks with my memory. Your pleasure, that once delighted me, is now an irritating whim of yours. Monday nights are for TV football; you knew that when you married me. Don't expect me to entertain your friends; they bore me; they're absolutely ignorant of corporation law. And stop rumpling my hair; I just combed it.

Of course love "rejoices in the right," rejoices in the truth; but lovers come to tears and tantrums on what is right, on what is true. Understandably at times; for right and truth do not come out of a computer. Paul is talking about truth that is the very heart of Christianity, truth that expresses itself in holiness. This can divide you, especially when you disagree on Christianity itself, on the person and meaning of the God-man.

Of course "love believes all things, hopes all things, endures all things"; but lovers doubt, lovers despair, lovers find one another difficult to endure. For the years take their toll of us. Sad experience can sour us. A dear one dies, in childbirth or in Auschwitz, and God dies too. The green years of youth and promise fade, and hope can wither as well. And how will you endure me when the firm lines turn to fat and I no longer remind you of Burt Reynolds?

Perhaps "love never ends"; but, dear St. Paul, ever since you wrote that lovely line, countless lovers have fallen out of love.

II

Now this is not a jeremiad against marriage, a salute to the single life. Quite the contrary. The flaws that can afflict lovers, the comedy of errors, the tragedy of dismembered love—all this is important and pertinent this afternoon because it leads into the second profound truth hidden in the passage John and Margaret Ann have plucked from Paul. The love Paul is lauding, the love that is patient and kind, never jealous or rude, the love that does not insist on its own way and rejoices in the right, the love that believes and hopes and endures simply everything, the love that never ends— this is not a love that bride and groom create. In this section of his letter to the Christians of Corinth, Paul is speaking of spiritual gifts—I mean gifts freely given by the Holy Spirit, given by God. And so he speaks of wisdom and knowledge, of faith and healing, of prophecy and tongues; he mentions apostles and teachers and administrators in the Church of God. In this context he suddenly cries: "And I will show you a still more excellent way" (1 Cor 12:31), a still more excellent gift, more excellent than any of the above. The great gift of the Spirit, the gift that surpasses all the rest, is the gift of love.

Here the crucial word is "gift." This kind of love Margaret Ann and John do not fashion by themselves, out of their natural talents, their native characteristics. High IQs they have, lovable personalities; generous they are, willing to share, anxious to please, touchingly concerned each for the other. But if on this alone they were to base their life together, I would be less than optimistic.

Fortunately for them, the love that links them in wedded oneness, the love St. Paul extols, leaps light-years beyond those splendid traits. God's gift to you today, Margaret Ann and John, is the love Paul proclaimed to the Christians of Rome: ". . . hope does not disappoint us, because God's love has been poured into our hearts through the Holy Spirit which has been given to us" (Rom 5:5). What makes your love for each other particularly precious, what lends high promise for love that never ends, is God's love. Not somewhere in outer space, but within you. God loves you; God lives in you; God ties your love to His, ties it to the love that led Him to give His own Son to a bloodstained cross for you.

Such love—God's love for you, God's love within you—such love is genuinely a gift. You may not demand it; you do not deserve it; you cannot buy it at Woodward & Lothrop. God gives it out of sheer goodness. It is His pledge that through the bittersweet years that lie ahead you need never be alone, that your love will endure all things, can indeed be endless, if you are not two but three, if your own wondrous love for each other is carefully, caringly cradled in God's love.

Therein lies my one word of caution: God's gift of love, though priceless, is not costless. Like all love, God's love makes demands on you. Perhaps His heaviest demand, His most constant demand, is the plea every lover wings to a beloved: Don't forget me. When you leave this chapel, this gentle reminder of crucified love, you will return to a fascinating world. I mean an absurd little earth, where a billion humans fall asleep hungry; a glorious globe that was freed from slavery by the crucifixion of its God; a paradoxical planet that nurtures love and hate, despair and hope, skepticism and faith, tears and smiles, wine and blood; a creation of divine love where men and women die for one another and kill one another. It is here that you must live your love, here that you must share your love, especially with so many who experience far more of Christ's crucifixion than of his resurrection. It can be an intriguing adventure in human love *if* . . . if you forget not the divine love that alone makes for endless love.

Knowing you, Margaret Ann and John, I have high hopes for your life together in love. One prediction seems safe enough: Your love will not be "a fuddy-duddy elephantine thing."

Dahlgren Chapel
Georgetown University
Washington, D.C.
April 13, 1985

28

POET, LUNATIC, LOVER
Baccalaureate Homily 1

♦ Acts 6:1–7
♦ 1 Peter 2:4–9
♦ John 14:1–12

It is not easy to preach to you today. For three good reasons. (1) In four years you have heard enough talk; millions of syllables have assaulted your senses; it's time to move from talk to action. (2) You and I are different people. You do not look at the world the way I do, use words the way I do, think quite as I do; certainly your music is not mine. (3) A baccalaureate homily is not a commencement address; it is not so much I you should hear, as the Jesus who promised to "guide you into all the truth" (Jn 16:13). So then, at this critical moment, when you itch to translate words into deeds, I shall not bore you with my wrinkled experience; let me touch the Christian gospel to your immediate future. Happily, today's three readings confront you with three pointed challenges: a challenge to your faith, a challenge to your hope, a challenge to your love. A word on each.

I

First, the challenge to your faith. It leaps from today's Gospel, from the breath-taking response of Jesus to Thomas: "I am the way and the truth and the life" (Jn 14:6). A challenge not only to Thomas but to each of you.

You see, BC, like Georgetown, has to be a paradox. You can enter a Catholic, leave an agnostic; come pious, go impious; start warm, end cold; find Christ, lose him. The reasons are legion, often hidden in the recesses of a heart. But one paradoxical reason is the

179

very education BC offers you. It reveals ways and truths and lives. In the classroom and outside. BC asks you not only to learn but to love learning, to fall in love with words and ideas, with numbers and letters, with macro and micro, with atoms and cultures, with amoebas and dinosaurs. She asks you to get inside not only safe folk like Aristotle and Aquinas, Plato and Augustine, Lonergan and Rahner, but unsettling minds like Kant and Camus, Nietzsche and Sartre, Lenin and Marx. She leaves you freer than you realize, exposes you to different ways of reaching reality; to truths that have more than a grain of heresy, to economic truth, historical truth, philosophical truth, legal truth; to living that lets you select and reject, feel as well as reason, face fat cats and the starving, every color on the human face.

The result? Faith can be shaken, obscured, lost. Or it can be splendidly deepened. In the midst of all these "ways," Christ proclaims himself *the* way. Not just a moral guide; not just a leader for disciples to follow. Through him you and I are to become fully human, be fulfilled in flesh and spirit. Why through him? *Because* he is the truth and the life.[1] He is *the* truth: I mean, he is the Father's revelation in flesh; he discloses God's mind to us. He is *the* life: Believe in his word, do it, and you live his life, God's life, now and for ever.

This can indeed raise problems, and it should. Not that the risen Christ is some outer-space threat to academe; not that faith is hostile to knowledge, the Christlife to human living. Rather because a loving faith is total openness to God, is total surrender to a Lord who makes difficult demands. Because it is not easy to uncover the truth God took flesh to unfold, not always easy to square it with what reason reveals. Because the truth that is Christ comes to you through imperfect vessels, through men and women as sinful and selfish as you are. Because God's truth can clash with our values. Because life in Christ collides with our culture—from J.R. to Knots Landing.

And still the struggle can be thrilling. For every bit of truth you uncover is a sharing in the truth that is Christ, a stage on the way to him. With this perspective, faith is stepping out on a journey of discovery—a long loving look at the real. With this perspective, you can search for truth in the spirit of that remarkable theologian-in-a-wheelchair Yves Congar: "As for me, I want to gather up every small fragment of truth, wherever it is to be found, with the same care that I would use in picking up a tiny piece of a consecrated host."² With that as an ideal, there can be "life after BC," life in and with Christ.

II

Second, the challenge to your hope. It comes, unexpectedly, from the second reading. I mean the apostles' choice of seven men to serve the community, men "full of the Spirit and of wisdom" (Acts 6:3).

More radically, the challenge to hope has its roots in today's hopelessness. We Christians call ourselves a people of hope; hope is a Christian hallmark. But what you are entering is a world where despair reigns as never before. Half the world is at war, hot or cold; refugees clog the earth's roads, huddle in inhuman camps; terrorism is a way of life; almost a hundred countries practice some form of torture; children starve to death in their mothers' arms; and atomic annihilation overhangs the globe.

Here too, in hope as in faith, BC has to be a paradox. Most of your four years have been lived under an unspoken presupposition: Education will make for a brave new world. Chemistry lab and philosophical stoa, supply-side economics and creative composition, international relations and bedside nursing, liberal arts and disciplined sports, computer science and communications, theology and the dance—here lies hope for the world. And so you study like mad (literally), turn God's night into day, panic and despair, play as if "This Bud's for you."

Now don't tense up! The clerical axe is not about to fall; this is not a jeremiad, a tirade, against "the wisdom of the world" (1 Cor 1:20). I am convinced that, as the Lord looks down upon what BC has wrought, He finds it good, at times "very good" (Gen 1:31). After all, you are not working with tools forged in the devil's factory; you are co-operating with God's own creation. You are responding to His challenge that you master the earth (Gen 1:28)—responsibly indeed and with reverence, but master it none the less, expose its secrets, harness its magic, release its powers.

I do insist, however, that your co-operation with your Creator will be half-baked, that the hope it generates will be inadequate to the challenge, if the human spirit is not infused with the Holy Spirit, if natural knowledge is not transfused with God's wisdom, if BC does not send forth men and women in the mold of Stephen, "full of the Spirit and of wisdom." Our Christian hope is not simply, with Isaiah, to make "the desert rejoice and blossom" (Isa 35:1), to "beat swords into plowshares" (2:4), to "extend prosperity" to the earth "like a river" (66:12). That much yes, but much more. Christian hope is our confident expectation that God will give us all we need to lead a risen life, the life of Christ, life in and with the risen Lord. And that, good friends, is not a gift you can buy at Filene's; it comes only from God's Spirit bubbling within you, the Spirit who alone can help you to hope against hope, to live pulsingly and passionately in the face of death.

Only if such is your hope can you carry out your Christian calling. I mean, to permeate your acre of God's world with a twin gift: your professional competence and your Christian confidence. Only then will those who experience so terribly much of Christ's crucifixion be touched by his resurrection: Through you they will begin to hope not only for the things of God but for the good God Himself, not from you but from Him.

III

This leads naturally to a third challenge, the challenge to your love. The first Letter of Peter proclaims you a "people," "God's people," a people "that has become God's own possession" (1 Pet 2:9–10). The challenge here is to *be* a people. Not simply because God has selected you to be such. Together with that divine call, the human society you are entering summons you mutely, needs you desperately, precisely as a people. Let me explain.

Sociologists have been describing a disturbing development, a frightening phenomenon. They see American society moving away from older character ideals, away from religious man/woman and away from political man/woman. Both these ideals were oriented to the public world, the community, the common good, the other. But when the central institution in our society is no longer religion or the political order but the economy, the ideal is now economic man/woman, man and woman in pursuit of private self-interest. Listen not to a dated Jesuit but to a distinguished sociologist:

> What is significant here is not the Moral Majority . . . but something that comes closer to being amoral and is in fact a majority. This new middle class believes in the gospel of success 1980 style. It is an ethic of how to get ahead in the corporate bureaucratic

world while maximizing one's private goodies. In the world of the zero-sum society it is important to get to the well first before it dries up, to look out for number one, to take responsibility for your own life and keep it, while continuing to play the corporate game. . . . [3]

Why float this before the class of '84? Because this new ideal finds its strength in the younger generations. Because the dominant theme researchers find in young economic man/woman is freedom, autonomy, personal fulfilment; your sole responsibility is to yourself; in the end you're alone. Because from the responses of your peers a central passion between 18 and 25 is money, and in consequence many in your age bracket confess themselves sexually unsatisfied, in worsening health, worried and anxious, discontented with their jobs, and . . . lonely as hell. [4]

Any solution? Yes . . . you, the people of God, what St. Paul called the body of Christ. The solution is suggested not by Rome but by the selfsame non-Catholic sociologist:

> . . . only the church as a type of Christian social organization can effectively combat the radical individualism and the managerial manipulativeness of modern society. . . . The church as the body of Christ can remind us that we will survive only insofar as we care for one another. As Christians and as citizens we might just possibly recover an idea of the common good, of that which is good in itself and not just the good of private desire. [5]

As Christians. Not by private piety but precisely as a people, as a living body where if I hurt, you weep; if I joy, you laugh; if I die, you are diminished. The tragedy is, sympathetic scholars tell us, our Catholic body has been more conditioned by the culture than an influence upon it.

How ready are you to resist the culture? In all the professions there are already individuals who do. But Don Quixotes will not change the culture. The culture will change only if educated men and women in massive numbers carry their Christianity into marketplace and countinghouse, into law court and genetics lab, conscious of their solidarity with every man, woman, and child "redeemed not with silver or gold but with the precious blood of Christ" (1 Pet 1:18–19). Not to fashion a Christian economics—that would be a two-headed monster—but to make economic man/woman serve the human person. Paradoxically, only thus will your profession be your servant, not you its slave.

A splendid Protestant preacher once said: The religious man or woman is "a queer mixture" of three persons, "the poet, the lunatic, the lover."[6] Such is my strange prayer for you as you descend from "the Heights." I pray that the poet may always find a place in you; for the poet is a person of profound faith, seeing beneath the appearances of things, seeing with new eyes—in your case, with the eyes of Christ. I pray that there may ever be a fair measure of lunacy in you: the wild idea, the foolishness of the cross, the mad exchange of all else for God; for herein lies your Christian hope. And I pray that, however radical the risk, however many the Judases who betray you, even on your cross you will always be Christ the lover, arms extended to your little world for its redemption—and yours. In this spirit I leave you, feeling much in tune with Rod McKuen when he sings:

> I make words for people I've not met,
> those who will not turn to follow after me.
> It is for me a kind of loving.
> A kind of loving, for me.[7]

Boston College
Chestnut Hill, Massachusetts
May 20, 1984

29

FROM WISDOM TO WONDER
Baccalaureate Homily 2

- ◆ Wisdom 6:12–20; 7:7–12
- ◆ Philippians 1:3–11
- ◆ John 15:12–17

Graduates of '84, you lay a heavy burden on this homilist. Almost half a century separates us. Not merely years and hairs; almost a cultural chasm: an Apple and a Wang, the Pretenders[1] and new genders, even your "soaps" and your hops. It makes for a double danger: canonizing the past and cannonballing the future. I could bore you with those 16 glorious years when the Cross conferred diplomas under the authority of mother Georgetown; and I could rant and rave against tomorrow's age of hard porn and soft morals, threaten the end of the world in ice or fire.

I shall do neither; I shall play not historian or prophet but theologian. In harmony with the Word you have just heard, and in tune with the Mystery you will in moments memorialize, let me share with you what it means, in a world humanized by Christ, to be at once human and Christian, what it means to be alive, alive specifically in the Spirit. As I see it, it has a ceaselessly recurring rhythm: Call it "from wisdom to wonder."

I

To be alive in the Spirit is to be wise. But this wisdom is not a commodity you purchase at the Galleria or Shakey Jake's, not the same as a 4.0. "I called upon God," the Wisdom of Solomon recalls, "and the spirit of wisdom came to me" (Wis 7:7). Not that unbelievers are condemned to be foolish. Hegel and Marx, Nietzsche and Camus were not out-and-out fools. I am simply saying that the wis-

185

dom which dots their life and work is not the wisdom which leaps from God's inspired word.

What is that biblical wisdom?[2] A homily is not a term paper; so let me risk your wrath and get uncomfortably concrete. I shall clothe *you* in the garments of Scripture's wise man/wise woman, hold the mirror up to you, let you judge if the suit or dress fits.

Biblical wisdom has two facets: the kind of person you are and the kind of thing you do. Who are you? You are experts in an art: how to live well. Oh, not "high off the hog"; you can eat "Kimball food" and still be reasonably wise. It is rather a matter of mind and spirit. Knowledge may fill your head: Shakespeare and Sartre, American history and religious mystery, social and physical science, accounting and anatomy, First World and Third. It fills your head but never puffs it up; sheer knowledge sits securely upon you, but lightly. Technical competence you have aplenty, but this you complement with artistic feel—with Don Quixote and e. e. cummings, with Michelangelo and Michael Jackson, with *Giselle* and . . . *Indiana Jones and the Temple of Doom.* You muse and mull over life's meaning, perhaps its absurdity, but not in abstruse abstraction, on the head of a pin or the pink of a cloud; you have a sixth sense of where you sit in this world, how you relate to it. Pious you are, but never syrupy or saccharine. Pious in its pristine sense: faithful, dutiful, reverent. Aware that, for all its mystery and madness, God still rules the world, you have a salutary fear of the Lord. Not slavish but salutary: healthy, the fear that leads to salvation, the fear that is kin to love.

What is it you do that is so wise? In harmony with the Hebrews, your wisdom is practical: You have a goal in view, and a technique for reaching it—through the pitfalls that peril the human passage. You are intimately interested in others—not only in "the people" but primarily in persons. And so your priority in an alphabet world is not so much CPA or CIA as SPUD and JVC: to serve the growing and the aging, the crippled in flesh and the broken in heart, the battered and the bruised—a new Mustard Seed, small to begin with, later a tree with many nests in its branches (cf. Mt 13:31–32). You know the human heart, its agony and its ecstasy. You sense our grandeur and our wretchedness, our loneliness, our fear in face of pain and death, our unease and disquiet before a God so often hidden from us. With all and each you yearn to share your wisdom.

Marvel of marvels, you know how to enjoy life: the dawning of a day or an idea, the love of man and maid, Fitton Field and a foaming Pub. Oh yes, you sense how imperfect and passing is the world that surrounds you, how sinful and selfish the human heart, how hostile the earth on which you dance, the air you breathe; but none of this shatters you. Through all of this you walk with sympathy and serenity; you enjoy being alive.

Where do you, like the wise of Scripture, get your wisdom? From three sources. (1) There is the accumulated wisdom of the past, the "tradition of the fathers." (2) There is your own experience. From openness to all that is real, you have grown in wisdom, never cease to grow. (3) It is, at bottom, a gift of God. Ultimately, for you the master of wisdom is Jesus. He is the Wisdom of God, in whom the sapiential texts of Scripture find their definitive meaning. He it is who, as Wisdom in flesh, communicates wisdom not to the wise in the ways of the world but to his little ones: those who, like young Mary of Nazareth, listen to the word of God and say yes.

I pray that, in some measure, this is what your Worcester mirror reflects back to you. If it does, you may well join "Solomon" and sing: "I preferred [wisdom] to scepters and thrones, and I accounted wealth as nothing in comparison with her. . . . I loved her more than health and beauty. . . . All good things came to me along with her. . . . I rejoiced in them all, because wisdom leads them; but I did not know that she was their mother" (Wis 7:8, 10–12).

II

Such, in sum, is biblical wisdom. Such, I hope, is your wisdom—to pun on St. Paul, the folly of "the Cross" (cf. 1 Cor 1:18). Happily, to be at once human and Christian does not stop with wisdom; wisdom moves in ceaseless rhythm with . . . wonder.[3]

When I say "wonder," I don't mean curiosity—the Hatter in Alice's Wonderland singing:

> Twinkle, twinkle, little bat!
> How I wonder what you're at![4]

I don't mean doubt or despair: I wonder if life is really worth living. I don't mean uncertainty, perplexity: I wonder if the Congress should vote 15 MX missiles or 40. No, in the grasp of wonder I'm surprised, I'm amazed, I marvel, I'm delighted, I'm enraptured, I'm in awe. It's Moses before the burning bush "afraid to look at God" (Exod 3:6), and Mary newly God's mother: "My spirit exults in God my Savior" (Lk 1:47). It's Magdalene about to touch the risen Jesus: "Master!" (Jn 20:16), Michelangelo striking his sculptured Moses and commanding him: "Speak!" It's Ignatius Loyola in ecstasy as he eyes the sky at night, Teresa of Avila ravished by a rose. It's doubting Thomas discovering his God in the wounds of Jesus, Mother Teresa spying the face of Christ in the tortured poor. It's America thrilling to footsteps on the moon, a child casting his kite to the winds. It's a new priest murmuring with the lips of Christ "This is my body. . . ." It's the wonder of a first kiss.

Such should be your reaction to living: to the life of spirit and senses and to God's own Spirit alive in you, to the word of God that brought you into being and the word of Christ in today's Gospel: "No longer do I call you servants. . . . I have called you friends . . ." (Jn 15:15).

But how do you get that way? I am convinced we are born that way. But as we grow older, most of us lose it. We get blasé and worldly-wise and sophisticated. We no longer run our fingers through water, no longer shout at the stars, no longer make faces at the moon. Water is H_2O, the stars have been classified, and the moon is not made of green cheese. We've grown up. Rabbi Heschel saw it as our contemporary trap: "believing that everything can be explained, that reality is a simple affair which has only to be organized in order to be mastered. All enigmas can be solved, and all wonder is nothing but 'the effect of novelty upon ignorance.' "[5] The new can indeed amaze us: a space shuttle, the latest computer game, the softest diaper in history. Till tomorrow; till the new becomes old; till yesterday's wonder is discarded or taken for granted. Little wonder Heschel concluded: "As civilization advances, the sense of wonder declines."[6]

This is not a tirade against technology. I am resonating to Heschel's alarm: "Mankind will not perish for want of information . . . only for want of appreciation."[7] To appreciate not only the new but the old, not only the miracle that shatters nature but the wonder that is every day. When did I last marvel not at *what* I saw—*The Big Chill* or the chilling Celtics, Rodin's "Burghers of Calais" or the two unconcealed ladies in front of Beaven—but *that* I see, that with a flicker of eyelids I can span a small world? Must I grow deaf with Beethoven before I touch my ears with reverence? Does it amaze me that I can shape an idea, tell you how I feel, touch my fingers to another's face, to a flower?

The enemy of wonder is to take things for granted. If, with Thomas Aquinas, I am to be "all lost in wonder" within this Renaissance chapel, I have to be lost in wonder outside of it.[8] I do not escape to church from a dull, unexciting, godless world to celebrate a solitary miracle of grace. I come *to* miracle *from* miracle. Despite sin and war, despite disease and death, I still must see, with Gerard Manley Hopkins, that "the world is charged with the grandeur of God," that even if all "wears man's smudge and shares man's smell,"

> . . . for all this, nature is never spent;
>   There lives the dearest freshness deep down things . . .
> Because the Holy Ghost over the bent
>   World broods with warm breast and with ah! bright wings.[9]

The divine milieu, as Teilhard de Chardin saw, is not only the mystical body of Christ; it is the cosmic body of Christ. The world, our world, is different because Christ is there. Not only here—there!

A dream world? Perhaps—when you look at the north of Ireland and South Africa, Afghanistan and the Gulag Archipelago, the Middle East and the middle of our own sick cities. You need little wisdom to wonder how Christ can be there. But he is—crucified again, face bloodied beyond recognition. There none the less, as he is on every Calvary. It only means that your wisdom has to descend from above, from a risen Christ who still bears in his flesh the wounds of his passion. It means that wonder is not the same as eyeing the world through rose-tinted glasses, not opium for the people, not an escape from the grime and the gore. To wonder is simply to see the world through the eyes of Christ, through the eyes of the Lord who first fashioned it with a word, then refashioned it with his blood.

III

A final word, passionately personal. Why this paean to wisdom and wonder? Because each of you has a challenging call from Christ: "You did not choose me, but I chose you and appointed you that you should go and bear fruit and that your fruit should abide" (Jn 15:16). In the context of this Gospel, in the framework in which Jesus himself has set the challenge, tomorrow's world will be more human than today's only if you penetrate it not only with your professional competence but with your Christian love.

I envy you your education—and still I am afraid. I fear much for the lawyer whose only life is corporate tax, the doctor whose whole existence is someone else's prostate, the business executive whose single responsibility is to his stockholders, the athlete who puts all his eggs in an 18-inch basket, the theologian who thinks the world can be saved by theology. It deadens feelings and sensitivities; it kills marriages and human relations; it makes for a society that lives in a thousand and one tunnels, with no communication and no exit.

I am not commending incompetence. I am simply insisting that, whatever your profession, the fruit you bear will be human and Christlike only if your life is charged with love—only if you love the things of God, the people of God, God Himself. Only if your education mirrors the remarkable insight of Aquinas: "There are two ways of desiring knowledge. One way is to desire it as a perfection of one's self; and that is the way philosophers desire it. The other way is to desire it not [merely] as a perfection of one's self, but because through this knowledge the one we love becomes present to us; and that is the way saints desire it."

It is with such knowledge in view—knowledge as love—that I have sung to you of wisdom and wonder. I ask only that, through the years that lie ahead, you will ceaselessly prefer wisdom to health and wealth, to beauty and power. Do that, and one day far into the third millennium you may murmur with Rabbi Heschel to the Lord of your life: "I did not ask for success; I asked for wonder. And You gave it to me."[10]

College of the Holy Cross
Worcester, Massachusetts
May 24, 1984

30

GRAZIE, SIGNORE!
Baccalaureate Homily 3

♦ Acts 2:1–11
♦ 1 Corinthians 12:3–7, 12–13
♦ John 7:37–39

To spark your Pentecost, let me do three things. First, I shall take you to the movies. Second, I shall move out from life on the screen to life in the Spirit. Third, I shall ask how all this touches a Hoya exiting the Healy gates.

I

First, a swift trip to the movies. Not surprisingly, *Amadeus*.[1] A powerful film. Not only the superb settings in Prague, not only the magnificent music of Mozart. More important this morning, two contrasting characters. Salieri, court composer to the Emperor, is a dutiful Christian, thanking God ("Grazie, Signore") for each laborious score. But he is "dull as scales, a technician . . . without a hint of inspiration." When young Mozart bursts on the Vienna scene, Salieri is stunned. "Through this foul-mouthed, bottom-pinching boor, Salieri hears 'the voice of God,' music more wondrous than he had ever imagined." He alone appreciates how God has visited His people in this crude adolescent from Salzburg, this boy "vulgar and vain, with the social graces of Caligula."

But how is it possible, he asks? How can one so gross and unworthy be gifted with genius? And how can God make Salieri yearn to sing for Him and at the same time make him mute? Coldly rational, he challenges God's wisdom. Tormented with his own limitations and the limitless talent of Mozart, he burns his crucifix in rebellion against an unjust God. Mediocre himself, he determines

191

to destroy genius. Unable to penetrate God's preposterous providence, Salieri is driven to murder and insanity.

And Mozart? Salieri's "obscene child" who never grows up. Upside down at a piano parodying Bach. A self-centered adolescent aware of naught save his music and his pleasure. "Wine, women, and song," someone commented, "and he didn't sing much." A nervous giggle that betrays his contempt for the less gifted. A strange sort of son, haunted by his memory of an intimidating father. A master driven by his Muse, but never a humble admission that his music is a gift, never Salieri's "Grazie" to God. Dying as he dictates a Requiem Salieri plots to play as his own at Mozart's funeral. Dumped at 35 into a rain-soaked grave. Covered with a lime that corrodes not God's music but man's giggle. Mourned by a handful of folk who loved the little boy who never grew up.

II

So much for the movie. How move from life on the screen to life in the Spirit? I suggest that the key is St. Paul's proclamation to the Christians of Corinth: "Now there are varieties of gifts, but the same Spirit; and there are varieties of service, but the same Lord; and there are varieties of activities, but it is the same God who activates them all in every one. To each is given the manifestation of the Spirit for the common good" (1 Cor 12:4–7).

Two realities basic to Christian living: "varieties of gifts . . . for the common good." Whatever it may mean that "all men [and women] are created equal," no men and women are created the same, without difference. It reminds me of Phyllis McGinley's perceptive verse "In Praise of Diversity."[2] She recalled that ever since the world's sixth day "one subversive grace/ Has chiefly vexed the human race." We feel there is something wrong with difference, diversity, unlikeness, heterodoxy, nuance. Her answer?

> . . . Yet who would dare
> Deny that nature planned it other,
> When every freckled thrush can wear
> A dapple various from his brother,
> When each pale snowflake in the storm
> Is false to some imagined norm?
>
> Recalling then what surely was
> The earliest bounty of Creation:

That not a blade among the grass
  But flaunts its difference with elation,
Let us devoutly take no blame
If similar does not mean the same.

Rejoice that under cloud and star
  The planet's more than Maine or Texas.
Bless the delightful fact there are
  Twelve months, nine muses, and two sexes;
And infinite in earth's dominions
Arts, climates, wonders, and opinions . . .

Praise the disheveled, praise the sleek;
  Austerity and hearts-and-flowers;
People who turn the other cheek
  And extroverts who take cold showers;
Saints we can name a holy day for,
And infidels the saints can pray for.

Praise youth for pulling things apart,
  Toppling the idols, breaking leases;
Then from the upset apple-cart
  Praise oldsters picking up the pieces.
Praise wisdom, hard to be a friend to,
And folly one can condescend to.

Praise what conforms and what is odd,
  Remembering, if the weather worsens
Along the way, that even God
  Is said to be three separate[3] Persons.
Then upright or upon the knee,
Praise Him that by His courtesy,
For all our prejudice and pains,
Diverse His Creation still remains.

What the poet said of nature, the theologian can say of the Spirit. Not only does nature shape the human with infinitely different strokes; the Spirit shapes the Christian with similar imagination. It is in varying degrees that the Spirit gifts us with Christ's own wisdom and knowledge, with God's own music and art. Gifts of nature and gifts of grace—the role of the Spirit in Christian existence is to direct these gifts beyond my private income, beyond my personal happiness, beyond my individual holiness, beyond a me-and-Jesus spirituality. For the Holy Spirit is not simply *my* Spirit; the Holy Spirit is the Spirit of a community. To live by the Spirit is to live all my gifts, high and low, in such a way that, as Jesus put it, "out of [my] heart shall flow rivers of living water" (Jn 7:38); in the power of the Spirit I become a channel of life to others.[4] To live by the Spirit is to live for the whole of Christ's body—so much so that, as Paul put it, "If one member [of the body] suffers, all suffer together; if one member is honored, all rejoice together" (1 Cor 12:26). By the power of the Spirit, if a Salieri suffers, each Mozart suffers; if a Mozart is honored, each Salieri rejoices. In this body—again Paul is powerful, pungent, pithy—"the head cannot say to the feet, 'I have no need of you.' On the contrary, the parts of the body which seem to be weaker are indispensable . . . " (vv. 21–22).

III

How does all this touch a Hoya exiting the Healy gates? Today, on Healy lawn, a new Pentecost has dawned. As in Jerusalem, so here, "devout men [and women]" have gathered from almost "every nation under heaven" (Acts 2:5).[5] From Afghanistan to Zaire, from every state in the Union, you have come "together" in this "one place" (v. 1). Why? Because, for all your dialects that could divide you like another Babel, here, in this Eucharist, you hear your sisters and brothers speaking your "own language" (v. 6). You are all one in the body of Christ; you have been "filled with the Holy Spirit" (v. 4). Here, as Paul phrased it, "There is neither Jew nor Greek, there is neither slave nor free, there is no male-and-female; for you are all one in Christ Jesus" (Gal 3:28).

Within this single body, a special reality should unite you, destroy the barriers of skin and tongue, of genius and mediocrity. It is Paul's twin affirmation: a variety of gifts . . . for the common good. It is all the more important if, as our President predicts, this is the age of the entrepreneur rather than the corporation, if yours is the era of the individual, the man and woman of initiative and risk. For here you are all the more likely to experience a promise and a peril.

The promise? A variety of gifts, from the plodder to the genius, from Salieri to Mozart. Among your generation, there will be the rare Einstein and the countless teachers of math; a handful of Bernsteins and Levines, a host of players of scales; the Iacoccas who revive a dying industry, and the second-level managers who keep it alive; the few in medicine who replace hearts, and the many who replace our placebos; justices like Burger and O'Connor to reinterpret our justice, and judges by the thousands simply to *do* justice; a charismatic pope, millions of unsung laity; the occasional Michael Jackson and Tina Turner, and the uncounted who just press their records; Olivetti's De Benedetti with his microchips, and those who simply make perfect pasta; the John Thompsons, and the young adults who play pickup with the kids on concrete. All of you have your charisms, your gifts from nature and the Spirit. All of you are needed, indispensable, if the Spirit within each of you is to transform the whole.

You see, if this is to be genuinely the age of the laity, each of you has a part to play. Your task, as Vatican II put it, is "to penetrate and perfect the temporal sphere with the spirit of the gospel,"[6] to shape this earthly city into a city of justice, of peace, of love. Such is your vocation—not by an ordination, a vow ceremony, a special adult commissioning. Such is your mission by your baptism.[7]

Where you fulfil your distinctive function, where you play your irreplaceable role, is not a sanctuary but our sin-scarred earth. Your apostolic turf is where you live and move and have your being: E. F. Hutton or the Pentagon, ABC or the F.B.I., Children's Hospital or the Washington *Post*, Harvard or the little red schoolhouse, wherever you are. For, with rare exceptions, only lay Christians can bring Christ to law office and legislature, to public school and private industry, to executive suite and union hall, to media and medicine, to the thousand and one areas of human living seldom open to the ordained. And here you are not replacing a shrinking clergy, not substitutes waiting for the first team to come back on. These are your home grounds; here *you* are the Church, by right and duty.

Such is the promise. Equally pertinent is the peril. From two directions: the fatal flaw in Salieri and the fatal flaw in Mozart. Of moderate talents, you can grow jealous of genius, challenge God's wisdom, burn your precious crucifix, live only to murder Mozart, and end with no shred of Christian sanity. Or, highly talented, you can wed towering triumphs to an adolescent giggle, a giggle of contempt for scale-players, miracle a music that changes everyone save you, forget that your genius is a gift, never recall the God who gave it, and end your days admired but unloved, the little boy or girl who never grew up.

The antidote to both lies in two simple, profound words. You see, each Eucharist, the liturgy of Pentecost, is literally the early song of Salieri. Literally, in this hour you are singing "Grazie, Signore!" Thank you, Lord, for this gift of yourself, this gift of your Spirit. And so I pray that, as you exit these gates, you will see these four years in Pentecostal perspective; see that, despite a host of Hoya inadequacies, ours and your own, the Holy Spirit has been astonishingly active within you with a variety of gifts; and seeing this, your GU swan song will be a resounding "Grazie, Signore!" I pray that, as the years roll on, and all sorts of people cross your paths with perhaps greater gifts, you will learn to live with your limitations, never lose sight of your own rich sharing in the Spirit, never cease singing "Grazie, Signore!" Do that, and one day, far into 2000, after "rivers of living water" have flowed from your heart, after you have become channels of life to others, your last whispered words on earth will be a eucharist, "Grazie, Signore!"

One final word. You may not think of us platform people the way I do. But the fact is, as we look out on you this morning, two words above all leap from our hearts, two words express what you have meant to us. We thank the Holy Spirit for letting us shape you, "rivers of living water"; and we thank the Holy Spirit for letting us be shaped by you. "Grazie, Signore!"[8]

Georgetown University
Washington, D.C.
May 26, 1985

31

PARTRIDGE TIME, PARTRIDGE!
Memorial of St. Teresa of Avila

♦ Galatians 4:22–24, 26–27, 31; 5:1
♦ John 15:1–8

By a happy coincidence, today's liturgy weds a text and a woman. More accurately, a man and a woman. A man of the first century and a woman of the sixteenth. A man who preached Christian freedom with graced eloquence, and a woman who lived it with eloquent grace. This evening, then, three brief words on the free Christian: (1) Paul of Tarsus, (2) Teresa of Avila, (3) you and me.

I

First, Paul. "For freedom Christ has set us free" (Gal 5:1). But what is this freedom to which, Paul insists, each Christian is called (Gal 5:13)? For him, it is a liberation of the human person that delivers from a fourfold slavery: from sin, from the law, from self, from death.[1]

The sin is an evil force, almost a personal force. It indeed entered the world through one man's rebellion, Adam's act of disobedience. But it is more than a single act; it is a malevolent power that tyrannizes every man and woman born into this world. It is a power hostile to God, a power that alienates from God. Because of it, Paul proclaims, "I do not do the good I want, but the evil I do not want" (Rom 7:19). It is Sin with a capital S.

The Mosaic law, good in itself, Paul found an occasion of sin: It instructed him in sin's possibilities and it incited his concupiscence. Though it came from God, it could not resolve the conflict each Jew experienced, "sold under sin" (Rom 7:14) as he was.

Though the law told him what he must do, it did not provide the power to do it.

The self is the existential human condition, what Paul calls "flesh." I mean my native self left to itself, the whole person tyrannized by earth-bound tendencies, man and woman in our contrast to God, subject to all that withdraws us from God.

Death, inherited from Adam, is a total death. It is not only the end of physical life here below; it stands over against eternal existence, resurrectional life, life with God days without end. The goal, the end, of what we do is death (Rom 6:21).

From this fourfold slavery, Paul preaches, Christ has set us free. How? By dying and rising for us. No longer are we slaves of sin; in bondage to Christ, we shake off the shackles of that dread tyranny. The new law is love: "Love fully satisfies the law" (Rom 13:10), specifically, the law that commands us to love others as we love ourselves. The self is no longer a schizophrenia; the Spirit within us is source of harmony between flesh and spirit, between the spirit of man/woman and the Spirit of God. And death? We die indeed, but we die unto life. "O death, where is thy victory? O death, where is thy sting?" (1 Cor 15:55).

Such is the freedom wherewith the dying/rising Christ has empowered us. Bound over to Christ the Lord, we are freed from sin and for sanctity, from law and for love, from self and for others, from death and for life.

II

Second, Teresa. I have known *about* her since my days as a Jesuit novice; I have known *her* only a decade or so. I came to know her through my friend and her confrere, the Carmelite William McNamara, whose spoken word sparkles with Isaian woe and Irish wit. One story he told captured me once and for all. Teresa and her sisters in religion are at table. The *pièce de résistance* is roast partridge. And Teresa is gorging thereon—yes, gorging. The nuns are scandalized. Teresa senses it, looks up from her partridge, laughs aloud: "At prayer time, pray! At partridge time, partridge!" No wonder Nikos Kazantzakis loved her so lustily.

The point of the story is that Teresa was a splendidly free Christian. It was not easy. She lived in an age when men were free and women were not, a sexist culture where to be effective she had to dissemble without lying, to function usefully she had to play games.[2] And she did. Not because she wanted to; only because she had to. Her movement to Pauline freedom—from sin to sanctity, from law to love, from self to others, from death to life—is too complex, too rich, for a weekday homily. But features of this movement merit mention.

Sanctity? The first 20 years of her adult life Teresa's heart was divided between God and the world. She manipulated people and rules, reached out to others not out of real love but from a need to be loved, approved, reassured. She was often not honest with herself and others. She "learned the hard way. She wanted instant mysticism but it took from ages 23–41 to realize that true growth is slow. Sanctity is learning to accept reality, being open to God's word."[3]

Liberation from limiting law? A ceaseless struggle for Teresa. To read Scripture in the vernacular was forbidden, and Teresa knew no Latin. It was God who opened the pages of Scripture to her, especially the Song of Songs; and then a confessor commanded her to burn her commentary because it was not fitting for a woman to write on the Song of Songs. "Learned men," she wrote, "are shocked at the things" the nuns at Seville "have been obliged to do for fear of excommunication."[4] A priest-confessor told her that her vision of Christ was clearly the devil, commanded her to make the sign of the cross and laugh at the vision. To establish a reformed convent, she had to suffer the fury of the townspeople, the rebuke of her provincial, a lawsuit. Her reform was harassed repeatedly— by a bishop, by her general, by a nuncio, by her own sisters in Christ. A new foundation was denied daily Mass by the bishop; Teresa requested daily confession! To her confessor's objections she retorted: "Don't be stingy with other people's riches." She was profoundly pained by ingrained attitudes and restrictive regulations that kept a whole sex from ministering the healing love of Christ to hungry men and women. She insisted that with her personal call to holiness was wedded a mission to lead others to perfection. Teresa was respectful of law but not enslaved to it.

Freedom from egoism? This came in a conversion experience before an image of "the sorely wounded Christ."[5] At the age of 39! The new Teresa delights in the vivid experience of God within her. She pays scant attention to the penances expected of her, and is no longer disturbed by it. The agonizing need to be loved gradually leaves her; she can go out to others without focusing them on herself. With this freedom goes a delightful sense of humor: "Tell Sister Jeronima, who signs herself 'dung-heap,' that I hope her humility is not merely a matter of words."[6]

Freedom from death? For Teresa, as for Paul, this meant transformation into Christ. "It is no longer I who live, but Christ who
lives in me" (Gal 2:20). In a favorite image, Jesus becomes the co-
coon in which we die and then are transformed—that marvelous
movement from the wormlike creature called caterpillar to the most
beautiful and graceful of insects, the butterfly.[7] The silkworm must
die. Freedom is, very simply, a ceaseless dying/rising in the image
of Christ.

III

From Paul through Teresa to us. No need to detail the four
facets of freedom; I commend them for your meditation. I would
stress not the fact of freedom but its purpose. I mean St. Paul's "You
were called to freedom, my brothers and sisters; only do not use
your freedom as an opportunity for the flesh, but through love be
servants of one another" (Gal 5:13). It is Dietrich Bonhoeffer's insight: "There is no 'being-free-from' without 'being-free-for.' "[8]
Free for the Other (capital O), free for the other (lower-case o).

If you want to know how free you are, ask yourself a single
question: How much of your life is service? Not slavery, but a service
of love. Teresa saw that love can err in two directions: We love too
much or too little; we want to possess or we don't really care. In
either case we are still enslaved—shackled to our small selves.

I am enslaved, shackled, imprisoned to the extent that life re-
volves around me: my sins, my laws, my self, my death. To be free
is to move out from all these, real though they are, terribly real. To
center on the Other, and in Him on the others. I know this not simply from Paul or Teresa; I know it from my own experience. When
have I been least free? When the center of my day is my sickening
sinfulness or my hiatal hernia; a critical review that pricks my pride
or loud applause for a lesser light than I; a slighting remark or no
remark at all; a restriction on my God-given rights from small-
minded superiors; my need to be loved, humored, approved, af-
firmed. The slaveries are legion (you know your own far better than
I) and awfully human.

But after seven decades of this, I beg you: Lift up your eyes
from your little navel! Let not seminary life lock you in; let it be an
eye-opener, thrusting your mind and heart out to a world imprisoned in sin and law, in self and death. To the refuse of the city and
the refugees of the world; to half the human family hungry for

bread or justice, for peace or freedom, for truth or understanding, for a God who does not seem to be there. A world that will only be free of its human bondage if privileged people like you are free. Free for the Other, free for others. They will come to life, to liberty, to the pursuit of happiness only if, like Paul and Teresa, you *are* a living gospel of freedom.

Who knows? It may even cure your heartburn.

Moreau Seminary
Notre Dame, Indiana
October 15, 1984

32

WILL NOT GOD VINDICATE HIS CHOSEN ONES?
Commemoration of Armenian Genocide and Jewish Holocaust

◆ Luke 18:1–7

This day, my friends, is not for passionate preaching; this day is for prayerful pondering. This day calls us to look back and to look forward, to remember and to resolve. Let me muse a while on each: on the days that have fled and the days that lie ahead.

I

First, a journey in memory. Some years ago I was worried. I found myself remembering. And that, they tell me, is a disease of the graying and the balding. To go back is to bore, to praise "the good old days." To remember is to bask in the past, to enter an Eden that never existed, a paradise as legendary as Atlantis. To remember is to start dying.

But then I began to see: No, 'tis not so; quite the opposite. I recalled Rabbi Abraham Joshua Heschel's startling affirmation: Much of what the Bible demands can be summed up in a single word—remember! I discovered in ancient Israel a community of faith vitalized by memory, a people that knew God by reflecting not on the mysteries of nature but on its own history. To actualize was to retain within time and space the memory and the mystery of God's saving presence. Christian existence, I recalled, is a living memory: Each day we Christians memorialize, we re-present, the passion and resurrection of Jesus Christ; we celebrate the death of the Lord until he comes.

Perhaps most importantly, Johannes Metz compelled me to distinguish my memories. There are memories that simply make us feel good, because they glide over all that is oppressive and demanding. And there are memories that are dangerous, because they make demands on us, reveal perilous insights for today, illuminate harshly the questionable nature of things with which we have come to terms.

My "Jewish memories" of the far distant past make no demands on me; they are delightfully simple, free of anxiety and complexity. I grew up in a multiracial Manhattan neighborhood, unaware of the Great Gatsby and the roar of the 20's, amid Italians and Irish, Jews and Germans. Where epithets like Dago and Mick, Kike and Kraut revealed not racial animosity but lack of imagination. Where Moishe was no more responsible for the crucifixion of Christ than I for a pogrom in Poland; Moische was my friend! Where this pre-teen sat with German mother and father in the rear of Jacob Rosenbluth's grocery and listened to two immigrant couples swapping very human anecdotes and trading in love, breathed the garlic and onions that hung from the ceiling and guaranteed Jew and Gentile against winter colds.

The Holocaust changed much of that, made for different memories, memories dangerous and demanding, memories harsh in the pitiless light they cast. I remember Marc Tanenbaum confronting Christians with a searing question: How was it possible "in a country which, when it vaunted its great values and its great moral traditions, spoke of itself as a country of ancient Christian culture, which was in fact the seat of the Holy Roman Empire for almost a millennium beginning with Charlemagne," how was it possible "for millions of Christians to sit by as spectators while millions of human beings, who were their brothers and sisters, the sons of Abraham according to the flesh, were carted out to their death in the most brutal, inhuman, uncivilized ways"?[1]

I remember that, as recently as 1965, the Second Vatican Council had to warn Catholics against blaming "the Jews" then or now for the crucifixion of Christ, against arguing from Scripture that "the Jews" are repudiated or cursed by God.[2]

I remember the anguished Jewish protest over the absence in Vatican II

of any note of contrition or repentance for the incredible sufferings and persecutions Jews have undergone in the Christian West. The Church's various declarations asked forgiveness from the Protestants, the Eastern Orthodox, from the Moslems, but not from the Jews. Many Jews, especially those who lived through the Nazi holocaust, asked with great passion, "How many more millions of our brothers and sisters will need to be slaughtered before any word of contrition or repentance is heard in the seats of ancient Christian glory?"[3]

I remember a 1974 symposium on the Holocaust in New York's Cathedral of St. John the Divine, where young Jew after young Jew assailed me with savage denunciations—and I realized it was not so much I that was under attack. My Roman collar was a symbol. It summed up every Jewish ghetto ever structured by Christians, every forced baptism, every Crusade to liberate the Holy Places, every Good Friday pogrom, every forced exodus like 1492, every portrait of Shylock exacting his pound of flesh, every accusation of deicide, every Dachau and every Auschwitz, every death for conscience' sake, every back turned or shoulder shrugged, every sneer or slap or curse.

I remember Arthur Cohen declaring that if "American society is . . . , as some Christian thinkers argue, an essentially Christian society . . . then Jews might . . . prefer a return to the ghetto which, however socially isolated, was spiritually free."[4]

I remember the seemingly hypersensitive young rabbi who took me to task after a public lecture because I had told an amusing story about Catholics and Protestants that took place in 1967. How could I joke about 1967? How could I mention 1967 without mentioning the Six Days War?

I remember that it is only a handful of years since Catholics stopped praying on Good Friday "for the perfidious Jews," substituted a warm prayer "for the Jewish people, the first to hear the word of God, that they may continue to grow in the love of His name and in faithfulness to His covenant."

I remember how the Holocaust has divided the Jewish people themselves. For some, "God died in Auschwitz." For others, after Auschwitz "How can you *not* believe in God . . . ?"[5]

I remember that a generation of Gentiles has grown up for whom Holocaust is a word and little more—as vague and transient as the War of 1812, or the Battle of San Juan Hill, or the San Francisco Earthquake.

I remember a letter from a Georgetown student to the school newspaper *The Hoya*. He claimed, seriously, that the Holocaust never took place; it is fiction, fabrication, pure and simple.

In this context I remember vividly Elie Wiesel's warning: To forget is to become the executioner's accomplice.

From "Jewish memories" I turned last week to my "Armenian memories." To my dismay, I discovered I have none—no Armenian memories. No one ever told me, and I never read, that parallel to the Jewish experience in World War II was an Armenian experience in World War I. No one ever told me, and I never read, that, on a prudent estimate, one million Armenians perished under the Ottoman Empire through deportation, starvation, and outright massacre. No one ever told me, and I never read, that 520 documents in our State Department files witness to a planned destruction of a people. No one ever told me, and I never read, that our then Ambassador to Ottoman Turkey, Henry Morgenthau Sr., testified: "I am confident that the whole history of the human race contains no such horrible episode as this. The great massacres and persecutions of the past seem almost insignificant when compared with the sufferings of the Armenian race in 1915."[6] No one ever told me, and I never read, that for seven decades the Armenian people have suffered to see their story rewritten by their enemies. Armenians must read that they themselves are to blame for their troubles: They were disloyal, treacherous, on the brink of a general rebellion when the fatherland was struggling for survival. And today they must squirm under a fresh strategy directed at the West. Not only is the "Armenian genocide" attacked as the greatest lie of the century; it is assaulted as a scheme to subvert Turkey and alienate it from its allies. A successful strategy. On March 29 our President asserted that he opposes a Congressional resolution designating April 24, 1985, as a national day of remembrance for all victims of genocide, especially the genocide of 1915. Why? Because such resolutions might "inadvertently encourage or reward terrorist attacks" and could "harm relations with an important ally."

All this, and so much more, no one ever told me, and I never read—till last week. A cram course in history, possibly good enough for a Georgetown C. But almost too late for memories—for memories that are dangerous, that make demands on me, that reveal perilous insights for today, that illuminate harshly the questionable nature of things with which I have come to terms.

More sadly still, I am not alone. For the vast majority of Americans, Armenia is a never-never land, somehow in the Soviet orbit. Armenians? Like the Jews, a wandering race; you meet them in the most unlikely places. 1915? It rings no bell; the First World War?

But you simply must try their pilaf, their shish kebab, and their baklava! No, I am not alone. . . .

II

So much for the days that have fled. What of the days that lie ahead? To remember is not enough, not by half. What matters is what we do with our memories. Pope John Paul II put the human problem and the Judeo-Christian perspective splendidly when he told all of us at the Museum in Hiroshima: "To remember the past is to commit oneself to the future."

The pregnant question is, what sort of commitment to what sort of future? On broad lines, we who remember commit our lives to a struggle—a vow that what has happened before will not happen again. No Holocaust or Hiroshima; no genocide, whether Armenia or Cambodia. But how? Memory can make for deathless division: between man and woman, husband and wife, children and parents, Christian and Jew, Protestant and Catholic, country and country. Memory can summon to summary vengeance: Kill the murderer, sterilize the rapist, chop off the hand that violated the law!

It is not for such commitment that we gather in a chapel, in a house of God. Please understand me. I am not saying, let bygones be bygones, let the dead past bury its dead. I am not arguing against reparations. I am not suggesting a statute of limitations for genocide. I am not implying that those who sin against humanity should not be brought to justice. If the civilized globe has no sanctions against genocide, 1915 and 1945 will rear their heads in 2015 and 2045. What I am saying is that the man and woman of faith, you and I, are committed to an even more radical future, a future that includes justice but leaps beyond it, a future whose hope rests not so much in us as in God.

What am I saying specifically? If our sin-scarred, teardrenched, bloodstained earth is ever to enjoy a measure of peace, justice must be joined to . . . reconciliation. Much as we must struggle for human rights, our eyes have to focus on a more distant horizon, where enemies are transformed into friends, where hands that have locked in hate are linked in love. For if our dearest, deepest yearning is not for oneness—the oneness of all God's children—then our memories will never reap their richest reward, we are unfaithful to the covenant God has struck with our peoples, and we might as well transport this gathering from Dahlgren Chapel to the Pentagon.

I realize how unrealistic it sounds, impractical, futile. What chance is there for oneness, for peace, for love, in the face of the insuperable: histories of hate, nations sworn to destroy Israel, a government that denies Armenian genocide ever happened? Is there any room for optimism, for hope?

Yes indeed! Precisely because our hope is not in ourselves. Jews and Christians alike, we sing with the Psalmist: "Thou, O Lord, art my hope,/ my trust, O Lord, from my youth" (Ps 71:5). If peace is ever to grace our war-wearied world, from Northern Ireland through the Middle East to South Africa, if genocide and holocaust are ever to be events of the past, it will be because the Lord, Yahweh, changes minds and hearts. He can, and we pray that He will. The Lord who parted the Red Sea for His people and returned His exiles from Babylon, the Lord whom Armenians have worshiped and trusted through centuries of peril and persecution, it is He who is Lord of history. We shall acknowledge this publicly this afternoon when we pray: "May God, who causes peace to reign in the high heavens, let peace descend on us, on all Israel, and all the world."

And still, Yahweh uses human instruments, uses us. How? Wherever we are. Reconciliation begins not in Ankara or Jerusalem; reconciliation begins right here. Where you and I can turn to each other and, without asking who the other is, clasp hands and murmur "Peace." On our campus, where we should be learning to deal not with imaginary universals, abstract generalizations—man and woman, white and black, Jew and Gentile, Armenian and Turk—but with living, breathing individuals: this man, this woman, this child.

Our memories should remind us brutally that hatred begets only hatred; our faith should remind us forcefully that only love begets love. On this level the 70 years I have lived have not been a roaring success—not if you remember Armenia and Cambodia, Dachau and Belfast, Johannesburg and Afghanistan, Iran and Iraq. It is on you and your generation that rest now the hopes and fears of today's Jew, today's Armenian, today's every victim of hate and power. Not alone, but under God.

Under God. The lesson from Luke (18:1–7),[7] the parable of the Dishonest Judge, is splendidly pertinent to our twin commemoration: "Will not God vindicate His chosen ones who cry out to Him day and night?" (v. 7). Vindicate. Will not God see to it that justice is done? Indeed He will—in His own good time. In the meantime, while God is seeing to it that justice is done for yesterday, will you see to it that love is not lost today?

Dahlgren Chapel
Georgetown University
Washington, D.C.
April 22, 1985

NOTES

Prologue

1. For a rich summary of the theology of Christian community, see Avery Dulles, S.J., *Models of the Church* (Garden City, N.Y.: Doubleday, 1974) 43–57. I am not denying that the Eucharistic liturgy creates invisible bonds among the faithful even when they do not recognize one another. I admit, with Jérôme Hamer, that what is distinctive in the Church is "the vertical dimension—the divine life disclosed in the incarnate Christ and communicated to men through his Spirit." But the communion given by the Holy Spirit is inadequate without the horizontal dimension, inadequate if it does not issue in "a network of mutual interpersonal relationships of concern and assistance" (Dulles 45–46; cf. Hamer, *The Church Is a Communion* [New York: Sheed & Ward, 1964] 159–64, 204).

2. William J. O'Malley, "Ten Commandments for Homilists," *America* 149, no. 3 (July 23–30, 1983) 47–49.

3. Constitution on the Sacred Liturgy, no. 2 (tr. from Walter M. Abbott, S.J., and Joseph Gallagher, eds., *The Documents of Vatican II* [New York: America, ©1966] 137).

4. References to a highly popular TV soap opera and two "deathless" night serials.

5. Augustine, *First Catechetical Instruction* 1, 15, 23 (tr. Joseph P. Christopher in *Ancient Christian Writers* 2 [Westminster, Md.: Newman, 1946] 50).

6. From "I Have Given You an Example," in my *Still Proclaiming Your Wonders: Homilies for the Eighties* (New York/Ramsey: Paulist, ©1984) 67–73, at 72–73.

7. Augustine, *Confessions* 9, 1 (tr. F. J. Sheed, *The Confessions of St. Augustine* [New York: Sheed & Ward, 1943] 183).

Homily 1

1. I am using "Isaiah" in a loose sense. The section in question here (chaps. 56–66) is known to scholars as Trito-Isaiah.
2. Quoted from William J. Byron, "Feeding the Hungry: A Decade of Inaction," *America* 151, no. 15 (Nov. 17, 1984) 321–23, at 321.
3. Quoted from *Time* 124, no. 22 (Nov. 26, 1984) 68.
4. See Byron, "Feeding the Hungry" 321–22.
5. Figures taken from a four-page piece, "Bread for the World" (10/84), issued from the organization of that name, 802 Rhode Island Ave., N.E., Washington, D.C. 20018.
6. Byron, "Feeding the Hungry" 323.
7. Ibid.

Homily 2

1. The inspiration for my approach to Ash Wednesday comes from a powerful sermon by Karl Rahner, "Ash Wednesday," contained in his collection of sermons *The Eternal Year* (Baltimore-Dublin: Helicon, ©1964) 57–63.
2. Ibid. 58–59.
3. From Gerard Manley Hopkins, "God's Grandeur," ed. W. H. Gardner and N. H. MacKenzie, *The Poems of Gerard Manley Hopkins* (New York: Oxford University, 1970) 66.

Homily 3

1. Here I am following the persuasive interpretation of Raymond E. Brown, S.S., *The Gospel according to John (i–xii)* (Anchor Bible 29; Garden City, N.Y.: Doubleday, 1966) 178–79, itself admittedly dependent on F. J. McCool, "Living Water in John," in J. L. McKenzie, ed., *The Bible in Current Catholic Thought* (New York: Herder & Herder, 1962) 226–33.
2. CD (= Cairo [Genizah text of the] Damascus [Document]) 19:34.
3. Cf. Carin Rubinstein, "Money & Self-Esteem, Relationships, Secrecy, Envy, Satisfaction," *Psychology Today* 15, no. 5 (May 1981) 29–44; see esp. 40–44.
4. Graham Greene, *Monsignor Quixote* (New York: Simon and Schuster, ©1982) 206–7.

Homily 4

1. Eugene O'Neill, *Lazarus Laughed,* Act 1, Scene 1; in *The Plays of Eugene O'Neill* (New York: Random House, 1955) 280. I have used this passage on several homiletic occasions; see, e.g., the baccalaureate homily "Look, Love, Laugh," in *Tell the Next Generation: Homilies and Near Homilies* (New York: Paulist, ©1980) 109–15.
2. On this division and interpretation of vv. 25–26 (two principal ideas: "I am the *resurrection*" and "I am the *life*"), see Raymond E. Brown, S.S., *The Gospel according to John (i–xii)* (Anchor Bible 29; Garden City, N.Y.: Doubleday, 1966) 434, himself admittedly dependent on C. H. Dodd.
3. Theodore Eustace Kalem, "O'Neill, Eugene Gladstone," *Encyclopaedia Britannica* 16 (1967 ed.) 965.
4. Eugene O'Neill, *The Great God Brown,* Prologue; in *Nine Plays* (New York: Garden City Publishing Co., 1940) 315.

Homily 5

1. John Chrysostom, *Homilies on 2 Corinthians* 20, 3 (PG 61, 540).
2. See Irenaeus of Lyons, *Against Heresies* 5, 1–16, and the synthesis fashioned from that section by E. Peterson, "L'Immagine di Dio in S. Ireneo," *Scuola cattolica* 19 (1941) 3–11.
3. On this profound text from the Letter to the Hebrews, see several brief but illuminating remarks in F. F. Bruce, *The Epistle to the Hebrews* (Grand Rapids: Eerdmans, 1979 [1964]) 102–4, and Hugh Montefiore, *A Commentary on the Epistle to the Hebrews* (New York: Harper & Row, ©1964) 99–100.

Homily 6

1. Elie Wiesel, *The Gates of the Forest* (New York: Holt, Rinehart and Winston, ©1966) 178–79.
2. I trust that the reader will realize I am using the verb "leave" loosely here; the Son of God can hardly "take leave" of His Father literally.

Homily 7

1. In this development, I am ringing the changes on a theme I have explored several times; see, e.g., "Let Go of Yesterday," in *Tell the Next Generation: Homilies and Near Homilies* (New York: Paulist, ©1980) 52–57, and "Behold, I Am Doing a New Thing," in *Still Proclaiming Your Wonders: Homilies for the Eighties* (New York: Paulist, ©1984) 45–50.
2. The Casa de Paz y Bien is the Franciscan Renewal Center in Scottsdale,

where this homily was preached; Camelback is an impressive local mountain.

Homily 8

1. Graham Greene, *Monsignor Quixote* (New York: Simon and Schuster, ©1982) 69–70.
2. For a similar (not identical) approach to the possibilities of redemption, see the homily "Why This Waste?" in my *All Lost in Wonder: Sermons on Theology and Life* (Westminster, Md.: Newman, 1960) 111–15.
3. Translation from Joseph A. Fitzmyer, S.J., in *The Jerome Biblical Commentary* (Englewood Cliffs, N.J.: Prentice-Hall, ©1968) 50:18.
4. Here I am stressing "the Johannine view, which tends to make of the ignominious raising of Jesus on the cross a majestic elevation to glory (Jn 3:14; 8:28; 12:34), so that the Father seems to glorify the Son on Good Friday itself (Jn 12:23; 17:1ff.)," in contrast to Pauline theology, which "saw the passion and death as a prelude to the resurrection itself" (Joseph A. Fitzmyer, S.J., *Pauline Theology: A Brief Sketch* [Englewood Cliffs, N.J.: Prentice-Hall, ©1967] 38).
5. At this point I am indebted to the dense but stimulating article on "Death" by Karl Rahner in *Sacramentum mundi: An Encyclopedia of Theology* 2 (New York: Herder and Herder, 1968) 58–62.
6. Ibid. 61.
7. Ibid.
8. *The Collected Poems of Dylan Thomas* (New York: New Directions, 1971) 128.
9. Francis Thompson, "The Hound of Heaven," in *Francis Thompson, Poems and Essays,* ed. Wilfred Meynell (Westminster, Md.: Newman, 1949) 112.

Homily 9

1. For similar approaches to letting go, with somewhat different rhetoric and examples, see my "Let Go of Yesterday," in *Tell the Next Generation: Homilies and Near Homilies* (New York: Paulist, ©1980) 52–57, and my "Behold, I Am Doing a New Thing," in *Still Proclaiming Your Wonders: Homilies for the Eighties* (New York: Paulist, ©1984) 45–50.

Homily 10

1. See, e.g., Marilyn Ferguson, *The Aquarian Conspiracy: Personal and Social Transformation in the 1980s* (Los Angeles: Tarcher, ©1980).
2. An appearance of the risen Jesus to his mother has a long, varied, im-

pressive tradition. See, e.g., the Spiritual Exercises of Ignatius Loyola, where the first apparition is to Mary: "He appeared to the Virgin Mary; and although this is not mentioned in Scripture, still it is considered as mentioned when it says that He appeared to many others, for the Scripture supposes us to have understanding . . . " (*The Text of the Spiritual Exercises of Saint Ignatius* [4th ed. rev.; Westminster, Md.: Newman, 1943] 100–101).

3. On this point, the meaning of fellowship in the text, I have profited much from Jacques Dupont, O.S.B., *Etudes sur les Actes des apôtres* (Paris: Cerf, 1967) 503–19.

4. The homilist should be aware that some interpreters understand "the breaking of the bread" here as ordinary table fellowship each day in the homes of the Christians, recalling the table fellowship Jesus had with his followers; so, e.g., Gerhard Kittel, *Theological Dictionary of the New Testament* 3 (Grand Rapids: Eerdmans, ©1965) 729–31, 737.

Homily 11

1. In 1964 the Congregation of Rites defined the homily as "an unfolding either of some facet of the readings of Sacred Scripture or of some other text taken from the Ordinary or from the Proper of the Mass of the day, taking into consideration either the mystery being celebrated or the special needs of the listeners" (*Inter oecumenici* [i.e., the *Instructio ad executionem Constitutionis de sacra liturgia recte ordinandam*, Sept. 26, 1964] 3, no. 54, in *Normae exsequutivae Concilii oecumenici Vaticani II [1963–1969]*, ed. Florentius Romita [Naples: D'Auria, 1971] 58). This definition has been incorporated into the "General Instruction on the Roman Missal" in the Roman Missal of 1970, no. 41. No need to belabor the ceaseless presence of our Lady in the Ordinary of the Mass; nor do I see a "text" from the Ordinary as an absolute requirement for a homily based on the Ordinary.

2. St. Augustine, *On Holy Virginity* 3 (PL 40, 398); *Sermon 215*, no. 4 (PL 38, 1074).

3. Constitution on the Church, no. 53.

4. Erma Bombeck, *Motherhood: The Second Oldest Profession* (New York: McGraw-Hill, ©1983) 176–77.

Homily 12

1. The reference is to a town in West Germany in whose cemetery are buried not only ordinary German fighting men but also 49 members of the *Waffen* SS, a branch of the elite Nazi guard that ran the death camps, although the *Waffen* SS did not serve in that capacity. The decision of President Ronald Reagan to lay a wreath at the cemetery as a

gesture of reconciliation with Germany sparked bitter protests and tense controversy.
2. See note 2 to Homily 6.

Homily 13

1. See Richard Kugelman, C.P., "The First Letter to the Corinthians," in *The Jerome Biblical Commentary* (Englewood Cliffs, N.J.: Prentice-Hall, ©1968) 51:11–15.
2. See Martin Buber, *Israel and the World* (New York: Schocken, 1948) 186, 193, 210; also Eugene B. Borowitz, "The Autonomous Self and the Commanding Community," *Theological Studies* 45 (1984) 34–56, esp. 45–48.

Homily 14

1. Francis Thompson, "The Hound of Heaven," in Terence L. Connolly, S.J., ed., *Poems of Francis Thompson* (rev. ed.; New York: D. Appleton-Century, ©1941) 77.
2. Ibid. 81.

Homily 15

1. See my homily "When He Saw Him, He Had Compassion," in my *Sir, We Would Like To See Jesus: Homilies from a Hilltop* (New York/Ramsey: Paulist, ©1982) 105–9.
2. See my homily "Who Touched Me?" ibid. 99–104.
3. See ibid. 100.

Homily 16

1. The movie takes liberties with the book, *The Leopard* (New York: Pantheon, 1960). The confrontation in question does not take place during the carriage ride (pp. 33–35) but back at the Villa Salina the next day; and the prince's remarks on worry (53–54) are more complex than the movie allows.
2. I have profited here from John L. McKenzie's Introduction in his *Second Isaiah* (Anchor Bible 20; Garden City, N.Y.: Doubleday, 1968) xv–xxx, xxxviii–lxvii (esp. xxiv–xxv), and 110–14.
3. See John L. McKenzie, "The Gospel according to Matthew," in *The Jerome Biblical Commentary* (Englewood Cliffs, N.J.: Prentice-Hall, ©1968) 43:46–47.

4. The meaning is disputed, some commentators interpreting the Greek of length of life, others of bodily stature.
5. William G. Thompson, S.J., "New Testament Communities in Transition: A Study of Matthew and Luke," *Theological Studies* 37 (1976) 571.
6. For the full legend, see Alban Butler, *The Lives of the Saints* 7 (rev. Herbert Thurston, S.J., and Donald Attwater; London: Burns, Oates & Washbourne, 1932) 358–64. I have developed the Christian implications of the legend at greater length in an earlier homily, "St. Christopher: Sanctity and Selflessness," in my *Saints and Sanctity* (Englewood Cliffs, N.J.: Prentice-Hall, ©1965) 117–27, where I also quote Ms. Lindbergh's poem.
7. Anne Morrow Lindbergh, "Saint for Our Time," in *The Unicorn and Other Poems* (New York: Pantheon, 1956) 45–47.

Homily 17

1. *Time* 123, no. 2 (Jan. 9, 1984) 28.
2. Ibid.
3. Such are, roughly, the equivalents in dollars of the 10,000 talents and the 100 denarii in the parable.
4. *Time* (n. 1 above) 31–32.
5. Ibid. 31.
6. In this section I have profited from the dictionary articles of Stanislas Lyonnet, S.J., "Sin," in Xavier Léon-Dufour, ed., *Dictionary of Biblical Theology* (2nd ed.; New York: Seabury, 1973) 550–57, and Jean Giblet and Marc-François Lacan, O.S.B., "Pardon," ibid. 404–6.
7. *Time* (n. 1 above) 28.
8. *Time* 123, no. 5 (Jan. 30, 1984) 8.
9. A supplementary note, written four months later, seems called for. In my third point, I observed: " . . . we cannot say that Agca was changed deep within." But according to an account from Rome by Andrew Nagorski a year after the Pope's visit, Agca "proclaimed that he was renouncing terrorism to become a man of peace. . . . He traced his transformation to a prison visit with the pope last year. . . . After close reading of the Koran, Agca said, he had become a devout Muslim with 'profound respect' for Christianity. And he promised that if he were freed, he would become 'a preacher, going to all nations of the world preaching good and the truth to all people' " (*Newsweek,* Jan. 7, 1985, 25).

Homily 18

1. See R. E. Brown, "Parables of Jesus," *New Catholic Encyclopedia* 10 (1967) 984–88, at 984.

2. Here I have been helped much by Joachim Jeremias, *The Parables of Jesus* (rev. ed.; New York: Scribner's, ©1963) 33–38, 136–39.
3. A popular TV prime-time serial, in the setting of vineyards, with an unscrupulous lady owner on center stage.
4. Jeremias, *Parables* 37.
5. Here I am following Jeremias (ibid. 136 and n. 16 there), who claims that the usual designation for this parable, Laborers in the Vineyard, obscures the fact that the central figure is the employer.
6. I have developed some of the following ideas in greater detail in a different context, the so-called Red Mass, a traditional liturgy that traces its history to the 13th century and invokes God's guidance and strength on the legal profession during the court term to come; see "As God Has Done unto You," in my *Tell the Next Generation: Homilies and Near Homilies* (New York: Paulist, ©1980) 121–26.

Homily 19

1. Here I have profited from Joachim Jeremias, *The Parables of Jesus* (New York: Scribner's, ©1963) 80–81, 125, 127.
2. Data taken from a booklet, *St. Mary's Celebrates 150 Years* (Rochester, N.Y.: no publisher given, [1984]).

Homily 20

1. A reference to a prominent landmark at the University of Notre Dame.
2. See "Partying in Christ," in my *Sir, We Would Like To See Jesus: Homilies from a Hilltop* (New York/Ramsey: Paulist, ©1982) 121–25.
3. Here I have profited from F. Schroeder, "Paul, Apostle, St.," *New Catholic Encyclopedia* 11 (1967) 1–12.
4. See J. B. Lightfoot, *Saint Paul's Epistle to the Philippians* (rev. ed.; London and New York: Macmillan, 1891) 163–64, and his dissertation "St Paul and Seneca," ibid. 270–333, esp. 304–5.
5. Karl Barth, *The Epistle to the Philippians* (Nashville: John Knox, 1962) 127.
6. Gerard Manley Hopkins, "God's Grandeur," ed. W. H. Gardner and N. H. MacKenzie, *The Poems of Gerard Manley Hopkins* (New York: Oxford University, 1970) 66.
7. *Time* 124, no. 15 (Oct. 8, 1984) 66.

Homily 21

1. See Raymond E. Brown, S.S., *The Book of Deuteronomy* (Old Testament Reading Guide 10; Collegeville, Minn.: Liturgical, ©1965) 41–42.

2. See Wolfgang Trilling, *The Gospel according to St. Matthew* 2 (New Testament for Spiritual Reading 2; New York: Crossroad, 1981) 164–67.
3. Homilists should also be aware that in Luke's version (Lk 10:25–28) it is the lawyer who quotes "what is written" in Deuteronomy and Leviticus.
4. Useful here is Raymond E. Brown, S.S., *The Gospel according to John (xiii–xxi)* (Anchor Bible 29A; Garden City, N.Y.: Doubleday, 1970) 612–14.
5. Brown finds "dubious the suggestion that the newness consists in the fact that Jesus commands the Christian to love 'as I have loved you' " (ibid. 613). For him (as I go on to say in this homily), "the 'new commandment' of John xiii 34 is the basic stipulation of the 'new covenant' of Luke xxii 20" (ibid. 614).
6. Karl Rahner, *Ignatius of Loyola* (London: Collins, 1979) 11, 12, 17, 13.
7. The reference is to Spiro Agnew.
8. Roger Wilkins, "Speaking Out," *Civil Rights Quarterly* 12, no. 1 (spring 1980) 2.

Homily 22

1. See Ceslas Spicq and Marc-François Lacan, "Faithfulness," in Xavier Léon Dufour, ed., *Dictionary of Biblical Theology* (2nd ed.; New York: Seabury, 1973) 164–65.
2. Here I owe much to Joachim Jeremias, *The Parables of Jesus* (rev. ed.; New York: Scribner's, ©1963) 58–63.
3. See a different approach in my homily for the same Sunday "Only If You Risk," in my *Sir, We Would Like To See Jesus: Homilies from a Hilltop* (New York/Ramsey: Paulist, ©1982) 137–42.
4. I have been unable to document this quotation, which I translate from the French in which I discovered it.
5. A reference to the four less than successful football seasons Notre Dame "enjoyed" (1981–84) under a coach with a five-year contract.
6. A metaphor from football, several hours after the Notre Dame–Penn State game.

Homily 23

1. I am aware that in the Sermon on the Mount "the Evangelist has given us a compilation of sayings of Jesus, some of which were originally uttered on other occasions" (J. A. Grassi, "Sermon on the Mount," *New Catholic Encyclopedia* 13 [1967] 119).
2. In preparing this first point, I have profited from Daniel J. Harrington, S.J., *The Gospel according to Matthew* (Collegeville, Minn.: Liturgical, 1983) 27–28; Friedrich Hauck, *"halas,"* in Gerhard Kittel, ed., *Theolog-*

ical Dictionary of the New Testament 1 (Grand Rapids, Mich.: Eerdmans, 1976) 228–29; Alexander Jones, *The Gospel according to St Matthew* (New York: Sheed & Ward, 1965) 76–79; M.-J. Lagrange, *Evangile selon saint Matthieu* (7th ed.; Paris: Lecoffre, 1948) 88–90; Xavier Léon-Dufour, "Salt," in Xavier Léon-Dufour, ed., *Dictionary of Biblical Theology* (2nd ed.; New York: Seabury, 1973) 518; Eduard Schweizer, *The Good News according to Matthew* (Atlanta: John Knox, ©1975) 100–103.

3. The title of a contemporary TV serial, in which various characters are allowed to live out their fantasies, regularly at great risk.

Homily 24

1. I have lifted this first point (save for the final paragraph) from an earlier wedding homily, "If I Have Not Love . . . ," published in my *Still Proclaiming Your Wonders: Homilies for the Eighties* (New York/Ramsey: Paulist, ©1984) 201–5, at 201–2, where I have a different theme in view: our need for a human person.
2. The title of a popular TV serial, where all sorts of "love" episodes crowd the tube.

Homily 25

1. The reference is to a long-lived TV serial whose replays continue to delight millions.
2. See Norman Cousins, *Anatomy of an Illness As Perceived by the Patient: Reflections on Healing and Regeneration* (New York: Norton, 1979).
3. *New York Times,* Dec. 9, 1984, 32.
4. Relevant examples because the groom was a dentist, the bride in the nursing profession.

Homily 26

1. The last reference is to the appearance of Georgetown University in the finals of the NCAA basketball tournament April 1, 1985 in Lexington, Ky. If any prayers were answered in the affirmative, it was Villanova University that profited, 66–64.
2. These references, and others to follow, stem from the fact that bride and groom were both at that time fourth-year students in the Georgetown University Medical School.
3. Sir William Osler, "The Master-Word in Medicine," in his *Aequanimitas* (3rd ed.; Philadelphia: Blakiston, 1932 [1st ed., 1904]) 347–71, at 366.
4. It is legitimate to use 2 Corinthians to exemplify what Paul says in the passage from Romans, since the two letters were written in close prox-

imity: 2 Corinthians "probably" in the autumn of 57, Romans during the winter of 57–58 (see *The Jerome Biblical Commentary* [Englewood Cliffs, N.J.: Prentice-Hall, ©1968] 52:6 and 53:2).

Homily 27

1. From Wilfrid O. Cross, "The No-New Morality," *American Church Quarterly* 5 (1965) 223.

Homily 28

1. I am following here one interpretation of the relationship between the three nouns: The way is the primary predicate, the truth and the life are explanations of the way. Jesus is the way *because* he is the truth and the life. Another approach has the way directed towards a goal that is the truth and/or the life. See Raymond E. Brown, S.S., *The Gospel according to John (xiii–xxi)* (Anchor Bible 29A; Garden City, N.Y.: Doubleday, 1970) 620–21, 630–31.
2. Yves Congar, *Challenge to the Church: The Case of Archbishop Lefebvre* (Huntington, Ind.: Our Sunday Visitor, 1976) 42.
3. Robert N. Bellah, "Religion & Power in America Today," *Commonweal* 109, no. 21 (Dec. 3, 1982) 650–55, at 652. I have not found it possible, within the time at my disposal, to include Bellah's remarks on the ideal of psychological man, who "pushes the logic of economic man one stage further" (ibid. 651).
4. See Carin Rubinstein, "Money & Self-Esteem, Relationships, Secrecy, Envy, Satisfaction," *Psychology Today* 15, no. 5 (May 1981) 29–44, esp. 40–44.
5. Bellah, "Religion & Power" 655.
6. Frederick Buechner, *The Magnificent Defeat* (New York: Seabury, ©1966) 23.
7. Rod McKuen, *Listen to the Warm* (New York: Random House, 1969) 112.

Homily 29

1. A popular rock group. Note also that at various points in the homily I make local (Worcester, Holy Cross) allusions that will be recognized only by those who have been there: shops (Galleria, Shakey Jake's), SPUD (Student Programs for Urban Development), the sculpture on campus of two undraped ladies.
2. Here I borrow, with some changes in rhetoric, from my homily "The

Man Who Lives with Wisdom," in *Tell the Next Generation: Homilies and Near Homilies* (New York: Paulist, ©1980) 100–101.

3. Here I borrow, with some modifications, from my homily "I Asked for Wonder," in my *Still Proclaiming Your Wonders: Homilies for the Eighties* (New York/Ramsey: Paulist, ©1984) 168–73, at 170–73.

4. Lewis Carroll, *Alice's Adventures in Wonderland*, in *The Complete Works of Lewis Carroll* (New York: Random House, [1936]) 79.

5. In *Between God and Man: An Interpretation of Judaism from the Writings of Abraham J. Heschel* (New York: Harper, ©1959) 40.

6. Ibid. 41.

7. Ibid.

8. The phrase "all lost in wonder" is borrowed from Gerard Manley Hopkins' translation of Thomas Aquinas' *Adoro te;* see *The Poems of Gerard Manley Hopkins,* ed. W. H. Gardner and N. H. MacKenzie (4th ed.; New York: Oxford University, 1970) 211.

9. Gerard Manley Hopkins, "God's Grandeur," ibid. 66.

10. Samuel H. Dresner, "Remembering Abraham Heschel," *America* 146, no. 21 (May 29, 1982) 414.

Homily 30

1. For this first point, I have profited greatly from the fine review of the film by Richard A. Blake, "God's Grandeur," *America* 151, no. 10 (Oct. 13, 1984) 210. Most of the quotations derive from him.

2. Phyllis McGinley, "In Praise of Diversity," in *The Love Letters of Phyllis McGinley* (New York: Viking, 1954) 12–16.

3. Only the pedant would complain that orthodoxy calls for distinct, not "separate," Persons. Anyhow, "distinct" would destroy the meter.

4. The preacher should be aware that exegetes do not agree on the question, who is the source of the rivers of living water, Jesus or the believer? For a succinct presentation of the two positions and their supports, see Raymond E. Brown, S.S., *The Gospel according to John (i–xii)* (Anchor Bible 29; Garden City, N.Y.: Doubleday, 1966) 320–21; see also 327–29.

5. This is something of an exaggeration. Still, students from over a hundred countries graduated from GU in 1985, though not all were represented at the Baccalaureate Mass.

6. Second Vatican Council, Decree on the Apostolate of the Laity, no. 5.

7. Note in this connection the insistence of Cardinal Léon-Joseph Suenens that the greatest day in the life of a pope is not his coronation but his baptism, the day of his mission "to live the Christian life in obedience to the gospel" (*Coresponsibility in the Church* [New York: Herder and Herder, 1968] 31).

8. In fairness to Mozart, it should be noted that the film focuses on the less attractive aspects of his character—and my homily uses the film for

its springboard. Neither film nor homilist suggests, e.g., that "Mozart was essentially a believing and practicing Catholic, as seems certain from many of his letters . . . " (R. G. Pauly, "Mozart, Wolfgang Amadeus," *New Catholic Encylopedia* 10 [1967] 61).

Homily 31

1. This first section has profited from Joseph A. Fitzmyer, S.J., *Pauline Theology: A Brief Sketch* (Englewood Cliffs, N.J.: Prentice-Hall, ©1967) passim.
2. In preparing this second point, I have learned much and used much from the essay by Sonya A. Quitslund, "Elements of a Feminist Spirituality in St Teresa," in John Sullivan, O.C.D., ed., *Carmelite Studies: Centenary of St Teresa* (Catholic University Symposium—October 15–17, 1982; Washington, D.C.: Institute of Carmelite Studies, 1984) 19–50.
3. Ibid. 34.
4. Letter to Don Hernando de Pantoja, Jan. 31, 1579.
5. *The Book of Her Life* 9, 2.
6. Letter to Discalced Carmelite Nuns of Seville, Jan. 13, 1580.
7. See *The Interior Castle* 4, 3, 5; 5, 3, 5.
8. Dietrich Bonhoeffer, *Creation and Fall: A Theological Interpretation of Genesis 1–3* (London: SCM, 1959) 38.

Homily 32

1. Marc H. Tanenbaum, "A Jewish Viewpoint," in John H. Miller, C.S.C., ed., *Vatican II: An Interfaith Appraisal* (Notre Dame: Univ. of Notre Dame, ©1966) 349–67, at 355.
2. See Declaration on the Relationship of the Church to Non-Christian Religions, no. 4.
3. Tanenbaum, "A Jewish Viewpoint" 363.
4. Arthur A. Cohen, "Notes toward a Jewish Theology of Politics," *Commonweal* 77 (1962–63) 11.
5. Elie Wiesel, *The Gates of the Forest* (New York: Holt, Rinehart and Winston, ©1966) 194.
6. Henry Morgenthau, *Ambassador Morgenthau's Story* (New York: Doubleday, Page, 1919) 321–22.
7. Verse 8, the last verse of the parable, was omitted from the reading at the service, apparently in view of Jewish sensitivities.